"...I found myself profoundly stirred, emotionally and spiritually... This Pile of Stones is a gripping and compelling narrative – much easier to pick up than to set down."

John A. Anonby, PhD.
Trinity Western University

"An incredible mixture of missionary endeavour, personal tragedy, and God's miracles. This Pile of Stones is a vulnerable look at one couple's journey with God in real life. It is encouraging and heart-warming, as well as challenging and thought-provoking in its openness and honesty. It is very readable and yet theologically sound. It deals with one of the key questions of earnest Christians: How can I reconcile, intellectually and emotionally, God's goodness and sovereignty with the pain and disappointments of life's experience?"

Duane Conrad, National Director
Campus Crusade for Christ
Germany

"Someone once said that trials will make us either better or bitter, it depends on where we go for the comfort and wisdom to handle the trials. We thank the Lord for the Jeske's testimony of God's faithfulness in the midst of really tough times. Their book, This Pile of Stones, is not a "how to" book on suffering. Rather it is their life journey told as an honest and compelling story of God's sovereignty and their faith. It will be a comfort to all who face the trials and tribulations that change us into His image."

Phillip R. Walker, PhD.
Continental Director
Africa and the Middle East
Walk Thru the Bible

THIS PILE OF STONES

THIS PILE OF STONES

Discovering Hope
Between a Rock
and a Hard Place

Phil T. Jeske
Nancy Jeske

Zinzendorf Publishing
Canada

*To all those who
have helped us in countless ways and
have been examples of Christ for us to follow –
We are indebted to you!*

*To the wife of my youth who,
in spite of my faults, has chosen to be my life's partner and
without whom I would be incomplete –
I love you!*

*To our daughter who
makes us look like better parents than we really are and
is already carrying the torch of faith for the next generation –
We are proud of you!*

Contents

Acknowledgements

We would like to acknowledge our appreciation and gratefulness to those who have influenced and impacted us along the journey of our lives thus far.

To our families and friends who are part of who we have become and have permitted us to publically peal back the curtain of their right to privacy, we hope we accomplished our goal with minimal infringements on this right. Thanks Hans for allowing us to mention your pain. We hope that the encouragement that you have been to us will be multiplied many times over as others view this pile of remembrance stones. With God nothing is by accident and nothing is in vain.

To those whom we have ministered with over the years and, in spite of our imperfections, have enabled us to develop through our various stages of growth, thank you. We apologize for any insensitivities we may have had, at times, as we focussed on the pursuit of our dreams.

To the many who have continued to be gracious with us over the years, even when we may have been less than gracious as we struggling to find meaning through our Jordan experiences. We appreciate your willingness to be God's instrument in our lives, especially during the dark times. Our prayer is that the return on your investment will be evidenced in the encouragement that this book is for others.

Of course such a project would not be possible without the invaluable practical assistance of many. Thank you to David Herrod, Candace Willis, Walter Rusnell and many others who read the initial manuscript and have offered valuable input. Particular thanks to John Anonby, for helping to hone the text and Christal Rusnell and Allegra Print and Imaging for your patience and expertise in getting our text and cover ideas into book form.

Most importantly, we want to thank our Lord and Saviour who has always been there, even when it seemed the waters of the Jordan would overwhelm us. Thanks for your nearness even when we were not aware of your presence. This story is not about us. It is a record of your grace and faithfulness in our lives. Thank you for the dreams, but thank you even more for patiently molding us into who You want us to be. Don't stop now, as you well know, we are still very much in need of your ongoing efforts!

Foreword

I first met Phil Jeske on the campus of Pan African Christian College in Nairobi, Kenya, where I had been serving as Academic Dean during an extended leave of absence from Trinity Western University in Langley, British Columbia. Phil shared with me his unique vision of Bible training for African pastors who desired to upgrade their qualifications without having to leave their ministerial responsibilities for extended periods of time. Little did I know that, some years down the road, I would be invited to join the Canadian Board of International Christian Ministries. Nor had I anticipated that I would be requested to write a foreword to Phil and Nancy's soul-stirring missionary autobiography.

When I began to turn the pages of this testimonial manuscript, I found myself profoundly stirred, emotionally and spiritually. These pages emanate authenticity, fuelled by a sincerity tinged with high hopes, deep disappointments, and a maturing faith in God's sovereignty over life's most challenging circumstances.

While reading these reminiscences and reflections, I had a strange sense that they resembled something familiar. Phrases such as "through much tribulation entering the Kingdom of God" (Acts 14:22) came to mind...referring to the Apostle Paul, of course! And Paul, as we all know, was the greatest of the earliest missionaries to take the Gospel from Jerusalem to Rome. Other passages came to me – all from 2 Corinthians, which depicts Paul's internal struggles more probingly than anywhere else in the New Testament. His list of painful experiences in 11:23-28 is both astonishing and formidable, ranging from brutal beatings and deprivation to almost unbelievable burdens of responsibility relating to his fledgling churches planted in hostile pagan territory. Why does Paul share his pain through this letter? The answer is crystal clear: to give glory to the "God of all comfort" and to "comfort others by the comfort we have received from God" (2 Cor. 1:3 – 4).

And this is where Phil and Nancy Jeske's *This Pile of Stones* comes into focus. All my life I have heard thrilling stories from missionaries who have shared their exciting experiences and narrow escapes from danger. Having served overseas, I too can share stories like these. What is much harder to express publicly are the petty frustrations, the bureaucratic red tape, the untimely illnesses (is sickness ever timely?), inexplicable delays of every variety....Yet, in spite of these uncomfortable realities – so frankly recorded in these pages – there is evidence of an irrepressible and tenacious conviction that God is greater than any circumstances.

The unmistakable sense of calling which Phil traces back to his childhood, the intractable griefs experienced within Phil and Nancy's family, the miraculous "coincidences" that testify to God's timely interventions, the hurdles that accompany every opportunity – all of this resembles the struggles Paul divulges to us in his frankest and most sensitive epistle.

Perhaps the most valuable feature of *This Pile of Stones*, with its ongoing implications that God leads all of us in unique ways in our individual lives, is the long-range perspective illuminated in this book. The title reminds us that we should not forget God's intervention and guidance in the past. As we share with others both the joys and pain in our lives, we become living proofs of God's grace and guidance. The long-range perspective is not, however, confined to reflections on the past – for we are also admonished to glimpse into God's glorious future plans for all the saints of all the ages. "The Final Stone" is the culminating and climactic chapter in this heart-stirring autobiography. The stone "cut without hands" (Daniel 2:34), God's great kingdom, will some day fill heaven and earth, and we can be a part of it as "living stones" strategically placed by the "chief corner stone," Christ Himself (1 Peter 2: 5 – 6).

This Pile of Stones is a gripping and compelling narrative – much easier to pick up than to set down.

John A. Anonby (Ph.D.)
Department of English
Trinity Western University

Preface

So often the busyness and activity of life crowds out any time for serious reflection and evaluation while we are in the middle of it. We are often just trying to survive day to day. Our experience has been that the realities of our obligations and responsibilities usually do not afford us the opportunity to review where we are at and where we are going.

It was a tragedy that touched a life of our friend that once again reminded us of some of the markers in our life which we knew were memorials of God's faithfulness to us. Over that summer as I reflected on these, it seemed time to commit them to paper. The desire that some of these experiences may not be "lost," but instead would help someone else in their lives, has led to this book. At the very least, taking the time to read these pages will provide you reflection time to review what God is doing in your life.

Over the years we have written countless newsletters and missionary reports. But we have never written down some of the deepest valleys that God has led us through and some of the real issues he has dealt with us on. Being able to explore all these through a writing project such as this has been an experience in itself. Throughout this journey we have found ourselves identifying with Winston Churchill who wrote regarding the process of writing a book, "To begin with, it is a toy and an amusement. Then it becomes a mistress. Then it becomes a master. Then it becomes a tyrant. And the last phase is that just as you are about to be reconciled to your servitude, you kill the monster and fling him out to the public." Though put in dramatic Churchillian fashion, it does in some measure reflect our own experience. We have made it to the "flinging" stage.

We hope that you may be able to identify with some of what you read in the following pages and be encouraged by some of the simple, though not easy, things we have learned as we have *stumbled* along. I choose the words, *"stumbling along"* very deliberately. For while stumbling along does not sound all that "spiritual," from our vantage point, it often seems that this is all we are doing. Even on our good days, there are times when we feel like we are doing nothing more than just faithfully putting one foot in front of the other. Of course, from God's perspective, He is bringing to pass his plans and purposes. As Proverbs 19:21 states, "Many are the plans in a man's heart, but it is the Lord's purpose that prevails." The Scriptures are full of examples of those who, with the benefit of hindsight, are now seen as "men and women of faith." Yet at the time, from their perspective, they were just doing what they knew to do with all the integrity they had; putting one foot in front of the other. They, like many of us, often did not always see the big picture.

We are well aware – actually *painfully aware* at times – of the fact that God is not finished with us yet; this is just a slice out of our lives to this point. It was this awareness that kept our initial scribbles and notes tucked away for several years. Then, as more time passed, a few more events would occur which would seem to confirm the apparent *wisdom* of not committing our thoughts to paper *quite yet*. Not only did the busyness and complexity of our life as missionaries seem to thwart each attempt at writing this book, but also the underlying question, "Would anyone actually want to read a book such as this?" So we wrestled for many years to come to the point of actually committing to paper a few of our experiences and thoughts. The initial outline for this book was initially filed in my notepad several years ago and travelled with me on my trips to Africa and Europe, with the hopes that one day we would actually find the time to put down some of these thoughts on paper.

During our second year in Berlin a tragic event happened to a friend which motivated us to take the necessary steps in order to finish the manuscript. This event gave us the last motivation we needed to begin the writing process. Then, as we were into the process, the terrorist attack of September 11, 2001 at the World Trade Centre in New York and the Pentagon occurred. The world-wide impact of such a large scale tragedy, made the events of our lives seem rather meaningless in comparison. Nevertheless, we continued to work on the book for we believed that the things we had learned in our personal lives were also applicable in a larger context and would benefit others.

It will soon become obvious, as you read this book, that much of what we share does not come from what would seem a position of strength, but rather one of weakness and imperfection. While at a discipleship school in California, over two decades ago, we were impacted by the necessity of sharing from one's own *life message*. Basically this means that we are most effective as we share, not just some great ideas or theories, but principles that God has taught us personally in our own lives. At the time, at the ripe old age of seventeen, we obviously had limited material to work with from our own life, but time has a way of changing that.

Little did we realize, then, how God was going to take the events of the following years to develop that *life message* in us (fortunately, He is not finished with us yet!). Little did we realize that much of what we were to learn would be gleaned from the wilderness times in our lives. I am increasingly convinced that it is God's mercy that we do not know the details of our future. It is only by his grace that we are able to face each new day. Yet grace, like the manna of old, does not have a very long shelf life. It must be received anew and applied in our lives every day afresh. We have discovered that it is only those truths which we have learned through the crucible of personal experience that brings *life* to others. This, of course, necessitates our obedience to share them with humility, openness and vulnerability.

Our ultimate desire is that this book will be an encouragement to you along the path that God has chosen for you to walk. Our prayer is that you may find the strength to continue on following the *Big Picture*, even though at times things may seem to be going sideways in your life and you may not fully understand what God is doing. As we share from the hard and dry times in our lives, may you also be able to see how God is working during even the desert times of your life. Though the lessons we have learned have been specifically tailored through our experiences, you have your own unique set of circumstances that God is using to mold you into the image of his Son. We hope that these simple thoughts, refined in the crucible of our lives, will serve to assist and encourage you as you reflect on what God has done and is doing in your life.

This book is for us like a *pile of stones* from the middle of the Jordan River. In Joshua chapters three and four, we see the children of Israel passing through the river Jordan, on dry ground, to the Promised Land. Once on the other side, God instructed Joshua to choose twelve men, one from each tribe, to carry one stone from the middle of the river. These stones were then to be piled on the Canaan side of the riverbank as a "memorial to the people of Israel forever." Figuratively, Jordan is also a type of passing from death to life; from where we are to where God wants to take us; from wilderness times to more fruitful times.

This book is a record of what God has done in our lives and is our *pile of stones* that we have taken from the river bottom of *our* Jordan experiences. It is not only a proof that we were actually there and saw God's works, but is also a testimony to others along life's journey. God has taken us through some *Jordans* and has more to take us through I'm sure. These are after all only remembrances of the journey thus far, not memoirs! But as with the Israelites, God's desire is not for us to camp by the stones or even become experts at rock piling; the point of the stones is to help us remember who God has been in our lives so that we may be an encouragement to others along this same pilgrimage. So this book is not just some theory, but a reflection of who we are – the good, the bad and, yes, even the ugly. We hope that you will not only find it interesting, but that our *pile of stones* will in some way help you in your journey.

The Apostle Paul reminds each of us that our lives are like open letters which can be read by all those around us. We hope that as you read our *letter,* you will be strengthened in your faith, encouraged in your walk, and deepened in your commitment to God and others.

Phil & Nancy Jeske
Berlin, 2002

Introduction

The sky was a bright blue that reminded me of the big blue sky I had grown up with on the Canadian prairies. Though living in the middle of Berlin didn't allow for a clear view to the horizon, as on the prairies, it was one of those days which showed the city off at its best. The wall to wall sunshine danced with the shadows created by the large green leaves of the majestic chestnut and oak trees that lined the city's many historic boulevards.

It was on days like this that the challenges of the fledgling ministry in Central Europe did not even seem as difficult. On such days, when the sunshine would stream though the window of my home office, the problems and struggles did not seem as insurmountable. It was also easier to ignore all the challenges still facing this once divided city on such days; to forget the divisions and ideological differences that the crumbling of a concrete *Wall* did not solve.

Our own journey to this city was anything but a straight line. After launching a missions society in Canada, we had lived in Africa and then had returned to serve the cause of world missions from Canada. It was during this time, in the mid to late nineties, that we had felt God begin to lead us here to Central Europe. Not unlike the *Macedonian Call* of old, we were responding to the plea to "Come over and help us!" The practicalities of this meant moving to Berlin to be catalysts in facilitating pastoral and leadership training with those that had invited us. But in the midst of this, while much of our energy, thoughts, and prayers were focussed in this direction, an event occurred which made us again take stock of our lives and our priorities – ultimately causing us to reflect on what God had done thus far in our lives and finally commit it to writing.

It all began with a phone call to our friend and fellow missionary in Berlin. I had first met Hans and his wife, Dee, on a ministry trip through Berlin years earlier. We shared the common vision of training leaders for the European church. It so happened that we had ended up moving a few blocks from them in the Steglitz community of Berlin. Not only did *we* hit it off, but our wives also became friends and were involved in various women's ministries in the city. To top it off, our daughters were close to the same age and had become friends. It seemed that God had placed us together to be a blessing to each other; sharing the ups and downs of the ministry together.

On this particularly sunny summer day, Hans' wife had gone into the hospital for some relatively routine back surgery. But events in the next few hours were to be anything but routine. I waited until the day after the surgery to call, as I wanted to find out how things had gone. But instead of good news, I heard from her thirteen year old son that, earlier that morning, his mother's heart had stopped for a time due to a blood clot. He continued to tell me that his Dad was now at the hospital, though he still did not know how his mother was.

As I quickly jumped into the car and raced to the hospital, the sun did not seem to shine as bright and the Berlin sky had seemed to lose some of its deep blue, as cloudy thoughts filled my mind. I managed to navigate the labyrinth of the large hospital and arrived at the intensive care unit where Hans was at the bedside of his wife. She had, by now, slipped into a coma.

Waiting on the single chair in the small cubicle that served as a waiting room, I was alone with my thoughts. To the slight flicker of the colourless flourescent light and almost inaudible hum of the hospital, I mentally began to retrace the steps to our *pile of stones* that we had labouriously placed by the shore of *our* Jordan river. Perhaps it was that many of these stones were pulled from the river bottom of the tragedies in our lives, or perhaps it was just the shock and gravity of the situation, but as I sat there praying for our friends and the dark valley of death which they were now passing through, some of the deep valleys that we had come through flashed before my mind's eye. "Why," I couldn't help wondering, "did so many of the most meaningful lessons of our lives need to be shaped through tragedy and turmoil?" Only the institutional hum of the hospital air-conditioning answered my rhetorical question.

As I mindlessly gazed at the medical posters that lined the walls, I flashed back in time to another hospital, another waiting room. This time it was *my* wife that was in emergency surgery. The large moving truck, which I had tried driving out of our driveway, had lurched backwards against our carport and the whole structure had collapsed on her and our two year old daughter. While I had waited in the hospital on that occasion, the surgeons had reattached her foot and determined the extent of her other life-threatening wounds. At the time it seemed life would never be the same again – and in some ways it never really was.

My mind then fast forwarded to almost one year exactly after that accident to the phone call we had received one night from my mother-in-law in California. She was the bearer of the shocking news that my wife's father had been brutally murdered by his own son – my wife's brother. Where was God in this senseless act that defied explanation? Another rhetorical question that had no easy answers. . .

Another hospital, another stone to carry as a remembrance from the riverbed, while crossing yet another *Jordan*. This time we were living in Kenya as missionaries. Repeated malaria attacks on our then four year old daughter, Alysia, resulted in a particularly long night as her body repeatedly convulsed from the feverish seizures, culminating in a frantic three hour helicopter flight later that night to a mission hospital in Kijabe, near Nairobi. Kenya, at the time, was going through its first elections as an independent country, which resulted in tribal turmoil and killings. The unrest, in addition to Alysia's health situation and the need of my wife to grieve for the loss of her father, eventually led to our earlier than anticipated return to Canada. This was to usher in a difficult valley in my life and ministry, which was to put incredible strains on our marriage. Yet another *Jordan*, yet another *stone* to add to the pile accumulating along the riverbank of our lives...each representing a memory of God's dealings in our lives.

One thing we have definitely learned through these and other valleys is that we will never be able to answer satisfactorily all the "why" questions this side of eternity. But we have personally proven that God does have a good plan for each of our lives, plans that include giving us a hope and a future (Jer. 29:11). While the circumstances of life may force some of us to our knees, in mere fatalistic surrender to the fact the we are not in control, God's purposes for his children are so much higher than this. For others, the circumstances of life do not lead to fatalism, but instead resignation. They reason, with or without realizing it, that since God *outweighs* them, they will just have to accept his will, albeit rather grudgingly.

But I would like to suggest that there is yet another alternative. We have discovered that in the midst of the storm, concrete answers are hard to come by, and even though God does not always answer our *why* questions, we can testify that He never gives up on us and continues to work in our lives according to his good pleasure and purposes. This is actually the greatest security there is. We are not so naive as to believe that every tragedy and circumstance has its source in God but, as his children, we are confident that everything that He has entrusted us to bear has had to pass by his desk first. If God has the confidence to entrust us with it, then we can be assured that it is his purpose to bring us *through* it. We must just remember to pick up a *stone* from the middle of our Jordan as a reminder of what God has brought us through.

Our goal is to encourage you to come to that healthy place in your life that our heavenly father wants to bring all of us to: a place of acceptance of his will in our lives – even including the *Jordans* that we must pass through. Yet we also desire to broaden your horizons so that you might perceive how you can participate in the Great Commission – to go into all the world – even though there are times in your life when you may just be trying to figure out what God is up to…those times when there seems to be more questions than answers, more clouds than blue sky. It is particularly then that we need to have the perseverance to carry on. For each of us these dark days may differ in intensity and duration, but they will inevitably come.

This book is not an answer book outlining all the reasons for evil or a systematic explanation of the big questions of life. While we do not believe that God is the originator of evil and is not merely playing celestial chess with his earthly pawns, the fact remains that *bad* things do happen to *good* people. We all need his grace in order to learn to deal with the thorns, while not forgetting to appreciate the roses along the way. In all these things we have found that God's purpose is to form us into the image of Christ, whatever may come our way. These events that we go through, then become our *memorial* by the shore of our Jordan. If we take the step to walk through Jordan, instead of just looking across at Canaan, we will reach the other side – the place to which God wants to bring us. Our pile of stones can then be used to encourage those who find themselves facing similar challenges and obstacles along the way.

Only those who have gone through the river can truly empathize and effectively assist those facing similar waters. That, in essence, is our *life message*. Without personal experience, our advice, and even Bible answers, are merely theoretical and lack the power that brings change. It is only as we participate in "the fellowship of his sufferings" (Phil. 3:10), that we are able to bring a message of reconciliation to a fallen world – a message that does not ring hollow or powerless. Someday, as we all join in worship around the throne – from every tribe, nation, culture and language – we will finally be able to fully share in his joy.

Our lives are not just our own; we have been bought with a price. God has a plan and purpose for each of us. As we are obedient, we will find the fulfilment and meaning we seek in our lives. In this life, this may even mean carrying what may seem like a heavy cross at times, though our natural man never enjoys that. While some experiences along our path are of our own making, others are strewn there by the enemy, and yet others have a divine origin to test our faith. But whatever the source, God has promised to walk us through each one, never leaving our side. They are not there to drown us, but to show us God's grace, love and power, so that we might grow stronger.

Our perspective is from those who have made it to half-time, as it were. We are not at the end of our race, but are still in the race. Yet we would like to encourage you that it is well worth it, not only for this life, but also for the life to come. As you read, we hope that you will be encouraged to finish the race that God has called you to in *your* life. He has a plan that spans beyond time into eternity, yet which is revealed in very down-to-earth, bite-sized pieces – our individual lives.

Join us as we describe a few of the stones which we have piled as a memorial of God's faithfulness. The first begins on what was to be as normal as any moving day could be, on that unforgettable September long weekend of 1988.

1

The Sawdust Trail

It was one of those beautiful – late summer, not quite autumn – days on the Lower Mainland of British Columbia. It was the September long weekend, which always seemed to be the official psychological transition from summer to autumn. Little did we know that it would be a day that would be forever etched in our minds.

As I awoke early that morning, however, my mind was on a million and one details, as we were moving from our home in Mission to Surrey, closer to the city of Vancouver in the province of British Columbia. As I wiped the dew (a telltale sign of the approaching change of season) from the windshield of the car, I continue to make mental notes of what I still had to do that day. Fortunately, we had already packed most things and so it was just going to be a matter of putting them into the moving truck, which I was on my way to pick up.

As I wound my way down the hills of Mission City, I could see that the fog was still settled in the valley. As the early morning sun began to break over Mt. Baker, located just south in Washington

State, its rays glistened off the top of the fog blanket. Not being much of a morning person, I was really appreciating the sunrise; after all, it was a rare occurrence for me to witness it! But as I heard someone once say, "If God had wanted us to witness every sunrise, He would have scheduled it later in the day!"

I descended into the fog on the valley floor, passing farmers' fields along the mostly deserted country road. The sun was beginning to cause the glistening moisture on the roofs to steam as it gained strength and burned through the morning fog. Yet, on this morning, as I was on my way to pick up the rental truck, I could not fully appreciate the beauty. My mind was too preoccupied and my emotions somewhat mixed. This particular move was more than just going from one house to another, or even from one city to another. We were actually only moving less than an hour's drive away, but this move seemed to carry with it more of a realization that this was a real transitional point – the turning of a chapter in our lives.

Since marrying my college sweetheart in California, some six years earlier, it seemed so much had already happened to us. A job offer, through a company my brother, Bernie, worked for, had brought us to the valley community of Langley, in British Columbia. At the time we had figured that it would be good to make some money and see what God would open up down the road. However, within a few months several things in the business had changed and there was no longer a job for me. So we found ourselves sitting at our kitchen table, which at that time was just an ironing board, wondering what to do next. Without a job we could no longer afford the townhouse, but moving would not be too difficult of a task for we had creatively covered our moving boxes to double as furniture. The more difficult issue was what to do next. My new bride was from California, and I had grown up in Edmonton, Alberta. Finding ourselves in the Lower Mainland of British Columbia was an unfamiliar experience for both of us. All of a sudden our townhouse seemed very empty and not very much like home. But on that day, on the ironing board in our kitchen, we prayed together as newlyweds, committing our lives into his hands again.

Over the following weeks God directed me to attend Bible School again in order to complete my Bachelor degree in Bible and Theology. Having just finished a two year program at *Genesis Discipleship Training School* in California a few months earlier, I was not too keen on more schooling right away. After all, I had left to go to college at the ripe old age of seventeen and now, two years later, I wanted to make my mark in this world as soon as possible. But as happened on many occasions, Nancy's gentle confidence and coaxing made me see the wisdom of the decision to take further schooling *sooner* rather than *later*. This decision led us to the community of Abbotsford, a stone's throw from Mission City, which lay just across the Fraser River. Abbotsford, where we were to spend the next couple years, was located along the edge of the coastal mountains, as they flattened out towards the west to form the rich farmland of the Fraser Valley Delta. Nevertheless, what felt to us at the time as a real curve ball and an unexpected change of plans, was actually God superintending our lives.

It was during those early days together as a newly married couple that we began to learn to hear God's voice through each other and experience how He began to lead us one step at a time. Little did we know, at the time, how many twists and turns that path would take. But God continued to have us in his school, making us into the people that He wanted us to be. While I had this desire to do great and powerful things *for* Him, He would gently, but firmly, remind us of his agenda – his desire to develop *who* we were, our character. It would be less than truthful to say that we were always willing participants in this process, but God continued to work patiently in our lives.

So, several years later, after more term papers, exams, and hours of housecleaning to pay the bills than Nancy and I care to remember, we both finished our degrees – mine a BTh and Nancy a PHT *(Putting Hubby Through)* degree. During my undergraduate studies I had done an internship with Pastor Roy Holmquist in Mission, BC, across the river from Abbotsford. Then upon graduation we had moved to Mission City to serve as Youth/Christian Education pastor in his church.

From a young teen through to my college experiences, it seemed that I had always had positions of leadership and had always volunteered in various capacities of ministry, but I was now finally able to give my full time attention to serving among a local body of believers. It was hard to believe that I was actually paid to do what I loved! To that point I had had to do tasks which I did not particularly enjoy in order to just pay the bills. My ministry involvement had often been in a part time volunteer capacity. It was a new experience to now be working full-time in the ministry.

Those early days of full-time ministry were both challenging and exciting days – good days. Working together with a seasoned pastoral team, who were also open to new fresh ideas, was a great experience. The love and affection we also experienced from the members of that small church are memories we cherish to this day and have made our frequent return visits particularly special. Working on our first fixer-upper home, the birth of our first (and as it turned out only) daughter, bucking and splitting wood in the bush surrounding the city of Mission, taking the youth on outings and being able to influence them to have a relationship with Christ – all these form a collage of special memories that we would hold dear for the rest of our lives.

It was the flood of all these memories that preoccupied my thoughts, as I left the country road behind and entered the still-sleeping town of Abbotsford to pick up the moving truck. But along with the good thoughts and feelings, there were also the mixed emotions of some of the more difficult times that we had been through during the last year there. Due to financial pressures, after only one year in the church, the assembly was no longer able to provide us with a salary. This sudden change of events forced us to pause and take stock again. By this time, however, we were at a *real* dining room table, as we were using our ironing board for its intended purpose! At the time we could not see how God could use this unexpected curve ball which facing us. We did not feel the time was right for us to be seeking to serve in another church, for we were just beginning to see some fruit from our efforts among the youth and we felt that we should stay to see a few of these things through.

So, as I had done at various times during college, I picked up my tool belt again to provide for the financial needs of our young family. Though I remembered hearing the saying, "If you are a jack of all trades, you will be the master of none," it actually seemed that my "jack of all trades" ability had come in rather handy over the years. Through all sorts of odd jobs, from tar and gravel roofing, wood window construction, siding installation, and renovations, God had always seemed to bless the work of my hands. This had enabled Nancy to be a stay-at-home Mom, which was important for us. So for that next year I worked construction during the day and in the church during the evenings and on weekends. And in between, I tried to do my best as a husband and new father. I am sure I must have slept at some time during that year: I just can't remember when!

But after a year of that schedule, it became apparent that I needed to make some changes. By this time things among the youth had stabilized and we had felt God release us from our responsibilities at the church. We had put our house on the market, and during the course of the one year that it took to sell, I continued to do construction work and we attended the church now as members with very few responsibilities. This, too, was a learning experience that God had designed just for us. Though I had let my name be known within denominational circles for another pastoral opportunity, we were increasingly becoming aware that our place was not to be in a typical pastoral setting. God had again begun to stir the same burden that He had placed in my heart as a young boy, which had been confirmed on several occasions since.

I had grown up in a Christian home, a home where prayer was important and following Christ was a priority. Though I grew up in a home where my parents loved and followed Christ, the pressures and complexities of my parents' lives resulted in them separating while I was still a pre-teen. Though there is always enough blame to go around in any family breakup, over the years it has become easier for me to view my parents as real people, and be able to place their struggles in an adult context, as opposed to seeing them only through a child's eyes. But in spite of all this, though I am not sure where or when it exactly originated, I found myself growing up with a sense of destiny and purpose.

In the Old Testament, the Lord came to Jeremiah and He said, "Before I formed you in the womb I knew you, before you were born I set you apart" (1:4-5). I remember hearing my mother tell how the doctor had advised her to not have any more children (which may explain something about me!), after having three daughters and one son already. She had just lost a baby before I was born and had prayed that if God would grant her another son, she would give him to the Lord. So I arrived to the planet as the last child of five and have been *the baby* ever since. But whether we know the details of our birth or not, God has formed each of us in the womb and has set us apart. No one's arrival is an accident or without purpose.

Yet we often have the same self-doubts as Jeremiah had. We remind the Lord of our frailties and our own particular liabilities, which many of us rehearse in our minds for years. In Jeremiah's case it was his youthfulness and his inability to speak. Ironically, growing up, these were also two negatives on the top of my list of excuses. I tried to use them so as to provide myself with some wiggle room for not doing God's will. But God has called all of us and He has given us not only general marching orders, but specific purposes to fulfill within his overall plan to reach the nations. Some of us are *goers*, others are *senders,* but we are all called to participate in reaching *all* people – from our own neighbourhood to the ends of the earth – with the love of the Father.

It was not until many years later that, as an adult, I heard from a cousin the innate sense of personal mission I must have felt from even a very early age. I say "must have" for I do not have personal memories of this at such an early age. However, I can still remember visiting this cousin's farm, which was at the end of a narrow country lane. Our visits there always coincided with going to Gramma's house, who lived close. Going to Gramma's house in rural Alberta was a Sunday tradition. I remember the car being packed and preparations made, as if this was going to be an African safari into the wilderness for forty days. In actuality, it was only an hour or an hour and a half drive from the city, depending on whether Dad felt like he needed to "clean the carbon out of the engine" that day! As a child, I could only imagine how much carbon the huge Ford Meteor "boat" with the large V8 engine could accumulate, for it seemed to need frequent "cleaning out." But *carbon* or not, we would soon leave the city behind and enter another world of farms and acreages.

Usually after visiting Gramma, there was just enough time left for a quick visit to my father's step-brother and our cousins. This was always exciting, for it meant going to what seemed to me to be a "real" farm – no electricity and no running water! Their little house was at the end of a long dirt road, bordered by crops on either side that were higher than the car. There was a *real* barn with all the *real* barn smells and the excitement of being able to explore the outdoors. Being from the city, this captivated my young imagination.

Claus, my cousin, had a drum set which seemed to fill his entire room. My memories of those late nights before returning home to the city were of jumping on the bed to the beat of his drums (which may explain my later interest in Africa!). After those childhood days, it was some twenty years before we would meet again. By then Claus would have a family and had developed a personal relationship with the Lord, as well as writing and performing songs as a family.

On one of my visits, after we had made contact again as adults, he told me of how at five or six years of age, I had clearly related to him that, "I knew what I was going to do with my life." Though I could not remember this, for all the intervening years he had distinctly remembered this young cousin from the city telling him that he was going to be a missionary overseas, apparently between bouncing on his bed while he played the drum set!

But God takes each of us on our own journey. Even though we may not recognize them as such at the time, it is important for each of us to place some stones by the side of the road to remind us of those times in our lives. This is not just for the "full-time minister" types, but also for each of us. God does not have the "A" plan for those in full-time ministry and a "B" plan for all others. *We are all ministers. We all have a call on our lives. We all have a purpose to fulfill.* It is a myth (and bad theology) that those in *the* ministry are the *really* called ones and all other Christians are only there to fill in the backfield. Scripture teaches that we are *all* ministers and we *all* have a God-given purpose. God has uniquely placed you where you are and has given you a specific sphere of influence. No one else can be as effective as you can be in that place that God has called you to be.

While the Lord had called Jeremiah, he too wrestled with this calling. Perhaps this is why, through this same prophet, God emphasizes, "For I know the plans I have for you," declares the Lord, "plans to prosper you and not to harm you, plans to give you hope and a future" (29:11). On that day in September 1988, little did I know how much deeper I would have to rest on this promise – not only later that day but also in the days to come.

Those childhood years inevitably melted into the teenager years. I am sure it would make interesting reading to recount all the wild oats I sowed as a rebellious teenager, but it never really quite happened that way. While I was no model child or particularly "saintly," I never did go through a period of abandoning the faith that was passed down to me. In spite of a less than perfect home-life, I found myself following after God and desiring to be closer to him. "Hardly a testimony worth repeating," or so I thought for many years. But particularly as I entered ministry and began working with youth, I began to see the blessing of not having dabbled in a sinful lifestyle. While it may seem as if it provides great fodder to make a spectacular testimony, it inevitably creates baggage and scars that need to be dealt with as an adult.

While we know that God forgives and restores, often there are issues that need to be dealt with that can become hindrances for years to come. As an adult, I began to realize that it was also a testimony to God's faithfulness to have been kept from a life of rebellion and destructive behaviour during those transitional teen years. If you have a Christian heritage, having accepted the baton of faith passed on to you from previous generations, recognize this as a privilege and realize that God has kept you and will use your strength in others' lives. It is as great a testimony to God's redemptive power that He also uses those who may have struggled in their faith as teenagers or came to a faith in God later in life. There are no second-class Christians; we are all on level ground around the cross.

The tightknit friendships developed within my church youth group were ones that would last into adulthood. Skiing and hiking trips to the Rocky Mountains were not only memories to be savoured, but times of mentoring by other Christian young men. Even before the word "discipleship" became popular, men like Wilf and Adey became those role models that we needed; showing us how to live a Christian life in a real, authentic, and fun way.

Perhaps some of the most memorable times as a teen were the times spent at family and youth camp at Alberta Beach. As any self-respecting teen, we did our fair share of pranks – simple but fun activities like throwing the girls off the end of the pier, clothes and all (something that their parents did not particularly appreciate). Then of course there was the occasional skipping of afternoon meetings to go waterskiing (and I thought I would never tell), and sneaking out of the dormitories in the middle of the night to play "Flying Dutchmen." But in spite of all the fun and games, I will never forget the summer when I was still thirteen years old. It occurred on one of those warm summer nights on the prairies, when the bugs and moths swarmed around every light and mosquitoes the size of birds feasted on any open skin.

As was common, the missionary speaker had called everyone wanting to dedicate their lives to God afresh to the front of the tabernacle. The old tabernacle at Alberta Beach Camp, with its original clap-board exterior siding and exposed interior wood frame construction, held many memories. Positioned next to the lake, with its large platform area and plain light bulbs which dangled from the rafters by long electrical wiring, it was the centre of spiritual life on the campground. Even after the new modern, multi-purpose building was built years later, it still held its own as the *place to be if you really wanted to meet God.* This continued to be the case, even after the wood chips and sawdust was replaced with indoor/outdoor carpet. Though we never really fully appreciated this as youth, there was something about that old tabernacle which seemed to prove the staying power of a faith that the preceding generation had proven. Looking past the worn wood with its accompanying aged odour, our annual pilgrimage to this site seemed to communicate the sense of stability that only comes from a faith that has been proven by past generations. A *pile of stones*, if you will, that previous generations could point to and explain the character of God and his dealings in their lives. It was as if this old *Tabernacle* was a public pile of memorial stones, there for all to see.

It was within that setting that I found myself as a young boy of thirteen. On that night I was on my knees at the front of that old tabernacle. The missionary had given the appeal and the altar area was full of people kneeling in the soft, albeit somewhat dusty, sawdust. On that warm summer evening I became consciously aware that God was calling me for service on the foreign mission field. In the following days, as I gazed across the lake with the sun casting its long shadows across the water, I could only dream of what lands I would see, and what adventures were ahead. While the possibilities seemed endless, I was still too young to envision how this little seed of a vision could, or would, ever become a reality.

Over the next few years, though, I continued preparing academically in high school, as if I were going to attend university. I took drafting courses leading towards a career in architecture or engineering, but I always had a sense that God would open up another door, before the eventuality of enrolling in university. I knew that I did not just want to make this happen myself, but given the opportunity I would walk through any door God opened. So when my sister, Christal, happened to leave a brochure for a discipleship school at our house during the last few months of grade twelve, I knew that this was the door God was putting in front of me. The motto of the school was "To know God and make Him known!" That is what I knew I needed and what I wanted. Regardless of what I would eventually do in life, to have the opportunity to take the time to seek him was what I knew I needed to do then. With that certainty, and the support of my father, I made the decision to take the step and leave the security of what I had known in Edmonton and go to college in the United States, which at the time seemed much further than the actual fifteen hundred mile drive. It was a fork in the road that was to affect the rest of my life quite profoundly.

2

One September Long Weekend

My thoughts of the past were interrupted by the present, as I geared the truck down, preparing to back down the driveway of our Mission home. By this time, the sun was already radiating its warmth, almost as if realizing that in a few short weeks it would no longer have the same power that it had had all summer. We had purchased a split level home for the amount that one could easily spend on a nice car these days. It was nestled on a lot which was lower than the front road with a downward slope from front to back. Though it had been a foreclosure that had required lots of work, it had been a fun and rewarding experience. This, our first home, had been a real blessing. It was with a certain amount of pride that I viewed the yard spread out below me, as I prepared to back the truck down the driveway. In only a couple of short years it had been transformed from what looked like an abandoned piece of property, into a home – our home.

I slowly reversed the large five ton truck down our driveway, stopping just in front of the carport. The carport, which was attached to the side of our home, was a trussed roof with no actual walls. The trusses and rafters merely rested on posts and beams on one side and were connected to the house on the other side. As I got out of the truck, I realized that the truck had no blocks to place behind the tires and so I found a use for some of those large maple burls that had been too big to burn in our wood stove the previous winter.

By this time, Nancy and Alysia were up and around and Nancy was making the final preparations before a few friends were to arrive to help us move. While in some ways this was a hard move for both of us, away from many good memories and friends, we also had a sense that we were embarking on a new chapter in our lives. But the reality was that we did not know exactly what that new chapter was. While from God's perspective there was a plan that He was unfolding, from our perspective it seemed that we were just stumbling along in the dark, doing our best to be faithful and live a life of integrity, but with no clear idea how the current events of our lives were part of the big plan. While we often see how his hand was clearly at work in our lives after the fact, during the process we are sometimes in the dark. Perhaps that is why it is called a life of faith. Our trust is in Him and his character, more than even our ability to figure it all out. We often read biblical stories, and God's ways seem so self-evident as the narration explains how it will end and offers God's perspective along the way. Unfortunately, in our own lives, we often feel we are making it up along the way and we don't always see God's hand. It is usually only at some later date that we finally gain God's perspective.

In this case, the process of selling the house and moving closer to the majority of my building clients had taken much longer than we anticipated and so we were really ready to move on. The house had been on the market for a year, during which time I had continued to apply siding on new and older homes; we also continued to attend the same church which we had been invited to serve in only several years earlier. Over the previous few months I had begun to purchase my own construction equipment and since there was more work than I could handle, I had also hired a couple of men. Yet in spite of the success of my newly formed company, there were nagging questions which seemed omnipresent: "How does doing this fit into your plan, Lord?" and "How do I reconcile spending most of my time wrestling with wood and siding, when I have a burden for the nations?"

Over the previous two years, as I had continued to serve in the church as a volunteer and focus on the construction company, nothing had opened up for us in the area of full-time ministry. Though I had graduated *Summa cum Laude* from the BTh program and was even Valedictorian (a real shock), my inquiries regarding a mission placement with the denomination of which I was a licensed minister had not borne any fruit. It seemed that it was either not God's timing or He had another plan. I must admit, instead of having noble faith, my attitude was more of resignation to just do whatever was before me. I had been instilled with a sense of the importance of providing for the needs of one's family and so, since it seemed that that was all I could do, I endeavoured to do it to the best of my ability. *Had I missed God by not pursuing architecture, instead being sentenced to a life of manual labour as a siding contractor? Had all the years in Bible School also been a waste of time, while my peers had made "real" careers for themselves?* These were often the questions that were just below the surface as I went through the routine of bidding on jobs, delivering siding and dangling off ladders and planks on the side of countless buildings.

But on that morning in September I had a more immediate concern. I had backed the truck down the driveway to within a foot of the carport and realized that I needed to drive it forward a bit so that we would have more headroom to get into the back of the truck. Our front door was the only door facing the driveway and so to load our things on to the truck we had to go under the carport. As I jumped into the cab of the truck to pull it ahead, it was with no comprehension as to how the events of the next few seconds were going to impact all of our lives so profoundly. As I released the clutch to pull the truck a few feet forward, up the driveway, I made what was to be a fateful error. With not enough engine speed to pull the heavy truck up in second gear, it stalled and lurched backwards. To my horror, instead of making progress in a forward motion up the driveway, I sensed myself lurch backwards, over the maple burls, making impact with the peaked roof of the carport.

The sickening feeling of no engine power, and then the devastating crash of several thousand pounds of wooden posts, beams, trusses and roofing material hitting the driveway are sounds that are forever etched in my mind. But there was another sound, more terrible than ripping lumber, that also was to become part of my permanent memory. That was the cries of my wife and daughter. As I jumped out of the cab of the truck and turned towards the carport, I saw that the twenty-foot structure was largely intact, but now it was laying on the driveway, having fallen back towards our front door. It was with the numbness of shock that I realized that my wife and daughter were underneath all that wood somewhere. As I searched for a way to get under the carport the sound of my wife screaming, "Phil!" and the cries of my daughter rang in my ears.

When I had gone to move the truck, Nancy had waited under the carport with our nearly two year old daughter on her hip. We were later to discover that the large main beam of the carport had travelled backwards, with the one end resting on the concrete step by our front door. This created about an eighteen inch space in which Nancy and Alysia were lying. Without this they would have surely been crushed. This was to be one of what was to be many miracles in the days and months ahead.

I crawled into this space and found Nancy and Alysia laying in this small area created by the beam. I less than ceremoniously pulled Alysia out by one arm, and though she was still sobbing she seemed to have no major visible injuries. I handed her to a neighbour, who had arrived on the scene, before going in after Nancy. It seemed that as the main beam had collapsed, it had just missed Alysia, who was resting on Nancy's left hip. However, it had landed on Nancy's right hip and had thrown her to the ground. As I went back under to be with my wife, the wail of the sirens announced the arrival of the fire and rescue crews. Nancy was still conscious and so we prayed together. She wanted to try getting up immediately, but I knew that that would be impossible. For as I had gone under the structure the first time I had noticed that her leg was at a strange angle. As I had tried to straighten it, it was with a sickening feeling that I noticed that her right foot had been severed at the ankle.

We were to find out that the technical medical term was a *Severe Compound Dislocation*. At the time, all I knew was that I could see the white inside of her ankle socket at the end of her leg. At those times, the mind finds it hard to accept what the eyes are telling it. Yet I had a growing awareness of the gravity of the situation as I attempted to straighten her leg from the strange angle it was in. But as I began to move it I realized that her foot was still attached to her leg by a flap of skin on the inside portion of the ankle. In order to move her leg I needed to simultaneously grab her shoe, which still contained her severed foot. As we were to also discover later, this small piece of skin was a life-link to the foot – a small detail which would turn out to be yet another *not-so-small* miracle.

———————◆◄———————

It was only one week before that fateful day in September and it was the second time my father had come to visit us in Canada. I am sure his main motivation was to see his first granddaughter, who at the time was nearly two years old! Phil and I had been married for about six years, and he had come for a visit along with my brother, Tony, and my Grandmother. Now that my sister was working for the Airlines, he was making good use of his flying privileges and, rather than coming alone, he chose to bring my Grandmother and brother with him. Looking back, I realize Dad knew it would be safer for Grandma to come along, instead of leaving her alone with Tony in California. By this time I had already heard stories from my younger sister of how Tony would still try to beat her up if she said anything to upset him. During his visit I found myself praying for our protection with Tony in the house. Even with his medicine, which my father made sure to give him, Tony would often pace the floors, deciding to eat after the meal was finished and the dishes were put away. Though we managed, it was very awkward to have him with us.

Meanwhile we took advantage of the warm August weather, seeing the sights around Vancouver. Because my Grandmother was eighty-six year old and would often be out of breath, we rented a wheelchair which worked out great. We were able to walk at a brisker pace and Grandma was happy too! I will never forget the time we were at a park as Alysia pushed me around in the wheelchair as she giggled. Although it was fun I could not help praying, "Dear God, please don't ever let me end up in one of these!"

Soon after my family had left to go back home, I had felt directed to go on a fruit and vegetable fast for three days. It was during this time that I had a sense that we were in a spiritual battle and that I should walk around the perimeter of our property and pray for God's protection.

The day before our move Phil had asked me to courier the contract papers between the lawyer's offices. As I was driving in the car, I felt as though the devil himself was sitting next to me in the car, tempting me with the power that he could give to me, if I would only surrender my will to him. I had a sense that he was attempting to tantalize me with this offer, but the offer did not tempt me at all and I quickly dismissed it in Jesus' name. As I continued to drive the Mission-Abbotsford highway, I sensed that the Lord was saying that it was He who had a purpose for my life. I somewhat flippantly thought, "Yes, I know, I know, you have a purpose for everyone's life." While I acknowledged this truth, I only did so superficially, for I was still waiting for God to share something more "profound" with me, during the third and final day of my fast. I had no idea what the next day would hold. I had never had an accident or traumatic event ever occur in my life. I had always imagined that life would be free of mishaps; after all, *God was on my side, wasn't He?* The Christian life was a protected life, wasn't it? Yet as it happened, the third and final day of my fast happened to be the day that we were scheduled to move from our home in Mission to another town about an hour away.

That morning there was really little left to do, as most of our things were already packed. Phil had already left to pick up the moving van and only the floor under the washer and dryer needed cleaning. "Things are going along well," I thought. By the time I had moved our car out of the carport, I could see Phil rounding the corner with the moving truck. With nothing left to do inside, Alysia and I watched Phil back the truck down the driveway. As he got out, he went rummaging around the yard looking for wood to put under the tires, muttering something about how they should have included some blocks for the tires of the truck.

As he opened up the back sliding door of the truck it was obvious that it was too close to the carport and so he again got in the truck to move it a few feet forward up the driveway. From my vantage point under the carport, all I could see was the large back of the truck. But instead of the truck pulling away from me and the carport – it lurched backwards! From then on, everything seemed to happen in slow motion, and fast motion, all at the same time. The few nails that were holding the carport to the house ripped out with a terrible screeching sound, like fingernails on a chalkboard. As I looked up, I could see the beam coming down, as it caught me on the right hip. With Alysia straddled on my left arm, it was as if I was frozen and could not move – only watch. It was as if I was detached from the scene, watching someone else's movie and yet somehow still a member of the cast. Though my eyes were open during those few seconds, for a moment I could no longer see what was going on around me; the seconds seemed to last forever.

"Was I going to go down that long tunnel with the light at the end, that I had heard others talk about?" "Was I already dead, in the process of dying, or still going to die?" "Maybe," I thought, "I would just wake up in heaven?"

When my eyes came back into focus, it was obvious that I was still in this world. I could not see too much, but I was aware that Alysia was on her hands and knees next to my side crying. In my state of mind, her crying seemed to be a good thing. "At least it meant that she was still alive and not fatally injured," I reasoned. By this time Phil had crawled under the carport and had dragged Alysia to safety. As for me, it seemed as if electricity was shooting up and down my arms and legs. It was unbearable. It made me want to scream. I felt a warm liquid trickle between my legs. As Phil tried to see if I could talk, I was trying to get up. "Yes, I'm gonna get up and walk away from here!" I told myself with great faith! But to no avail. As we prayed together, all I knew was that my back was aching unbearably.

After we prayed together, it seemed Phil was gone and replaced by a stranger, who began asking me a lot of questions. "Why was he asking me if it was my time of month?" I couldn't help but wonder. That trickle must have been blood, but I didn't feel any pain. While I was still conscious, I was not all there. I noticed lots of activity as jacks and inflatable bags were put under the carport, trying to raise it, so that they could get me out. After what seemed like an eternity, but what was actually closer to forty-five minutes, they had dismantled, moved, or whatever they did to the carport, so that I could be put on a stretcher. As for the stretcher it felt like it was only a hard piece of wood and I kept asking for some padding. While the paramedics were kind enough, my continued pleading for more padding must not have seemed like a high priority to them! Once out from under the carport, I was quickly put in the ambulance and whisked the short distance to the hospital.

———————◆———————

After getting Alysia out from under the carport and praying with Nancy, the next thing I knew a firefighter was asking me to leave my wife and come out from under the carport. Though I protested, he led me to the ambulance so that I could be with my daughter. There are times when it is really obvious that there is nothing really to do but pray. I mean nothing. We had committed ourselves to God during the good times and now was one of those gut check times when we had to commit our lives in his hands – during a bad time. In some ways it is easier to do that when you have no real choice, while it is often more difficult to do when there seem to be other options to choose between. It seemed that at this point Nancy still had her life, but as to the use of her leg, being able to walk again, and any other details, there were far more questions than answers.

I must confess that I have never felt comfortable in hospitals. For that matter, I have never even liked watching the popular medical emergency television shows. I have always appreciated those who have chosen this profession and know the necessity of hospitals, but I have always tried to spend the least amount of time as possible in them! However, over the next few years I would see more than my fair share of the inside of these institutions. As I sat in the back of the ambulance on that morning, tightly holding my daughter, I would have exchanged anything – a successful career or ministry, life itself – all to turn the clock back a few minutes. It is at those times that the truly important things come into focus. While trying to comfort Alysia, I could not shake the image of my wife laying like a raggedy-Ann doll under the carport of our home. It was almost too much to bear. Along with dealing with the realities of her physical situation was the realization that it was I who had caused the events.

But rarely do the times of tragedy afford a person the opportunity for measured reflections. Within minutes we were at the local hospital of our small town and decisions needed to be made. As Nancy's clothing was cut away and a large tube was jabbed into her abdomen to determine if there was internal bleeding, it seemed we were again spectators at an event that somehow included us, yet at the same time did not. While we were the centre of the activity, it was as if we were somehow detached from the important events taking place around us.

During that next hour, things seemed to move at a frightfully slow pace. Though it was by now turning into a nice warm summer day, Nancy could not get warm enough, even with a pile of blankets on top of her. Her body was obviously in shock and the doctors were first trying to stabilize her vital organs, while still trying to determine the full extent of her injuries. The most obvious was her still detached foot, which lay at a weird right angle to her leg. A thoughtful nurse had by then propped it up on a pillow, which only seemed to accentuate its unnatural position. Nancy had begun to complain about her "sore foot" and one of the attending nurses, who happened to be from our church, even began to massage her detached extremity.

"Have you seen your foot?" she asked. And though Nancy looked in the general direction of the x-rays hanging on the wall, without her glasses, which had flown off along the way, she could not see the condition of her leg and foot.

"Just rub my foot, it is really sore!" was Nancy's reply. Though it seemed unbelievable, the nurse rubbed her detached foot to Nancy's grateful, "Thanks, that feels better!"

For me, nothing seemed to be moving fast enough. "When are you going to attach the foot? How long do we have, before it will no longer be possible to reattach it?" I asked the attending doctor privately. These were the questions that were uppermost in my mind, which I repeatedly queried anybody that looked *official* and would listen. But nobody was willing to provide any answers at that point. As we were to find out later, most blood vessels to the foot are located on the instep side of the ankle, the exact flap of skin that still attached her foot to the rest of her leg. While her foot injury was serious, she had other injuries that we were not aware of, which were of an even more life-threatening variety.

As my wife's vital signs began to stabilize, the x-rays began to come back. The report was that it seemed that her back was not broken, but that they had discovered a large wound between her buttocks that ran internally to the base of her tailbone. While more tests would have to be done regarding her back, this soft tissue injury by her tailbone, which had occurred as the beam hit her hip and caused her to sit down hard on the asphalt, was potentially more life threatening than any of her other injuries.

By now more family had arrived at the hospital and we prayed regarding what that next step should be. We were currently at a rather small hospital and there was a large hospital within an hour's drive that had a large trauma unit. After some discussion, we decided that it would be best to move Nancy to a surgeon who had the greatest amount of experience possible. Though local surgeons insisted that the operations could be done there, I insisted that she be moved to this large trauma unit. It was nearly lunch time before we drove by ambulance towards New Westminster and the trauma unit of Royal Columbian Hospital. The drive was a bit surreal. I sat in the front seat of the ambulance, making small talk with the driver, while it seemed we meandered at a leisurely pace towards the hospital. As in the emergency room which we had just left, everyone seemed to have all the time in the world. All I could think about was getting my wife into surgery and have her put back together. It seemed to me that full lights and sirens would be more appropriate, a fact that I mentioned to the driver.

"Not necessary," was the reply, "it goes almost as fast this way" ... hmm. Let just say, I was having trouble reconciling the facts as I knew them regarding my wife's condition and this *logic* of the ambulance driver.

Eventually we arrived at the trauma unit of Royal Columbian Hospital. Things seemed to begin to happen at a much more rapid pace, more typical of what one would expect to see in a movie set of an emergency room. Almost before her stretcher had stopped rolling out of the ambulance, I was signing forms of release and who knows what else. It did not seem to make much sense to read them too closely at that point. After all, what was my choice – to fix her up on my own!? After several hours of uncertainty, it was just reassuring to know that her injuries were going to be attended to. There was nothing more I could do but wait and pray.

A rather sombre surgeon met me just before the operation and explained the obvious, "There are no guarantees as to what we will find and what will work, but we will do our best." That much I had assumed.

As I sat in the waiting room for the surgery to end, other family members began to arrive, as did Miss Clemo whom we had served with together at the Mission church. It was now early afternoon and I heard, almost as if from a distance, that Alysia was with an Aunt and doing well... another brother-in-law had rented a second moving truck (as the first one had been impounded by the police as evidence) ... part of our fence adjacent to a neighbour's driveway had been removed in order to move our things from the rear of the house, this being necessary as the carport had collapsed in the driveway by our front door and the police would not allow it to be cleared until the next day. But all this information, various details, other voices, and even the typical hospital noises seemed to fade into the background, as my wife went into surgery. As for me, I was again alone with my thoughts.

3

Marriage and Montezuma's Revenge

As I sat numbly in the waiting room, the day's events churned over and over in my mind. Regardless of how I reviewed the day's events in my mind, it seemed that I could not escape the personal blame and recriminations.

The list of "If only's" was loud and long. *If only I had not backed down the driveway so far the first time. If only I had not tried to pull ahead. If only I had told Nancy to go inside while I pulled ahead.* But it *had* happened and that was that. Nothing could or would change that now. Perhaps the more difficult questions to answer were the deeper ones. *Would Nancy ever walk again? Would she ever have use of her bodily functions? Would she be able to have more children? How was I going to look after our daughter, while finishing the houses I was working on?*

But the most difficult question of all was directed to God. *How did this fit into God's plan for our lives? Had we not done our best to follow Him, even at personal sacrifice?* These were not questions regarding his existence or even his sovereignty. Rather they were anguished ones questioning his goodness and control in our lives.

While I knew it was only our faith in Him that would get us through this dark valley, this did not eliminate the *Why* questions. And while God does not always answer the *Why* questions, He also does not condemn us for asking them. *How could the frustrations of having our ministry on the shelf over the last few years and now this tragic accident, ever turn out for good and fulfill God's purpose in our lives?* It was hard to believe that life, which had seemed so full of promise and hope only a few short years earlier, seemed so bleak now.

As I waited for the results of the operation, my thoughts took me back to the time when I was only seventeen. I could still feel that sense of hope in the future, as I had bid farewell to the city of Edmonton, to go to college in the States. I had left with a longing to experience more of God and learn to make Him known. It had been only several months earlier that I had seen a brochure from the school, *Genesis*. Its focus was to help the student develop a strong personal relationship with God. Though I had grown up in a Christian home and had never turned from my personal faith, I had a burning desire to get to know God even better. I wanted to make my life count and so wanted to determine what his specific purpose was for my life.

I had not left Edmonton alone, but along with a van-load of family members who had accompanied me to the small town of Corvallis, Oregon, which was to be home for the next ten months. The excitement of new adventure seemed to increase as we travelled from the flat prairie surrounding Edmonton, through the Canadian Rocky Mountains and finally to Vancouver on the West Coast. From there, we crossed the border into Washington State, passing through Seattle and finally Portland, Oregon. After the family dropped off "the baby of the family" in the sleepy college town of Corvallis, it was time for them to head back home to Canada. As the van pulled out of the cul-de-sac, I turned to go into the townhouse unit that was to be my new home, along with six other students. Barely two months out of high school, I was really on my own for the first time. The next few days and weeks were full of new experiences and meeting new people. The combination of classes and the emphasis on practical application of biblical truth in every relationship, encouraged much personal growth in the following months. These lessons built upon pre-existing spiritual foundations which I had received at home and growing up in a church. But it was during this time, as an early adult, that spiritual life disciplines were formed.

Yet I was also going to gain something else from my time at college which I would have for the rest of my life. It all had a rather inauspicious beginning as a roommate and I took Lynette and her friend, Nancy, to the country fair. Being from the city, the nuances of the country fair were lost on me, though I was later told that I kept up a steady stream of repartee and witty comments. Actually, as Nancy tells the story, I was fairly obnoxious and loud, as well as talking incessantly about the girl I was dating from back home. . . so much for first impressions! While in those early weeks my heart continued to beat for a girl I had left in Canada, time had a way of confirming that this high school relationship was no more than just that.

Over the next few months, dating and "finding a mate" was definitely low on both of our priority lists. I was feeling God stir within me that call that I had first consciously responded to in what seemed a far away place – something that had been deposited in my heart while on my knees in an old tabernacle next to a lake on the Canadian prairies. My youthful zeal to reach the world for Christ did not seem to leave room for such *earthly* matters as marriage! No, that would definitely have to wait until I had tamed a few lions and slain a few dragons. Those initial dreams, which had been birthed in my heart at a camp during my youth, were soon to become very practical. Though I was now far away, geographically, from that camp, the dreams seemed as real and close as ever. Little did I know that by Christmas of that year I was going to be even further from home – though closer to my dream.

It all began with a guest speaker one morning in chapel. He was a rather unassuming man from an organization called *Operation Mobilization (OM)* and gave a simple appeal to anyone wanting to go to Mexico for a Christmas Outreach. After his presentation it was as clear to me as handwriting on the wall that I needed to join what I was sure would be a whole group of students going on this outreach from the school. The OM plan was fairly simple: first, get permission from one's parents; next, don't tell anybody except God about the financial need; and, finally, read a ton of books by the founder of the organization, George Verwer.

With some reservation, my father gave permission, perhaps not realizing what I was getting into. As I continued to make preparations it also became clear that I was the only one from the whole student body that had decided to go, something I hadn't quite bargained on. But since I had already begun my preparations, I continued, thinking that somehow all the details would work out. Years later I discovered that there had been one other student who had wanted to go, but could not get the necessary permission from her parents. You may have guessed – it was that dark-haired, dreamy-eyed girl that I had so *impressed* at the country fair (though I was not going to notice her in any serious way till several months later, after that Christmas).

As November of 1980 turned into December, not only did I turn eighteen, but I was busy reading the mountain of books from this radical missionary, George Verwer. My initial impression was that this guy was out of balance in his passion to serve God and reach the world, but I found my heart also began to be gripped by this same passion to reach the world for Christ. It was as if his words not only reflected what I felt in my heart, but also motivated me to press on to give my life to the Lord on an even deeper level.

Although I continued with my preparations for the Mexico trip, the details did not seem to be coming together. First, there was nobody going from my region in Oregon with whom I could get a ride. Then there was the issue of not having enough funds. After I had paid the registration fee, I had no extra funds left at all. While my Dad would have wired me some funds, I felt the need to prove God in this on my own. I needed to see Him as my provider. While the unknowns remained unknown, I continued to finish reading all the necessary books. This principle of continuing to do the only thing I knew to do in the face of unknowns was a principle that was to become a life habit in the years to come. With only a few days left before I had to leave I found an anonymous envelope in my mailbox with some cash for the trip! This coincided with a phone call from the local OM representative, informing me that there was a carload of three Canadians coming down from Surrey, British

Columbia. All I had to do was get the few miles to the I-5 freeway and they would pick me up from there.

Well, as most students had already left for the Christmas break, my choices to hitch a ride from Corvallis to the interstate freeway were very limited. But as I finished packing my backpack, my roommate agreed to drop me off at the interstate diner where I was to meet a "white Plymouth" coming south from Canada. Even for a "hey what could go wrong" idealistic youth, as I waited by the diner in the dark and 10:30 pm. came and went, I sure hoped that I had not miss some important rendevous detail. But eventually a car fitting that description with Canadian license plates drove into the diner. With only a few introductions, I joined the three other zealous youth and we were off down the road heading for Mexico.

The next night we made it as far as southern California. Someone in the car knew a certain missionary whom we could stay with. All I remember hearing at the time was that his first name was "Don." They knew he lived somewhere in Pasadena, though they did not have his exact address. "But, after all, how hard could it be to find it anyway?" we naively thought. Never having been in the Los Angeles area, we were just glad that he lived in the *smaller* suburb of Pasadena. But as soon as we read the first freeway exit sign, "Pasadena, Next 8 Exits," it began to dawn on us that this would not be as easy as we had thought! After a few hours of searching and several detours, we eventually arrived at his home. Once there, it was hard to miss the many foreign artifacts that decorated the home. The most notable in my mind was the unique zebra foot lamp on the coffee table. It was obvious that this guy had been there, done that, and had the T-shirt to prove it! Not having read his book *Peace Child* at that time, I was unaware that our host was none other than *the* Don Richardson, a modern day mission hero and respected missiological thinker. Years later I would regret not having taken the opportunity to pepper him with many more questions that night in his home!

With four drivers, we were able to drive non-stop from LA, across Arizona, New Mexico and Texas. As I had never been to these states, I wanted to be awake every minute to absorb every cactus, every town, every city. I wanted to drink it all in. Several sunrises and sunsets later, we eventually arrived in El Paso,

Texas and crossed the border into Mexico. This was also my first experience to be in a developing nation. It all seemed so strange, and yet at the same time exhilarating. The next ten days were spent witnessing, praying and sharing our testimony in churches. As with most short term missions endeavours, I am sure we learned much more than those we had come to serve. (Not much consolation to the nationals or full time workers on the field, as I would discover later in life!). As many before us, who had had their first mission experience in Mexico, we were following in a tradition that still continues.

After basically only eating bread all the way down from Oregon, the local food that the church provided tasted great. For one particular meal, they had apparently even raided the local farms and provided us with green beans. "Ah yes, a common vegetable from back home," I thought. Mind you, after the first bite, I quickly discovered that these "green beans" tasted nothing like the ones back home! They were in fact jalapeno peppers and I learned to give them a wide berth for the rest of the trip!

I don't know if it was the diet of jalapenos, the meal in the village that looked like chicken, or the mistake of trying the local candy sold by the roadside vendors, but by Christmas Day I was not feeling so well . . .actually I felt quite sick. Most of the other team members had gone to local churches for festivities, but under the circumstances, I thought it would be best to stay within eyesight of a bathroom facility. As the jalapenos and other local delicacies began to work their magic, wisdom won over valour, and my decision to stay close to the facilities proved a wise one. These "facilities" were conveniently located in the centre of the walled compound where we were staying. Our accommodation was a room in which thirty of us slept side by side in our sleeping bags on a concrete floor. Since everyone else was gone, I was alone and found myself tossing and turning, unable to sleep.

As I got up to pace around the courtyard in the eerie light of the vintage street lamps, it was only the yelping of stray dogs fighting over their Christmas meal that interrupted my thoughts. In between my frequent trips to the facility, thanks to *Montezuma's Revenge*, I continued to pace back and forth on that dark, somewhat crisp night. I felt a bit like Jacob of old who wrestled with an angel.

But in my case, I seemed to be wrestling more with myself, my feelings, and coming face to face with what the ramifications of this *call* might actually mean in my life.

The camp meeting altar, where I had made that commitment, seemed a long way away and the grandiose dreams seemed to be turning into more of a nightmare. The realities of what missions was all about began to become more clear on that night. *Was I really ready to give my life away and embrace a missionary lifestyle?* As I continued to wrestle that night, in this strange place with its strange sounds and smells, God walked me back to that *sawdust trail,* and I began to see more clearly the obedience that that call would demand. I never saw any visions that night, nor an epiphany – just a clearer realization of what this walk with God may mean and what answering "Yes!" may entail.

Would I be willing to limit my rights to the "good life" and creature comforts so that others may hear this same Good News... News that for me had come so easily in the comfortable setting of a Christian home, a caring church, and youth camps next to a prairie lake in a far away place?

While the diet was not agreeing with me, and I would have liked to be with family on that Christmas Day, there was an even stronger yearning. God began to place a burden on my heart for the nations. But this time instead of an abstract, theoretical calling, I was being asked to make a more informed response, having a clearer understanding of what the cost could be. Would I still be willing? Pacing by myself on that cool night in Monclova, Mexico, I again reaffirmed my commitment to pursue what I had felt God say to my heart as a young teen. But this time it was on a deeper level.

Several days later, it was time for us to leave Mexico. We had made many new friends and had developed several relationships with other Mexican youth. I will never forget one young teen, whom I only knew as *Alex.* As our now "not so white" Plymouth headed out of Monclova, I saw Alex for the last time. He was standing on the dusty street corner waving to us as we left. As I turned to wave to him, I saw tears rolling down his face. I quickly asked the driver to stop and I ran back to give Alex a hug. It did not take much Spanish to understand the emotions of the moment.

He was feeling the imminent loss of some new found friends who had told him of Jesus, but who were now leaving. Even though I did not want to leave, I knew we had to, but the pain of having to leave new friends on the mission field would be something I would have on multiple occasions over the years to come. But on that day, as I jumped back into the car, I also choked back a few tears knowing that, if given the opportunity, I would be back on some mission field someday. In spite of the challenges, it was where I would feel most at home.

As we crossed back over the Mexico/Texas border, we were transported into another world. Only a few hours after leaving Monclova, somewhat tired and subdued, we rolled into the official sign of *real* civilization. I am, of course, referring to those famous *Golden Arches*. Unfortunately this coincided with the realization that I had no money left! But since we were only a two to three day drive from Oregon, it did not seem to be that big of a deal. "After all," I figured, "I could last that long." As it was, my *internal plumbing* was still getting back to normal.

But as I waited for my travelling companions, a total stranger approached me and, without any introduction, pressed ten dollars into my hand and said, "God told me to give this to you." With that he turned around and I never saw him again. A few minutes later, ordering a Big Mac and chocolate milkshake (I trace my love affair with this culinary delight back to that very day!), I was still a bit dumbfounded as to how God had chosen to provide for my need. There was even enough money left over (ah yes, the good ol'days!) to buy some bread for the rest of the trip back to Oregon. Over the next years God provided in many other more *natural* ways, but the message was clear: when God wants to provide, He can do so in any way He pleases.

A few days later I was dropped off back in Oregon, which had become "home." I dropped my backpack by the door and had the first warm shower I had had in some time, perhaps one of the best that I had ever had in my life thus far! In the following days and weeks I began to realize that this short trip to Mexico had been a pivotal experience in my life. But it was only years later that it become apparent to what extent it had crystalized the direction that my life would take. There were also many simple lessons that

God had begun to teach me – themes that he would continue to work on, and principles such as committing to step out even before all the "i's" are dotted and "t's" crossed, being willing to count the cost associated with obedience, and no matter how dark things may seem, recognizing that He is always present along the way.

But there was another *little* matter that was going to have an even bigger impact on my life... but this one *snuck up* on me.

As the dense Oregon fog of January gave way to longer days of sunshine and the spring of 1981, I found myself *bumping* into the same girl that I had first met at that country fair in October. While we had had very few conversations since, before Christmas I had been aware that there were plans for her to be married after graduation to a man she knew from her home town of South San Francisco.

Yet as the days of spring turned longer and warmer, I seemed to keep seeing this young lady out of the corner of my eye – regardless of where I sat in class. During coffee breaks we always seemed to be in the same area and soon we began to strike up more conversations. There was something intriguing and appealing about her. Beside her obvious good looks, with those big beautiful eyes and gorgeous hair, I was attracted by her shy composure, as I would incessantly tease her. As we developed a friendship over the weeks and months that followed, I discovered that she had broken off her relationship with the man from California. She also discovered that the relationship that I had had with the girl from my home town had long since failed the "separation" test. Yet, above all, we began to get to know each other and develop a growing friendship.

It was through this process that God began to teach us important lessons that would be the foundation of our relationship. Both of us had had a history of having many relationships with the opposite sex that were of a more romantic nature. While they had not necessarily been immoral, many had been less than God's best. Through teaching, we began to discover a new perspective on co-ed friendships. We began to see that it was not only possible, but preferable, to develop a friendship without all the complications that premature romantic feelings can produce. Of course, in time, some of these friendships with the other gender came to the inevitable fork in the road, but we saw the wisdom in not making a commitment based on the romance of the moment. During those last few months of our first school year we developed a good friendship, as we discussed issues, went for walks and got to know one another. This friendship was to stand us in good stead in the years ahead, especially during those times when the romantic feelings waned.

After our first year of studies, the school moved back to its roots in Santa Rosa, California. This would mean that, if we were accepted, our second year of college would be back in Nancy's home state. Since the second year of the program included taking on many leadership roles in the school, the process to be accepted included a personal interview with the staff. *Interview Week,* as it was called, was always an anxious time for students who felt they wanted to return to complete the second year. Initially it was unclear as to whether Nancy or I would be returning. Yet over time, quite independent from each other, we had both applied for the second year. During *Interview Week,* as others we knew were not accepted into the program, we were not sure if either of us would be. Yet we both did "pass" our interview, ensuring that we would be returning after the summer. As we said goodbye to each other that summer, we each seemed to know that in the fall we would have to make a decision regarding which direction our relationship would go. We promised to keep in touch over the summer and with that I headed north to spend the summer in Edmonton and she went south, to the *City on the Bay,* San Francisco.

A wise, and probably lonely, person once penned, "Absence makes the heart grow fonder." Well, that axiom pretty much summed up my summer of '81. *To ensure that we fully appreciated this truth,* Canada Post strategically scheduled a postal strike which lasted the whole summer of 1981. So much for keeping in touch (unfortunately e-mail had not yet become available). This curtailed any further communication we might of had over the summer, yet, as it turned out, this was to be a cloud with a silver lining. In an odd sort of way it caused each of us to evaluate our friendship and where it would lead once we were in school again. It was almost as if we were given eight weeks to determine this for ourselves, without direct personal contact with each other.

As the summer drew to a close, I picked the right moment to ask my father if I could take my little Pontiac Astre to college in California. I must have caught him at a weak moment, for he agreed! The downside, which I had not contemplated, was that once I got it there I never have enough money for gas! But perhaps the greatest miracle of all was that it actually made it there and back!

It did not take long to pack a few things into the back of the car as I began the journey to Santa Rosa. This time, however, I was not leaving Edmonton with a vanload of family, but accompanied only by my father, who was going to travel with me as far as Vancouver. From there I was on my own, travelling down the now familiar Interstate 5, through Washington and Oregon State and eventually arriving in northern California. What faith my father must have had to allow his eighteen year old son off on his own!

It was still summer as I arrived for the first time in the beautiful Napa Valley. The days were still warm, well past the time a northern Canadian boy was normally used to. Throughout that year, I never did tire of seeing the palm trees and vineyards which lined the country lanes and boulevards.

The intervening two months of separation had proven to both Nancy and me our desire to deepen our relationship. After having developed a good friendship the year before, as second year students it almost seemed strange to be one of the "official" couples at school. While the school's dating policy was strict, we found this beneficial, as it enabled our relationship to grow slowly and with accountability. The latter may be a bit of an understatement, as college life had the transparency of living in a fishbowl. But this intensity caused much growth in our personal lives as well as in our relationship.

In addition, to our personal growth, the second year program emphasized "making Christ known." As staff teachers and guest teachers, such as Winkie Pratney, Juan Carlos Ortiz, the Dawsons, and Judson Cornwall, shared from their hearts, we were taught that the real focus of ministry was *people*. It has little to do with the particular *position* one holds in a church, but rather our function of serving within the Body. Coming from a "churched" background, these were invaluable lessons and formed my philosophy of ministry for the years ahead.

The intensity and busyness of the program caused the months to fly by and before we knew it the Christmas break was just around the corner. Yet for an "official" couple, Christmas break brought pressures all of its own. It seemed to be school tradition, however unofficial, that the Christmas vacation was *make or break time* for the "official"couples of the school. It was either the time when the *wheels* would come off or the engagement ring went on! While it was not a hard and fast rule, the pressure was inevitable.

While I wasn't sure we were ready (or perhaps more accurately, if I was ready) for this, I also knew that I did not want to miss the opportunity the Christmas break afforded. So, confidently taking only half a step forward, we both decided to just *visit* Edmonton over Christmas. At the very least, I reasoned, Nancy would be able to see my *neck of the woods*. Over the last few months I had also met Nancy's family as we had periodically visited San Francisco, so it seemed only natural that the next step was for her to meet the rest of my family.

It was hard to believe that it had only been one short year earlier that I had been in Mexico, where I had renewed my obedience to the Lord in whatever He had for my life. While I did not want anything to stand in the way of this decision, I also wanted to be open to what God's plan was for Nancy and me as a couple. Though neither of us – at nineteen years young – was in a big rush, the end of the school year was only six months away. At that time each of us would go back to our respective corners of the world. So without being sure exactly where the road would lead, we found ourselves taking off together from the rain soaked San Francisco International Airport.

What I may have failed to mention to Nancy was exactly how cold it could be in Edmonton in the dead of winter. I had also not anticipated how small the Edmonton airport would seem in comparison to the one we had just left in San Francisco. But that would not be the end of the surprises. Instead of taxiing to the terminal, the plane stopped about one hundred yards away, which meant we had to walk to the terminal in the snow, as the ice crystals shimmered in the orange hue of the lights illuminating the apron area. Though we Canadians often, euphemistically, called this weather "fresh" (which is defined for all others as just plain cold), after a couple of winters away at school in southern climes, it felt much colder than I could even remember. I couldn't imagine how cold it must have felt for Nancy. *So much for positive first impressions.*

But over the next two weeks there were many good times, as my Californian girlfriend put on a brave face against the bitter arctic front that gripped Alberta that year. Being alone in this northerly environment must have seemed a stark contrast with her growing up experience, yet it was an opportunity to visit with my family and friends. While we had taken this step, as hard as it might seem to believe, I was still wrestling with whether I should be asking her hand in marriage. My sister, Anita, had already offered to loan me the money for an engagement ring and so I did not have that as an excuse. My wrestling with the decision did not originate from any reservations regarding Nancy as a person, or as a future wife, or mother. It was more of a struggle with my own preconceptions and wrong thinking. I had read enough missionary biographies to know the horror stories that many of their families had endured. Knowing my own zealousness, I did not want their experiences to become our own. While, on one hand, it seemed an easier solution to stay single, I knew deep down that I was not cut out for that kind of lifestyle.

Having come from a broken home myself, I also wanted to make doubly sure that this was the right decision. As I would pray, it was as if I expected God to give me a guarantee that this young lady was the right one and therefore our marriage was guaranteed to work. Yet on one of these nights, in my father's home in Edmonton, it became clear to me that God could not give me such a guarantee. The strength and longevity of the relationship would depend on us, albeit with God's grace and under his direction. As I reviewed how God had brought us together and how He had led us over the last months, I began to see his sovereign direction up to that point. But it would still require our decision – and continued good decisions – in the years that followed. This cleared up a lot of bad theology that I had picked up along the way; theology that indicated that there was just "one" right person for every person and when you find that "one," your life will be peaches and cream, living happily every after.

Even in our relationship with Jesus, *who is definitely the right one for each of us,* there is the requirement of ongoing discipline and cultivation of the relationship. So, I finally came to a place of peace, knowing that I would have a hard time living *without* this young lady and that God had graciously placed her in my life. Before going to sleep that final night I talked with my father, and then phoned Nancy's father in San Francisco to ask him for permission to marry his daughter. Though he was rather shocked that I would even bother to ask, he had no reservations and gave his blessing. As for others, they seemed to see what I had not even wanted to admit to myself: that Nancy and I were a good fit for each other.

With the finality of my decision behind me, the next day dawned bright and beautiful, with a deep blue sky like you can only get on a cold, clear day in the middle of winter on the Canadian prairies. Perhaps it was because I had finally decided to ask Nancy to marry me, but the day seemed even sunnier than normal to me. We spent the following days visiting my old haunts, such as my high school, just as she had already done with me as we had visited where she had grown up in "South City" (South San Francisco). She even braved the bitter cold ("The inside of my nose is frozen, Phil!") to go ice skating, tobogganing, and even a skiing trip to Sunshine Valley, by Banff. This latter perhaps tested our relationship more than any other. But then how was I to know that it might not be the best way for everyone to learn how to ski by going right to the top of the mountain on the first run? My rational seemed flawless: "Start at the top and by the time you get to the bottom, you will know how to ski!" Needless to say, it did not work out quite like that. Let's just say that the learning curve was a bit steeper than anticipated – hers with skiing and mine with relationships!

Yet in the midst of our activity, I knew that the time had come to pop the question. When and where were the only questions remaining. My plan was to propose on New Year's Eve – kind of an "out with the old and in with the new." But finding a restaurant was virtually impossible at that late date and so we decided to order in Chinese food for a romantic candlelight evening in the basement of my father's home (dining at the ping pong table!). After finishing our meal, and doing as much gazing into each other's eyes as is possible, I began my little speech. In a rather matter of fact manner,

I began to detail the very real likelihood that I might be martyred before I was thirty, would most likely live in abject poverty on an insect-infested mission field, far from family and friends. I know that it is hard to imagine a young lady refusing such a romantic, appealing offer! But in spite of my proposal sounding more like the reading of a riot act, when I was all done, she accepted! It's good she never believed half of what I had to say!

Days later we lifted off of a cold prairie runway to the whine of jet engines – whining as if to say that they too had almost had enough of the cold. We had arrived in this land of white two weeks earlier as individual friends on separate paths, but we left preparing to take on the challenges of life together. The next few months were filled with the busyness of school, discussions over our life together as our relationship deepened, as well as preparations for the wedding, which was to be held close to Santa Rosa where we went to school. Between all these activities, we also explored the sites of San Francisco together – from the Golden Gate Bridge, Pier 39, Alcatraz Island, Lombard Street, and Coit Tower, to watching sunsets over the Pacific Ocean at The Cliffhouse Restaurant. . . pictures of which we filed away in our photo album, yet memories that we would treasure in our hearts forever.

I not only left college with a bride and a whole life ahead of me, but also with key truths that would be foundational for my life. During those months of engagement we continued to grow in our love for each other and the Lord. It was during this season of our lives that we began taking one day a week to fast and pray together for various concerns and challenges facing us, a habit which we continued throughout our lives and ministry in the years ahead.

June arrived and with it both our graduation from college and our marriage to each other. Nancy's family came up from various parts of California and even some of my family and friends made the long journey from Canada. Our wedding was on the Sunday after our Saturday graduation from college. As my bride was accompanied down the aisle by her father, she never looked more beautiful. The following week was a special time of enjoying each other with the pressures of school behind us and our dreams ahead. The beautiful drive to Vancouver, British Columbia, served as our honeymoon. We meandered our way up the scenic coastal highway through the massive Redwoods of northern California, along the rugged coastline of Oregon, finally arriving at the blue waters and green evergreens of the Northwest.

4
_____

"Assemble My Pieces!"

As I sat in that waiting room, those joy-filled days seemed more like an eternity away — not the mere six years that had passed. The balloon of our dreams seemed to have lost much of its air. It was the sight of the approaching surgeon which jarred me back to the seriousness of our present situation. From the joyful memories of our wedding day and the beautiful sights of the Pacific Ocean on our honeymoon, I was brought back to reality by the surgeon telling me how the surgery had went. The vibrant young lady that I had promised to love and protect, was now lying broken in a hospital bed.

"The surgery went well," explained one of the two surgeons involved in the multi-hour surgery. We were to find out later that two of the top surgeons had just *happened* to be in the hospital on the day we had arrived at the trauma unit. This was particularly remarkable as it was the last of the summer holiday weekends. Rather than coincidence, this was another one of many *God-incidences*. The orthopaedic surgeon, who had realigned her left leg and reattached her foot, was the same surgeon who had worked on Terry Fox, the well-known one-legged Canadian who had run across Canada raising money for cancer research. He was one of the best in the business. Though he could not say for sure, he figured that there was a good chance that she would have some use of her foot, though we would not know until the cast came off six weeks later.

The abdominal surgeon then went on to explain that she had not sustained any internal injuries, but that the large wound on her bottom was very susceptible to infection and consequently life-threatening. The large tear was a very unusual type. It began about one inch from the rectum and went clear to the tailbone. The surgeon explained that it was large enough for two fists to fit into the cavity. It also *just so happened* that he had had a similar case before and knew exactly what had to be done. We later learned that he *happened* to be one of the top abdominal surgeons in the area. Another God-incidence.

With his slight British accent, he continued to explain that this kind of wound had to heal from the inside out. This meant that he had to fill the wound with gauze. Then over the next two months, first in the hospital and then at home, it would slowly be pulled out. Left to itself, the wound would heal on the outside first, leaving a cavity on the inside. This would be fatal. Due to the high risk of infection they had also put her on four different strong antibiotics. While life-saving, these would eventually cause an imbalance in her system, which caused her to struggle with her health for years to come.

Finally, the doctor mentioned that, due to the proximity of the wound to her rectum, they needed to give her a colostomy. This, he explained, meant that they had made an incision on her side from which they opened her lower intestine. In this way, her bodily wastes would drain into a colostomy bag which was attached on her side, thereby keeping the area around the wound sterile. He hoped that this would only be a temporary measure, but tests would have to be done in several months after her wound had healed to determine if the sphincter muscles of the rectum would function normally again.

While still trying to absorb all this information, I and my brother-in-law, who was also a minister, were then allowed to visit

Nancy, who had just arrived in the recovery room. As I saw her frail looking body lying amidst all the white sheets, it was hard to believe that this was the same strong woman that had been packing boxes and cleaning the house only hours before. Now she lay there attached to various monitors, with tubes and lines running in her arms and nose. To the background sounds of hospital equipment, we prayed together again, as we had under the carport hours earlier, this time thanking the Lord for the wisdom of the doctors and for a successful recovery.

It was still hard to believe that only hours before we had been preparing to move; only hours since I had heard the wrenching crash of the collapsing structure and heard the cries of Nancy and Alysia from under the carport. But now there was also gratitude that my wife was still alive, and that our daughter had survived with only a scratch – a physical memento to God's faithfulness. Though life might never be the same, or the way we had anticipated it would be, we would be able to go on together.

For me the first couple of weeks after the accident were a blur of very early mornings and late nights. My schedule meant getting ready for work early, taking Alysia to relatives, then working all day, and finally visiting Nancy in the hospital late in the evenings. After this I would often try to unpack some of our things that relatives had moved into our rental home on the day of the accident.

Due to the nature of the accident, there was also the need to obtain a lawyer. The litigation process following the accident would continue for the following two years. Within two days of the accident I had to appear at the Mission branch of the RCMP *(Royal Canadian Mounted Police)*, who had the jurisdiction over the small community. While on that first visit the more serious charge of *Reckless Driving* was dropped, out of leniency that it had been a family member affected, I was assessed with the traffic violation, *Driving Without Due Care and Attention* – an obvious understatement. While the legal case never proved exactly what occurred, it was obvious that the vehicle never ended up where it should have. The case also eventually proved that the building was not built up to standard, for if it had been it never would have collapsed as it did. It was determined that the impact by the truck was just not great enough for this to have occurred.

All these background matters that ultimately involved lawyers, litigation, enforcement authorities, home and vehicular insurance companies, were an added burden on top of dealing with the unknowns of Nancy's prognosis for the future, looking after Alysia, and somehow keeping my contracting company going. Over the course of the next year Nancy would have to relive the event many times over in front of lawyers on *Days of Discovery*. These were emotionally draining days for Nancy as she had to go over every detail of the accident in front of several lawyers from various insurance interests in order to determine the claim.

But while this was happening in the background, the dailyness of life was complex enough that it took all my energy. For the two weeks that Nancy was in the hospital, I would visit her every evening after being on the construction site all day. Often driving back late at night, I would pull into the driveway and not really remember the details of the drive. Life took on a vague blur. The tyranny of the immediate did not allow for too much introspection or reflection during those first few weeks. But as time passed, the full reality of our situation began to dawn on us. Actually, it was initially something I had to deal with, as Nancy had plenty on her plate just to get well. While her recovery became both of our priorities, the accident, with the backdrop of the previous few years, caused me to ask some further questions of myself and of God. *What was He up to? How did this tragedy fit with the preparations we had felt He had directed us to make? How did it fit in with his purpose for us in the years to come?* None of it seemed to make any sense from our vantage point. Even before the accident, things had seemed to be getting darker, not brighter, as all of our own plans and dreams seemed to be laying around us in ashes. Now the future seemed even more unsure.

After attending the training school in California, and then finishing my Bachelor of Theology degree, I had served as a youth pastor. Throughout this time, there had been periods of tentmaking in order to make ends meet, from tar and gravel roofing, landscaping, working in a fish processing plant, and various and sundry construction jobs. But during these times it was still easy to connect the dots. Each one of these jobs was merely a means to an end; something necessary to fulfill the big picture. But during the last few years, as my position in the church had dried up, I had needed to look for other full-time work in order to make ends meet. After all the preparation for the ministry, I struggled with the feelings of rejection and not being needed. It seemed even God had forgotten where He had left us. It was even worse to have experienced the joys of full-time service, only to then be put on the shelf again. *Where had I failed? Where had we missed it?* These were some of the questions that seemed to preoccupy my mind and heart.

I could still clearly feel what I had felt as a teen at camp, what I had experienced on that Christmas night in Mexico and the renewed commitment I had made then. *But were all those years of preparation wasted time and effort?* As I got up every morning in the dark, put on my work clothes, made my lunch, only to spend another day slogging in the mud of a construction site, it seemed as if this were the case. Perhaps I had missed God and I really should have pursued a career in architecture, instead of the constantly closing doors that I seemed to run into as I tried to pursue ministry. During those times of questioning there was also the temptation to manipulate circumstance to make something happen. But on each occasion we knew it was not the right thing to do. It had to be something that God orchestrated, not us just pushing our own way through. It was exactly at this low point of confusion that the accident had occurred. The dreams that had been fading, seemed to now be snuffed out by the accident.

While those were dark days from our perspective, from God's perspective there were lessons he wanted to teach us and character he desired to build in us. Often we feel we are just stumbling along, in the dark as it were. Yet this is not such a bad place to be, as long as we remain faithful, and keep stumbling forward! The life of faith is much more than having all the answers; it is a life of moving forward, however slowly it may seem at times – doing the right things, in spite of not knowing how it is all going to turn out. The Scripture says that a flickering reed He will not snuff out. Since God will not snuff out the weak and tired, neither should we. We have discovered that it might not seem, from our perspective, that we are on top of our game, but God's perspective may be quite different. This is why we must be careful not to judge others according to their outward circumstances. We do not know the path they are walking and what God is doing in their lives. It might seem as if they are only *stumbling*, but don't be fooled, God is doing something very special in their life.

We had already learned some foundational lessons, but God still had us in his school to refine us and plant these truths in our hearts so that they would bear fruit one day. Jesus, predicting his own death suffering in John 12:24-25, states, "I tell you the truth, unless a kernel of wheat falls to the ground and dies, it remains only a single seed. But if it dies, it produces many seeds. The man who loves his life will lose it, while the man who hates his life in this world will keep it for eternal life." This difficult period in our lives is best described by Jesus' analogy of the seed. The seed may have had much potential, but it was covered over in a dark and damp place. It had the potential to produce other fruit, but in order for that to happen a process needed to begin to take place. From the seed's perspective, it was in the dark – uncomfortable and useless. But from the grower's point of view, it needed to be right where it was, so that its outer husk could be softened and broken away. Eventually this would expose the life within it to the outside world. We could identify with that seed and could testify that it did not *feel* all that good. And as is often the case, the seed does not usually recognize the process of which it is a participant. If, however, the *seed* does not submit to this process, it is destined to remain only a single seed, never multiplying and becoming many seeds.

The temptation during these times of anonymity and seeming lack of movement, is to try by our own means to *wrestle* our way above ground, to *prove* that we have something on the inside. But this is not the process of true life, which only grows in the *fullness of time*. Being willing to remain in the shadows, "on the shelf," as it were, is one of the most excruciating places to be in. Yet paradoxically, it can be the richest of learning times. The deciding factor is our attitude and perspective. We need to have the attitude of Christ (Phil. 2). He did not need to grasp at his rights or a position, for He knew who He was and had a sense of God's timing. Even the Son of God learned obedience in humility, even though it meant death on a cross. From an earthly perspective, this seemed the most unlikely of scenarios.

Joseph, who was a type of Christ in the Old Testament, had this attitude. He was a young man of many dreams and visions. But things did not get off to a good start in his life – from the dubious beginning of being sold into slavery by his very brothers, to being falsely accused and sent to prison. Every time he seemed to catch a break, whether working in Pharoah's court or the remarkable *coincidence* of helping out the Pharaoh's baker and butler, his *good fortune* always seemed to evaporate. Knowing the end of the story, it is tempting to read the narrative with the assumption that Joseph knew all along how it would all turn out. But it stretches the imagination to believe that he sailed through these setbacks with never a waver or question. Surely there were times that it must have seemed, from his perspective, that he was merely stumbling along. Yet he lived a life of integrity, doing the right things, even though it seemed that he was not getting any further ahead.

I am sure that there were days at the bottom of that damp, dark, rat infested Egyptian cell when Joseph could not clearly see the end from the beginning and how all things would fit together. On those days, he may have asked some of the same questions we ask at those times: *"God, what are you doing? Don't you realize that you are wasting all this potential?"* I have discovered that we can express this level of honesty without threatening God and his sovereignty in the universe or, for that matter, his sovereignty in our lives. But questioning is different than taking matters into our own hands and thwarting what God wants ultimately to accomplish through us. The enemy in those times often presents many *good* opportunities to sidetrack us from God's *best*. At those times it is a test of our willingness to wait for God's best for us (signified by Isaac) or opt merely to make something happen to help God fulfill his plans in our lives (signified by Ishmael).

Those who accept God's will and have Job's attitude, *though you slay me I will serve you*, will learn those lessons that can only be learned in those dark, lonely, seemingly forgotten places in the wildernesses of our lives. Often these are not even places of our own making, but places which we are willingly, or unwillingly, led into. Will we remain faithful while we are only a seed in the dark, as it were? At those times when it does not seem to matter to anyone what we do, will we remain faithful while invisible and outwardly ineffective? Even during the times when no one but God knows and sees our inner motivations and attitudes? It is precisely during these times that God, by his Holy Spirit, is seeking to develop the character of Christ within us. The degree that we allow him to do this is the degree to which we will one day be effective at bearing fruit for the Kingdom. The capacity to bear fruit is encoded in the very *DNA* of that buried seed, but it is only as it undergoes this process that its potential can be unlocked. It is during those times that we really discover that God is always more interested in the *process* than the *destination*. His will in all of our lives is that of the pure worship of obedience. This always takes the form of an ongoing process; it is not a destination that we arrive at.

The promise that God had given to Abram was about as big a picture as possible: "I will begin a great nation through you, and I will bless you." (Gen 12:1-3). This is the basis we still have for being a blessing to all nations. Yet after Abraham received this promise, his life seemed to take a convoluted path. Again, knowing the end of the story, it is possible to paint the narrative with a broad brush, eliminating his humanity, with the inevitable moments of uncertainty. But the text seems to indicate otherwise. We seem to see a paradox in Genesis chapter fifteen. Abram believed God and it was credited to him as righteousness. Yet less than a verse later we read, "But Abram said, O sovereign Lord how can I know that I will gain possession of it?" He was much like us, some days strong in his faith and other times weaker. But we read further in this chapter that God comes to him and his faith is strengthened by the awesome promise that the fulfilment would not come through his servant, but actually his own seed. But, as is so often the case in our lives, there is yet another twist and turn. In chapter sixteen we see this man of faith, Abram, having relations with Hagar, his concubine, seeking to fulfill God's purpose in that way.

For those who have committed their lives to God, I do not believe that the biggest struggle is *knowing* God's will or even *doing* it. Instead, I think the greater challenge is to have the patience to do his will, in his *time* and in his *way*. If the enemy cannot keep us from believing we are *children of promise*, he will often switch tactics and bombard us with the encouragement to, figuratively, have relations with Hagar instead. The fruit of this union was not (and never is) *Isaac,* "the promise," but *Ishmael,* or "misery." The consequences of our own hasty solutions can haunt us and conspire against God's best in our lives, even after we are on track and have later experienced the birth of our own *Isaac.*

The most important prayer, while living as a seed in the obscurity of the dark should not be "Deliver me from here, Lord!" but instead, "Give me patience and divine perspective to believe your promise so that I may not miss what you want to do in my life right now." That is a much more difficult prayer, but more likely to be answered with a divine, "Yes!"

Ishmael represents the visible result of the self-strength and impatience that causes us to try to fulfill God's call and will in our lives in *our own way.* The temptation is not so much a rebellion against God's will, but rather the temptation to fulfill his will in our lives with our own ingenuity and strength. We inevitably give into this temptation if we do not allow him to fulfill his processes in our lives, as Joseph did. If we do not accept his will for us *on his terms,* then, as we begin to have greater responsibility and influence, we continue a pattern of manipulation in order to achieve our own ends. Instead of taking on the attitude of Christ and learning through obedience, we never learn to embrace the dark, uncomfortable times in our lives. The working out of this from theory into practice is one of the greatest challenges of the Christian walk; unfortunately, it is most often not accomplished without some pain. Painful, for though we believe we heard what God has said to us, we often do not understand what God is doing during the dark times; painful, for often other Christians have much more unsolicited advice than understanding.

Standing next to my wife, lying there in that hospital bed, the seed kernels of our dreams, hopes and aspirations seemed to be crushed and covered. What the events of the last few years had not stolen of our hope and faith, this tragedy was trying to extinguish.

Phil was the first person I saw as I slowly came out of the fog of the anaesthetic after the surgery. He was by my bedside, holding my hand and next to him was our brother-in-law, Walter

Rusnell. It was remarkable how quickly I felt my head clear. While it is typical for a patient not even to recognize, or be cognitive of their surroundings, I heard myself jabbering away to Walter about a book he gave us and how much it had meant to me. On and on I talked about how during the few days before the accident God had seemed to prepare me through my fast. I was to later find out from the doctor that this fast, in which I was eating only vegetables, probably saved my life. It meant that my body was better able to deal with the shock and my digestive system was clear, which was important as the life-threatening wound affected that region of my body the most. But the doctors would not be able to tell for some time if I would be able to walk again without assistance of some sort, or if they would be able to reverse my colostomy.

I was just thankful to be alive and especially to see my smiley little girl, who seemed all back to normal. But in those dark days in the hospital, I could not help but cry to God, *"I have followed you as close as I know how, and now this is my reward?!"* In those days, I needed not only assurance that He was there with me, but also that He would put me back together again. One day during my devotions, my eyes fell on Micah 2:12 where God was promising to gather all the remnant of Israel together again. In the New American Standard Bible it is translated, *"I will surely assemble all of you."* This became a specific promise to me and was what I needed in order to hang on during the difficult days of rehabilitation that lay ahead.

The next seventeen days in the hospital took on a certain routine. Every few hours I needed to be turned over by the nurses, usually all of them, as with a full leg cast and damaged buttocks I was rather helpless. Perhaps the worst was the lack of privacy with regard to virtually every bodily function and having to adjust to my bodily waste being deposited in a plastic bag at my side, instead of where God originally intended it on the backside of my body. The end of the day was punctuated by Phil's visits, as we spent the last few hours of the day together. In time I was able to get into a wheelchair, which meant we toured the deserted hospital corridors late at night. On one occasion he made a wrong turn and we found ourselves in the morgue – not exactly the turn we wanted to take, even as a harmless tour!

Finally the day arrived when I was able to go back home. As I tried to get from the wheelchair into the car, it soon became apparent how much strength I had lost (and how heavy the cast really was). It seemed to take all the energy I had just to make it up the stairs of the little bungalow that we had rented. Phil had hung up some of our pictures and made it seem like home, though I had not yet seen it. Though it was a small, older home, with green carpet and orange walls, anything was better than the institutional feel of the hospital.

The following weeks and months consisted of seeing Phil leave early in the morning, at which time a homecare worker would arrive to take care of Alysia and me, while he was gone. I would position myself on the couch and could not move much from there, even taking up needlepoint for the first time in my life! There were also the daily visits from the nurse who would dress my wounds and slowly begin withdrawing the gauze from the wound in my buttocks. The realization that things could have been a lot worse did not totally soften the reality of our situation. Our lifestyle had totally changed, as I needed care for everything – I mean everything. At times it was very humbling, but Phil did not complain. Not only did he work, he also then took a greater role in taking care of Alysia, as well as my personal care when he got home. Due to what we had been through emotionally, we grew closer to each other, even though during this time we were not able to be intimate with each other. The proximity of my wound in this area meant that this would be the case for some time. Having a bag attached to my side also did not do much to kindle romantic feelings! As much as I recognized our needs for intimacy, having a colostomy was definitely something that I had to overcome in order to bring some normalcy back to our personal life.

It was six weeks before it was time for the doctor to take the plaster cast off. What I had not been aware of was that there was a long eight inch metal pin which needed to also come out. It had been screwed through my heel and ankle and up into my leg to hold it together. With the bedside manner only a surgeon can possess, and without saying a word, he quickly grabbed the steel pin at the bottom of my foot and before I knew what he was doing, firmly pulled the pin from my leg – all eight inches! Fortunately I did not pass out from the pain, but my feelings could not quite match his enthusiasm as he announced, "Wasn't that better than having to go through surgery again to get this thing taken out!"

While the cast had been on, I had been able to wiggle my toes, which the doctors all seemed to be quite pleased about. But once the cast was off, the next step was to see if I could move my foot. With a painful effort I tried to move it, but with only limited results. As the white plaster came off, it was a shock to seeing my purple, bruised leg. As I began to realize that I could hardly move my foot and leg, I could not hold back the tears. Tears of frustration; tears anticipating the rehabilitation ahead. My leg would just not do what my mind was asking of it! On top of this, the pain and throbbing seemed even greater now that the cast was off. Phil had waited till some days after the surgery to inform me that, except for a bit of skin, my foot had actually been severed. Until the cast came off, this had been mere theoretical knowledge, but now looking at the still-bloodied scars, and not being able to control the foot as it flopped downwards, the stark realization of what had occurred fully struck me. *"Well, Lord, you promised you would assemble my parts, but will they ever work again?!"*

The weeks and months of therapy that followed seemed, at times, to be more painful than the actual accident! As for my soft tissue wound, as the nurses daily withdrew the gauze, it seemed to be healing well without infection. As the wound closed I was also able to exercise my leg and foot more. Then as the cast came off, I was able to get around more with crutches. After months of living in a blur since the accident, it seemed we were coming back to life. From the first day in the hospital so many had brought flowers, had prayed, brought meals, and had helped in so many other ways. But more and more we were having to figure out our life on our own.

While I was still in the hospital I had received a Hibiscus plant from some friends. It now was full of buds and was in our livingroom where I could see it every day. One day it seemed as if God whispered to me that once all the flowers had bloomed and dropped off, I would be walking again. But it was such a full plant, with so many buds that it seemed it would last forever; there must have been over thirty blossoms! Some days two would bloom at a time, and on other days a blossom would fall off and only one new one would bloom.

On the morning of one of my last visits to see the orthopedic surgeon, the last blossom had fallen off. *"Oh dear, my foot is still too painful to walk on,"* I thought. Once at the doctor's office I asked him, "When do you think I will walk again?"

In the *sweet, sensitive* style of a surgeon he retorted, "It won't do you a bit of good to just rely on your therapist's treatments, YOU need to walk on it!"

Back home again I decided to throw my injured leg forward and put all my weight on it. Somehow I began taking those first steps. It was excruciating, as the muscles had been so damaged, but I kept on going, though at the time there was only one speed for me to walk – *very, very slowly!*

Day by day, my wound healed more, and I was slowly able to put more weight on my leg. The final looming decision was to determine if it would be possible to reverse my colostomy. By mid-November the wound by my tailbone had closed completely and so it was just a matter of determining if the sphincter muscles were still functional. From personal experience, let me confirm that the exploratory tests may be even worse than the injury! The results of these tests indicated that it was worth trying to reattach my intestines, so that they could again function as God had originally intended.

The surgery to reattach my digestive system was scheduled for December 6, exactly three months after that dramatic long weekend in September. After waking from the anaesthetic, my senses became aware of the intense burning on my left side, where the open ends of my intestines had been stitched for the last three months. It was a procedure that had undoubtedly saved my life, but which I must admit I was glad was in the past. As everything healed, I was able to eat the foods that I loved. This was truly a blessing as Christmas was approaching! It was also no small matter to have my *plumbing* system working in the normal manner. God had truly shown his mercy and had re-assembled my parts.

Little did I know that within a few short weeks something was going to happen that would perhaps change our lives as much as the accident ever had.

5

Light at the End of the Tunnel

After I had finished my undergraduate degree, while still serving in a local church, Nancy and I attended several of the first Missions Fest Conferences. These had started during the mid-eighties by several church leaders in the Vancouver area. The purpose was to gather those involved in missions and provide a forum to inspire and motivate others to take part in the Great Commission worldwide. Originally held in a local church, it began rather small with only several thousand attending and a handful of churches involved. Yet before the millennium would close, there would be over 200 agencies involved, with over 100 participating churches and an attendance of 35,000. By the nineties Missions Fest was being held at the Vancouver Trade and Convention Centre, and had become one of the largest annual Mission Conventions in North America.

Our desire was to hear from God and see if there was somewhere that we could participate in a cross-cultural ministry. I had felt this call to missions as a teen, and on my trip to Mexico I had sensed that God was continuing to lead me in this direction.

As I had by then finished both my schooling in the United States and my degree at WPBC, we continued to gravitate to missions. Interacting with other missionaries, I had begun to recognize that the need on many mission fields was the training of leadership. This also was my area of interest and so it seemed one of the most effective ways that I could personally serve on the mission field. This was the burden that God began laying on our heart.

During those years we continued to visit Missions Fest annually, though by this time I was no longer pastoring and was working full time as a siding contractor. Every time we went, there was the hope that perhaps this was the year when we would be taken *off the shelf* of *apparent* inactivity. Simultaneously, I had also made several inquiries to the denomination of which we were affiliated with at the time, but in spite of my efforts it seemed that there were no openings. While we understood ministry was more than just a full-time position or being involved in traditional church work, there was a burning desire to be involved more directly. Ministry is something all believers are called to in our daily lives, be it construction, office work, our families – wherever God has place us. But while we continued to be faithful, we could not shake this inner desire to serve the Lord in a more full-time capacity. There were even times that we wished we could be freed of this inner passion if it would not be able for us to be able to fulfill it.

My previous experiences had caused me to go through some personal changes in terms of my perspective of the Body of Christ. Since my experience at the interdenominational school in California, I had discovered the joy of working with people from a variety of denominations, church traditions and organizations. This had impacted me and would influence my future ministry. From my early days of ministry, when we as youth pastors across denominations monthly joined our youth groups, to my involvement in the planting of a community church, I developed a greater awareness of the need to bridge denominational divides. Missions Fest had not only a global perspective on the needs and opportunities around the world; it also was comprised of a cross-section of churches and groups, which mirrored my own interests. So every year, we would visit the booth of every organization, being open to God's voice, hoping that there might be an organization that we could serve with.

So when January of 1989 rolled around, it was not that unusual for us to consider attending the missions conference again. Though it seemed even more impossible than ever that we could ever go (after the accident), we wanted at least to hear God's heart again, as expressed through the mission speakers. Of course it had only been five months since the accident and Nancy was still hobbling around on crutches, so I initially planned on only going for one day on my own, but then at the last minute Nancy decided to come along. Though we were beginning to believe that the light at the end of the tunnel was not an approaching train, we were still in more of survival mode than eager anticipation of the future. *After all, how could God use us overseas now?* If He had not opened up anything before all this had happened to us, it seemed unlikely that anything would happen now. Not only was Nancy's body still recovering, but our somewhat fragile emotions were still healing and our faith seemed weak.

Yet, as in past years, the conference was exciting as we heard what God was doing around the world. Also, as in past years, we visited the scores of mission displays, but we did not really make any connections with anyone. But as we were ready to head back home, I bumped into someone I knew from the *Open Doors* organization. Ever since reading *God's Smuggler* as a teen, their work of smuggling Bibles behind the Iron Curtain fascinated me and we had an ongoing interest in their ministry.

In January of that year, 1989, the Iron Curtain was still in place, but was beginning to show the initial signs of weakening. As we chatted together at their booth, neither of us could have anticipated the global changes which were to occur in the coming months. While in Budapest, Prague, and other once isolated cities, there were sparks of political change beginning to take place, little did we realize that it would be in that very same year that the Berlin Wall would fall. The resulting domino-effect would eventually reach to the very doors of the Kremlin. Not only was this going to affect the ministry of *Open Doors;* it would directly affect our ministry in the coming decades.

As we continued to talk I shared with my friend the need I saw of training nationals so that they might be effective in discipling their own people. He agreed that, on many fields, particularly where there was some sort of church already established, one of the greatest needs was to equip these emerging leaders. While traditional missionaries were still necessary, those from within the community were often much better at evangelizing in their own culture than even the "outsider." Those involved on these fields were beginning to see the need to rethink the typical role of the missionary. On many fields, discipleship needed to catch up with evangelism. It was beginning to become apparent to some that missionaries from the west could be more effective as "facilitators" not just "doers." Effective missions work meant investing in the lives of nationals.

The *Open Doors* representative mentioned that he had just had a similar conversation with someone from another organization who seemed to have this attitude and were doing something in the area of training. By now, Nancy was getting pretty tired from hobbling around all day on crutches, but on the way out I thought we could quickly drop by their booth. My first impressions of the make-shift booth were not exactly negative, but neither were they that terribly encouraging. The brochures were of the photocopied variety and it seemed like a rather small group. At the time there were only two couples involved and their emphasis seemed to be training missionaries from the west on the mission field. They had initially begun in Israel, but were now in transition to being based in East Africa. A representative at the booth mentioned that the Director from the US was attending the conference and was still up by the seminar rooms, if I wanted to meet him.

With Nancy in tow, I took the long way back to our car, hoping that I might *bump* into this man, Phil Walker. We did not have much time to talk, but did share a few minutes together. It seemed that they were still a rather small group and that their primary work had been taking teams to work on the Kibbutzim in Israel. Within the last couple of years they had moved the missionary training program to Kenya in East Africa. They were initially looking for those who wanted to take part in their on-the-field missions' training program, in which they used the *Perspectives Course* (from the *US Centre for World Missions*). Things still seemed to be in the early stages of development and I was not really too keen to enroll in another training program.

While I had not been thinking at all about being involved in missionary training, I was interested in the emphasis of discipling a generation of leaders in practical, life-changing ways. It brought back memories of my college days at a discipleship school and it seemed that perhaps it would be a good fit with my interest and gifts. The international and interdenominational approach, as well as the openness to working with others, was also very appealing. I had not really thought specifically about service in Africa or for any particular part of the world, for that matter. While I had previous applied for service in Liberia and Iran Jaya with my denomination, my focus had never been on only one region or country. What had always been of greater importance to me was working with those of similar vision and direction and being able to utilize my gifts within the context of a team ministry.

On the way home, there was no overwhelming sense that this was the connection that we had for years been looking for. But over the next few days, as I reread the very brief info I had on this ministry, I had the same feeling that I had had exactly ten years previously, as my sister had placed a brochure for a discipleship school in my hands. As I had looked at that brochure in 1979, I had not been able to shake the idea that this is where I was to spend my first year after high school. Now as I looked at this brochure, it too raised more questions than it answered, but I had that same sense that I needed to pursue this. In January of 1989, it was hard to imagine travelling far from home, let alone halfway around the world, but as Nancy and I discussed it, we felt that I needed to send my resume in and see what God would do.

Over the next few weeks, I continued to be very occupied with my business, as it seemed that I had more clients than I could handle. Though I had just launched out on my own a few months earlier, somehow the phone continued to ring with more home owners wanting me to give them a quote to put siding on their house. So my days were consumed with putting in bids, getting enough jobs to keep the crew working, and then in the evenings doing the paperwork. At night I was also trying to help Nancy with tasks around the house, as she was still limited in what she could do.

In spite of this busyness, there was a growing excitement about the possibility of *finally* being directly involved in missions overseas. Yet, at the same time, it seemed almost incomprehensible that it could be possible for us to go. In my weaker moments I wondered if I was just fooling myself by trying to fulfill a dream which was not grounded in reality. After all, the fact was that Nancy was still mending, and the issues surrounding the settlement of the accident were still grinding their way through the legal system. Moving overseas seemed far removed from my daily life of getting up early to set up the equipment on the job site, so that the crew and I could put siding on yet another home. The hot sun of Africa seemed far away from the grey overcast skies of a Vancouver winter and the knee-deep mud of the construction site.

Nevertheless, several weeks after the Missions Conference I again talked with Phil Walker by phone. During the initial conversation with Phil at the conference, it seemed that the only real avenue would be to enrol in their missionary school. After nearly six years of college I was not too keen on attending yet another school, but I also knew that this would be practical training and at the very least would be a step closer to *real* missions work. So it was a bit of a welcome surprise to hear the voice on the other end ask me if we would be interested in joining as staff members, instead of as students. After receiving my resume, the two couples who were involved with ICM, USA at the time had discussed things and were wondering if we wanted to join the team for a two year commitment. *Well, as they say, is the sky blue!?* Of course my answer was, "We would love to!"

At the time, the only staff members were Phil and Debbie Walker and Myron and Carol Goodwin. Both had worked in Israel together and were now in Kenya. As I would discover upon our arrival in Africa, I had connected with them just as they were transitioning from facilitating a missions course in Kenya, which was primarily for North Americans, to focussing on training local national pastors and church leaders. This transition actually occurred during the year and a half since I first met Phil Walker at Missions Fest in Vancouver and when we arrived in Kenya. So upon our arrival in Kenya this became our new focus. It is remarkable how God prepared a place that would fit so closely, not only with my skills and giftings, but also with the burden which He had placed on my heart so many years previously. Instead of enrolling in another missions course, I was helping develop the initial stages of a pastoral training program that would grow, throughout the decade of the nineties, beyond any of our expectations.

During our time of preparation in Canada, we also found ourselves participating in planting a new church. This was exciting, but necessitated many evening meetings, on top of my construction work. Yet all the activity could not drown out the growing sense of God doing a new thing in our lives. He had spared the life of my wife and daughter and now, after years of seeking and praying, He was releasing us to fulfill a dream that had been birthed in our hearts many years before. What the enemy had meant for harm, to destroy us and the vision, God seemed to be turning for good. That sinking, devastating feeling that I had experienced as I had jumped out of the truck, only months earlier, was now being replaced with hope. *Perhaps God did have a good plan for our lives yet?* In the dark period after the accident, the enemy had bombarded my mind with the lie that God did not have a good plan for our lives. Yet as a new light was beginning to dawn, this lie was being dispelled by the recognition of God's hand of faithfulness in our lives.

Since there was no existing structure in Canada to facilitate our dream, we began to take steps to organize and incorporate a new missions society. At that time, the team in the United States was still fairly loosely organized and consisted of only two couples. In light of this and other factors, we decided that it would be better to use another name for the society in Canada. Over the next few months, we gathered a board of directors and incorporated under the name, *Global Outreach Association (GO)*.

But then the real challenge was, How were we going to support this work? We had no experience overseas, and we could not hide the fact that all we had was a vision and a dream within our hearts. Neither Nancy or I were then living where we had grown up, and so our friendships in the area were relatively few. Our other contacts were spread out from Alberta to California. Also, since I was not going on the field with our denomination and most of my contacts were within this circle, the challenge was even greater. But we slowly began to approach relatives, friends, contacts, basically anybody who would listen! Our goal was to be in Kenya by the summer of 1990, one and a half years after first beginning the process. Looking back, I am not so sure I would have supported us in those early days! No track record, lots of dreams, but few real ministry successes. Those early supporters of Phil and Nancy and *Global Outreach* were the real men and women of faith and vision!

Perhaps one of the hardest things to do was to ask others to support us financially. Yet in those early days, we established what was to be the *modus operandi* for the mission: simply making our needs known and then trusting God to speak to those He would have partner with us; no guilt, no manipulation. The inherent challenge which we faced was not original with us. Our experience was similar to many who had gone before us. Everyone wants to give to something that they feel will be successful. Yet we were just starting out, with only our dreams and visions; we had no proven track record and no guarantee of *success*. It was humbling to have those who trusted us enough to put their funds on the line to see us sent out.

In spite of our own insecurities in having to ask others for funds and the fact that in those early days it seemed we were just *stumbling* along, at best, responses began to trickle in. Having been instilled with the value that a man looks after the needs of his family himself, it was excruciating to ask for funds and then see those whom we knew, willingly give to us and the fledgling ministry. I had always provided for the needs of my family through all types of jobs, even starting my own ventures when there just were no other jobs around. But as we embarked on this new journey, every cheque that arrived seemed like a miracle and helped to dissolve my misplaced pride. The interdependence of the Body of Christ which is reflected each time someone chooses to partner with us has never become routine. Seeing God's faithfulness year after year was something we never would take for granted.

While the cheques began to trickle in, God was simultaneously blessing the business. Even in the first year of the company, there had always been money left over at the end of the month after paying our bills. By the end of the first year our tithes and offerings were more than our total income had been just a few years previously! Yet it was right at this point that we were making plans to go to Africa. While some thought we were making a mistake to leave during the booming economy, we knew that God wanted us to go. *I also knew who was blessing the work of my hands.* We knew that the increase was not just due to our own ingenuity, but that it was God who was blessing us. But his blessing was for a specific purpose. In a consumer driven society, even some in the church have proclaimed that God's blessing is primarily a means to make our life nice and easy. While He does promise *not to withhold any good thing from us*, Scripture clearly tells us the purpose of this blessing: it is so that we might be a blessing to others.

In our lives, God's provision has always been coupled with our willingness to get our hands dirty. This was the case during our time of preparation. I continued to do the contracting work, while sending out support letters. As it would turn out, it would be our savings from the business, together with a few supporters, that would finance our first two year term.

So spring turned into summer, of that year of new beginnings for the Jeske family. Nancy was mending and continued with the painful task of rehabilitating her leg. There were *Days of Discovery* with the lawyers to settle outstanding insurance issues. Our daughter was doing well and growing and I was keeping a crew of four to five men busy, slapping on more siding than ever. In the evenings there were letters to be written and all the details of preparing for our upcoming move to Africa.

Yet, before leaving for Africa, we were going to go through yet another unexpected valley. It would even have the potential to change all of our plans and thwart our preparations for Africa. It happened in the fall of 1989, almost exactly one year after our accident. Enough time had passed that we were not cringing at the sound of every ambulance that went by and we were gaining perspectives on how God works during even the toughest experiences of life.

Though we did not recognize it initially, the family crisis on our horizon was going to test us and these principles in ways that we could not even have imagined at the time. While the accident had left physical scars, this valley was going to leave emotional ones.

6

The Shadow of Death

October can be very beautiful on the Lower Mainland of BC, with clear skies, the changing leaves and cool, clear nights. On the other hand, it can also be very wet and just plain miserable! Of course, the greenery and beauty of the Vancouver area has a lot to do with the amount of rain that it receives each year. Unfortunately, it does not all come in one or two months, but is instead evenly distributed throughout the year – which usually translates into long, unbroken periods of the wet stuff.

In October of 1989, while we continued making preparations to leave for Africa less than a year away, I was still installing siding. This meant working outside in the fresh air every day. During the warm, sunny days of summer those with inside jobs would look out their windows with envy at those of us working in the sun and fresh air. But once fall and winter rolled around it was a different story. Having to put on our rain gear to work in the dampness and mud of yet another water-drenched day became an unpleasant daily grind. Listening to the weather report was a matter of survival, even if it was only to be able to psychologically prepare oneself for the next wet day! (Having to work in the elements every day invariably turned one into an amateur meteorologist!). I believe this explains my *addiction* to the weather channel in those days!

That autumn, I and my crew were working on a particularly difficult job. I had submitted a rather high bid, knowing that it would be a miserable job. I was kind of hoping that we would not get it but, as it turned out, we did land the job. This particular house was made from modular walls and so instead of a solid plywood exterior it had staggered 2x6 framing with styrofoam in between. The meant that we first had to install plywood sheets over the whole exterior, necessitating lifting 4 x 8 foot sheets of plywood up our ladders and planking system, which was precariously perched on the side of this three story home.

The endless rain of that particular month just added to the nightmare scenario. The dirt that had been used to backfill the foundation had long since been saturated. We struggled to set up our long ladders only to see them sink deeply into the mud. Walking around the goo, trying to haul the sheets of plywood up our planks, meant a very frustrated crew. As the job began taking longer and longer to finish, my profits were also evaporating, which even made me question the sense of this muddy fiasco.

Yet it is what I heard one day on our jobsite radio that sticks even more firmly in my mind – more than even all the mud and frustrations. It was October 17, 1989 when we heard the breaking news of a major earthquake in the San Francisco area. Since Nancy's family still lived in the Bay area, I quickly called her and let her know of the news. Though we were unable to get through to them that evening, her family was eventually able to contact us and let us know that they had all survived the quake, though shaken. Over the next few days we saw on television the incredible damage as a deck of the Oakland Bay Bridge collapsed, as well as entire sections of the freeway. The devastation that occurred due to gas fires and sandwiched decks of freeways captivated us, and the world, for weeks. Little did we know then that within ten days we also would be in the Bay area.

Nancy's mother had been on a bus in the middle of the city as glass from the skyscrapers showered the sidewalk next to her. Her sister, Mary, worked at the San Francisco International Airport and saw the massive walls shake like jello. Nancy's father, who was a French-trained tailor, was on the third floor of Macy's, as the floor began to slide and roll. It was a relief to hear that they, along with Nancy's other sister and two brothers, were fine. Although a bit shaken, they were, after all, long time Californians and were used to earthquakes. But this one had really gotten everybody's attention.

It was one week later that *the* phone call arrived. I had returned home from the *job-in-the-mud* that we were beginning to refer to with more derogatory names. After a nice warm shower and supper, I was at my desk doing some paperwork. As the phone rang I thought it was just another homeowner wanting us to bid on his house, or worse yet, the general contractor of *the mudhole* house wondering when we were eventually going to finish! Instead, I heard the shaky voice of Nancy's mother on the other end of the line.

As I listened to her relate the news, I had that same sinking feeling that I had had one year earlier as I had jumped out of the cab of the truck to the screams of my family under the carport. It was the kind of news that has such devastating impact that it takes your breath away. My mother-in-law proceeded to explain that Nancy's father had just been murdered. As tragic as this was, in and of itself, it was even worse – he had been murdered by her own son, Nancy's older brother, Tony.

After Nancy got off the phone that evening, we were just dumbfounded and sat shell-shocked. As the impact of this event and what it meant began to sink in, Nancy began to cry. After what she had endured over the last year, the senselessness of this act seemed incomprehensible. As we prayed together I could not help but think how devastating this must be for her. She had not only lost her father, but would also have to live with the ugly reality that it was at the hands of her own brother, someone that she had known, trusted and grown up with. The next day we left Alysia with relatives and boarded a plane to San Francisco. As the plane lifted off the wet runway on a dreary October day in Vancouver, our emotions seemed to match the weather. We were not sure what awaited us, and there was really not too much to say, so accompanied by the drone of the jet engines we held hands and were lost in our own thoughts.

As I had hung up the phone, though I cried, the full impact of what my mother had told me did not sink in. That night, as I read Alysia her good night story and prayed with her before tucking her in bed, I saw a picture in my mind as I knelt next to her bed. It was a picture of a silver goblet filled with a dark black liquid. I felt that God was saying to me, "Nancy, you will be able to drink this bitter cup." Though I was not sure what that meant, the following years were going to make it clearer. I had not yet even experienced the death of a close loved one, let alone one under such tragic circumstances.

Actually, I always thought that my family was fairly normal. I was raised in a middle class family in the San Francisco Bay area by parents who tried their very best to raise us, a family of three sisters and two brothers – with me right in the middle. They were not perfect, but good, honest people who did the best they could with what they had. It is only as we are adults and have children of our own that we begin to realize the struggles and obstacles that they must have been dealing with. But this fact is largely lost upon us while we are children. My mother grew up in Pennsylvania, the daughter of European immigrants. There was only one childhood trip back to this eastern State, to the location of the Pennsylvanian farm where my mother had grown up. It remains one of those great childhood memories of playing with our cousins, in such a different world than was ours in our South San Francisco suburb.

My father's parents had fled Armenia during the Turkish genocide at the turn of the century. He had grown up in France and eventually emigrated to America when he was in his twenties. Other family members also followed, some settling in Fresno and others in southern California. Trips to Grandma's house in Fresno were another one of those highlights of childhood that will never be forgotten.

Years later my parents met in San Francisco and eventually settled in a small house in a South San Francisco suburb. As children, we could never quite grasp why this location was chosen, as it seemed to be in the wind and fog year-round! How many times, as kids, we had tried to save our pennies to help initiate a move, even if only ten minutes south, where the weather was better. Yet this never happened and so, in retrospect, perhaps God was already preparing me for the colder climes of Canada!

Growing up in a Catholic home, I went to Catechism every Tuesday and Mom took us to Mass on Sundays. It was this background that formed my belief that there was a God. But this general knowledge never had a personal impact on my life. While growing up, no one had told me that I needed a personal Saviour and that I could chose to make him Saviour and Lord of my life. It was only as a sixteen-year-old that I had a personal experience with God at a youth camp. From then on my life was forever changed. During the following years I hungered for more of God. This eventually led me to attend *Genesis*, where I would eventually meet and marry Phil.

But amidst all the joyous memories of home, there were also some dark foreboding ones. Though we all had our own challenges growing up, it seemed that my older brother always took the brunt of things at school. As an adult I seemed to remember only the positive memories from my family, but this act of brutality by my brother forced open the door to ask some hard questions about my upbringing. *What in the world happened in my family? Had our upbringing been really so bad, that it caused Tony to do this?* These questions turned over and over in my mind. It forced me to deal with the pain which I had felt as a child over my parent's relationship. While they were honest, hardworking people, who really loved us children, it seemed to me that they had difficulty making their relationship work. With the luxury of hindsight, I am sure that this was due to a multitude of varied factors and reasons. While this caused us to grow up in a home with high levels of stress at times, this in and of itself was not what caused this event to occur. After all, the rest of us siblings had made good life choices, though we had grown up in the same home. Others with worse families have been successful, and others with better families have turned out worse. Ultimately it was choices that my older brother made that were going to affect all of us in many life-changing ways.

As a family we had enjoyed eating together and it was actually a form of entertainment. But for Tony it also became a way of coping and, while he was always a big fellow, by his early teens he had become obese. From a very early age, it seemed Tony was overweight. Right from the first grade, others would pick fights with him and tease him for being fat. On more than one occasion, in elementary school, the class bully would kick him in the belly and crotch. Other than his weight, it is hard to determine a specific reason why Tony was their target, for he was very smart in school and, surprisingly, considering his weight, even pretty good in sports. Perhaps what I found most heartbreaking at the time was the fact that none of Tony's friends ever stuck up for him. Though he tried to avoid confrontations and did not start fights, he had to learn to fight back. It was perhaps this lack of aggressiveness that was perceived as a weakness and somehow, in the rough and tumble of San Francisco schools, he was continuously picked on.

In junior high school, it was horrible to see my older brother running to his locker, getting his things as quickly as possible, and then scurrying to his next class chased closely by an even larger boy. Scenes like this were daily occurrences. I am not sure if my parents knew, but it was never discussed in our home. It was not like Tony to complain about it to Mom and Dad. He didn't steal, smoke or drink, or fall into any of the other common vices of youth, and he had even saved a rather healthy bank account from his regular paper route.

By the time he entered high school it seemed that he was no longer the victim that I had seen while he was in junior high school. Strangely, his former tormentors would now even talk to him. While attending high school, I and a few others, started a Christian Club. It was during this time that Tony also made a decision to follow the Lord and attended our Christian Club. Though we saw others come to Christ, there was also some weirdness, as one member of the group began to try controlling the behaviour of the others. Yet in spite of this, Tony at one point spoke of Bible School and perhaps going into full-time ministry.

But as time went by, it seemed that he became disillusioned with other Christians and began to withdraw from others. Ironically enough, during this time Tony remained closest to my father. When he had been younger he had played catch with Dad and now that he was older he would often go on business deliveries with him. To the rest of us, it seemed that, of any of us children, he was the closest to Dad. As the years of his early adulthood progressed he seemed to develop, or at least begin expressing, more anger. And though a gifted mechanic (he would keep all of our cars working!), he could never keep a job. At any criticism or negative comment he would just walk off the job and never return. In time this made him virtually unemployable.

The breakup of my parent's marriage at that time, only months after Phil and I were married, seemed to affect his emotional state deeply. Though he was a young adult, chronologically, by that time, his emotional maturity could best be described as adolescent. After my parent's separation, he continued to live with Dad and, though Dad would always help him get a job, he could never keep it. Though we were by this time establishing our own home in Canada, the situation with Dad and Tony remained a matter of prayer. It was during this time that Tony had even struck and threatened Dad and Grandma. Though the rest of us were trying to help Dad get professional intervention, Tony's stays in mental care institutions were usually short lived, only providing him a wider variety of contacts with stranger and stranger people.

It would only be after my father's death that we were to learn more about these days, through various legal and medical papers that were found. We discovered that Dad had even been admitted to an emergency room with broken ribs and a bloody nose on one occasion. Throughout this time Dad was trying to get Tony counselling and admitted to a psychiatric hospital on the grounds that he was showing schizophrenic tendencies. Tony was beginning to hear voices and seemed to even be involved in the occult, listening to the suggestions of voices in his head. His lifestyle had deteriorated to living in his room, which was often dark and surrounded by out-of-context scriptures from Revelation, scrawled on pieces of paper.

It seemed like such a waste of a life compared to the potential of what could have been.

The thump of the large plane landing safely on the runway of the San Francisco International Airport, jarred us from our thoughts back into the present. The one and a half hour flight from Vancouver to San Francisco had been rather uneventful. As several of Nancy's siblings gathered in their Father's home, it all had a bit of a surreal feeling to it. By this point Nancy's parents had been divorced for several years and only Tony and their Grandmother Buyuklian had been living in the small fifties-style home. Over the next hours the details of what had happened began to unfold.

Apparently her father and grandmother had been watching television in the living room on that Monday evening, while Tony was in his bedroom. While Dad had been trying to get help for Tony for years, during that week following the San Francisco earthquake he had been seriously trying to get him, now 27 years old, admitted to a psychiatric hospital. On the night of his death, Dad had been talking with his mother in Armenian in the living room. This seemed to aggravate Tony, so much so that he had told them to stop. Of course, since Grandma Buyuklian understood only Armenian and French, after Tony went back to his room, they continued with their conversation which was most likely a combination of both languages. Then, without saying a word, Tony had gone to the attached garage, taken a shovel and returned to the living room, swinging it in a rage at his father.

Tony was a big man of over two hundred pounds, while Dad was only a short man barely over 5'4". Even if he could have known what was coming, he never would have had a chance. Years of frustration, rage and confusion were released as Tony repeatedly delivered blows with the blunt object to the outstretched arms, back and head of father. As Tony went back to his room, Grandma ran to the neighbour yelling, which eventually brought the paramedics and police. Dad's life expired moments later in the ambulance. His mother was also deeply traumatized by what she had witnessed and was never the same again, till she passed away several years later. Tony, who had gone back to his room, was quickly taken into custody by the police.

Everyone in the family had seen signs of potential disaster and we had all tried to get help, but the authorities repeatedly had said that nothing could be done, unless Tony actually did something against the law. Being unstable, and even threatening someone, was not reason enough to be institutionalized. *Now* there was reason enough to incarcerate him, but for Dad and the rest of the family it would be too late. They would have to live with the scars that this moment of rage had produced. There was slight comfort in the fact that at least Dad did not survive the brutal attack with horrendous injuries. We knew that he had gone to a better place of perfect peace.

We all stayed in the family home for that night, but sleeping in the same room that held such gruesome memories proved too much and so for the rest of the time we stayed with other family living in the area. The days following our arrival were a bit of a blur – consoling one another and making the necessary funeral arrangements. These were further complicated by the fact that the coroner did not want to release his body, as they wanted to insure the exact cause of death. After much pressure by Nancy's older sister they finally relented and gave up the body so that the funeral could take place as scheduled. After all, the blatant nature of the attack was never questioned nor was there any question as to who had committed the crime. While the details for the immediate were beginning to sort themselves out, it would take years for the executor to sort out some of the other family matters.

Since we were already in the Bay area, Nancy and I decided to visit some friends from our college days. Santa Rosa was only about an hour away and so one sunny afternoon we headed north up the US 101. The hour drive north from the city was therapeutic. Accompanied by a glorious autumn sun, we drank in the beautiful scenery as we crossed the magnificent Golden Gate Bridge, wound through Marine country, with its luxurious estates, finally reaching the vineyard country of the Napa valley. It was almost as if by retracing our steps, we could turn the clock back to the good ol' memories of college and our courting days – back to a time when our dreams were still fresh, before having to deal with the realities of dashed expectations, Nancy's accident, and now this ugly murder. It was almost as if the autumn sun could melt away every hurt in our hearts.

But it was only God who could soothe and bring answers to our hearts. It was the very biblical principles we had learned nearly ten years earlier in this place that had helped us through many of the hard times. Perhaps retracing our steps was an opportunity to pause by our pile of stones that were reminders for our lives: reminders of the truths we knew; reminders of what God had said in our young hearts; reminders to apply his Word to our situation, now that we were in the middle of the battle.

We pulled into the driveway of the Andersons, looking forward to our time together. Rich and Beth had been staff members when we had attended *Genesis* and Rich had been my mentor. Rich was not the kind of guy who said very much – there were actually occasions during our weekly meetings when I wondered if he was there at all! But in time I discovered that he was very engaged and was a good listener. When he did say something it usually was important and something I needed to think about, like the time we had sat in his van years before, preceding the Christmas break of 1981.

"Well, Phil, what are you going to do over Christmas?" had been his approach to the subject. Of course what we both knew he really meant was, "You've been dating Nancy seriously for some months, God has led your relationship, now it is time for you to make a decision. Over the Christmas break would be an opportune time to decide one way or the other." It was his apparent laid-back attitude that was disarming, but very effective for my kind of personality. If he had been too direct, I would not have been able to learn as much as I did from him.

But now, years later, we were again with the Andersons. It was comforting to be with them during this week of grief and turmoil. Now Rich still did not say too much; just an appropriate nod and that knowing smile, as he would lean back in his chair and fold his arms over his chest. Now it was we who were the ones straining under the yoke of responsibility and service. While we had been in college they had modelled a godly marriage and principles of ministry for us, yet now we were the ones having to live them out for ourselves and be that model for others. The afternoon passed by quickly and as the sun set in the west over the Pacific ocean, it was time for us to drive back to the Bay area.

The family did not seem to have many other options, on short notice, and so it was arranged that I would preform the funeral service. As it was the first funeral that I had ever officiated, I was a bit apprehensive, particularly in light of the circumstances. Though Dad was not an orthodox believer, some in the extended family were, and so the funeral service was held at the *Armenian Orthodox Church* in San Francisco.

Before marrying my bride to be, who was of Armenian heritage, I had read with fascination of the history of Armenia. It is a small country sandwiched between Turkey, Georgia and Azerbaijan, straddling Europe and Asia, with a very interesting history. Perhaps its greatest claim to fame, even before it was a nation, was the fact that Mt. Ararat, the traditional resting place of Noah's Ark, was located within its borders. But perhaps more noted in history books, is the fact that around 300 AD it was the first country to formally adopt Christianity as its official religion. This even predated Constantine's declaration in 312 AD that the whole Roman Empire would follow the Christian faith. Throughout the ebb and flow of history, there has always been an Orthodox Armenian Church which, at least on paper, held to many of the doctrines of Christianity.

Given the setting of this historic church, it only seemed appropriate for the Armenian priest to have an opportunity to say a few words in the Armenian language. Those *few words* took over forty minutes, which for ninety percent of us who knew no Armenian seemed much longer. From my vantage point on the platform, I could see that he had lost most of the audience, but he was a real trooper and did not let that stop him! Finally it came time for me to say a few remarks and I knew that they would have to be abbreviated as time had slipped away. *What could I say that would make any sense and would help to sooth the wounds?* So as briefly as possible I tried to direct the audience to a God who is in control, even during the unexplainable, and of a God who can comfort, even during the unbearable. I then directed my final remarks to those who, as of yet, had no personal peace with God, and I shared the Good News that through the life, death, and resurrection of Jesus Christ we all could have the same eternal hope that Dad Buyuklian was experiencing right now.

After the service, family members who had travelled from various regions of the Golden State had the opportunity to become reacquainted and share each other's grief. Yet even in the face of tragedy, everyone remembered the good times with this man who some knew as friend, others as neighbour or work colleague, still others as brother or father.

Whether it was a co-worker, friend, or relative, the common memory seemed to be that of a likeable man who was very jolly and liked to laugh. Everyone could remember seeing his body shake with laughter, eyes shut, mouth open, even though no sound was coming out! This would usually be enough to get everyone else laughing. The family also discovered just what he had meant to so many people. Details such as his favourite pastries were also discovered from co-workers. He had worked many late nights at his sewing machine in the attached garage, doing jobs on the side to pay the bills. He was remembered by many of these loyal clients as a nice man who was willing to help them with any and every tailoring job.

He had been trained in France as a custom tailor, but would often sigh, "No one needs that skill anymore, in a world of picking a suit off a clothing rack." This fact had led him to spend his days being the main alteration tailor at the large Macy's store in the City, only doing custom tailoring on the side.

Even I, who at the time had been part of the family for only the last seven years, had my share of good memories. I could still remember first meeting this short, somewhat hunched over gentle man. My first contact with Nancy's family happened while we were still in our first year at college in Corvallis, Oregon, a small town about eighty miles south of Portland. Mary, Nancy's older sister, had her pilot's licence and had flown up in a small plane together with her Dad. Nancy and I had waited for their arrival on the tarmac of the small airport. Once they landed and introductions were made, Mary offered to take us up for a little spin. She seemed to know what she was doing and so I agreed. "After all," I reasoned, "it would only be a short flight, one takeoff and one landing. How bad could it be?" The beauty of the rolling hills surrounding Corvallis and the Willamette Valley almost made me forget how much more this felt like *real* flying than being in a commercial jet as I was accustomed.

I will never forget the almost nonchalant question Mary posed after about half an hour of flight, "Phil, do you have any idea where the airport is?"

"Do I know where the airport is!" *I could not remember being asked to be the navigator!* I had assumed that that was the pilot's job! But trying to be cool, and make a good impression on my girlfriend's family, I just as nonchalantly replied, "Ah well, I am not sure, I am actually not from here."

Meanwhile I was starting to look at the ground very intently, study it for anything that may look like an airport, or for that matter any flat piece of land! I began imagining my first flight in a small plane ending in a farmer's field somewhere. Fortunately it did not come to that and Mary, with the aid of the map that she had spread out on her lap, got her bearings and found the little landing strip and we landed uneventfully. For my part, my faith in small aircraft pilots around the world was restored, as well as in the sanity of my girlfriend's family. Mary stayed in Nancy's townhouse and her father in mine and over the course of the weekend I was able to get to know him on a more personal level.

Over the next year, I met him on several occasions. His ability to discuss any subject with breadth of perspective was always interesting. I was to discover that there was a whole lot more than met the eye with this man, who was to later become my father-in-law. For instance, the way he could navigate his small Pinto car up and down the steep streets of San Francisco, or the way he would listen to the ideas and opinions of a young eighteen year old whipper-snapper and seem interested!

An incident occurred a year and a half later on the occasion of our marriage that I will never forget. My father, brother and sister and their spouses had come down to California. The night before the wedding, together with Nancy's family, we had all gathered for a meal following the wedding rehearsal. As it came time to pay the bill, everyone contributed their portion of the bill in cash. Once it was all added up, it became clear that there was too much money. Someone had obviously over contributed. For some reason Dad Buyuklian was accused of being the generous one by putting in the extra cash. Against his protestations that he had not, his kids tried to make him take it back. Meanwhile, I continued to *impress* my family with my "greenback knowhow." I was explaining how easy it was to mix up the paper bills since they were all the same colour, unlike Canadian bills which had different colour schemes. I waxed eloquently as to how I used to make this mistake, but after living for two years in the USA, I never made that error anymore.

Meanwhile the voices were getting louder trying to convince Dad Buyuklian of his silly "mistake" of contributing too much money. As was his manner, he never got angry, just had his jovial smile and laugh ready. "Okay, if you want me to take some back then I will," though he knew he had put in the right amount.

It was not until later that night that I discovered that it was indeed I who had put in a $50 bill instead of a $20 bill. When I told Nancy's father the next day, he just smiled and had a good chuckle, without any mention of the obvious abuse he had taken the night before. Just a knowing chuckle. That was George A. Buyuklian – my wife's father.

These are memories of a man whose life had been snuffed out too early for our liking. But we consoled ourselves with the realization that we knew that he was in a better place. His eternal home had a lot to do with Tommy, a young man who also attended the funeral. Nancy had talked to Tommy about Christ during her zealous days in high school, but at that time he had brushed off her attempts. While these efforts seemed fruitless, Tommy eventually did accept Jesus as his Saviour and even became a pastor. Unbeknown to Nancy at the time, Tommy had continued to hang around her father quite a bit. George was a fatherly influence on him and Tommy, for his part, would talk about Christ with him. He continually encouraged him that "church" or "right living" in and of itself could never save one's soul. This was only possible through Jesus Christ and regardless of what age we were, it was never too late. But whenever Tommy would ask George if he wanted to receive Christ into his life, he would always shake his head. Yet on one occasion, while they were shopping together in a Christian bookstore, a salesclerk asked George if he was ready to turn over the control of his life to someone that loved him more than anybody else ever could. Then and there he was ready and said yes, only three short years before he was whisked away to see his Lord face to face! Nancy, the first in her family who became a Christian, had planted the seed which Tommy had watered, but it had taken a virtual stranger to see the fruit of their labour and prayers.

So it was on a cool, but clear, October day that we wound our way up the hills of the city of Colma, to the cemetery to bury the body of Dad Buyuklian. As we all circled around the grave side, there was a brisk autumn breeze blowing off the Pacific Ocean. Standing on the edge of the rolling hill, I repeated the words of the Apostle Paul, in 1 Corinthians 15:51-51, to those gathered:

> "Listen, I tell you a mystery: We will not all sleep, but we will all be changed–in a flash, in the twinkling of an eye, at the last trumpet. For the trumpet will sound, the dead will be raised imperishable, and we will be changed. For the perishable must clothe itself with the imperishable, and the mortal with immortality. When the perishable has been clothed with the imperishable, and the mortal with immortality, then the saying that is written will come true: 'Death has been swallowed up in victory.' 'Where, O death, is your victory? Where, O death, is your sting?' The sign of death is sin, and the power of sin is the law. But thanks be to God. He gives us the victory through our Lord Jesus Christ"

As the sun from the clear azure sky reflected off the white surf of the ocean that afternoon, these words seemed to ring clearer and truer than at any other time that I had ever read them. It had been a senseless act, an event that would take years to emotionally come to terms with and one that would deeply affect our life, marriage, and ministry. But the truths that the Apostle Paul penned were never more comforting, more profound. Regardless of the tragedies on this side of eternity, we know that God is still on the throne. Through his victory, Christ defeated death and we can now share with others that there is a future hope. Regardless of the tragedy or seemingly desperation of the situation, this same power that raised Christ from the dead is also at work in us. Perhaps this is the greatest comfort that can be given to mortal mankind. Knowing that Dad Buyuklian had made his peace with God during the last years of his life gave us the strength to take the last step and lower the casket into the ground. For we knew that it contained only his earthly "tent." The *real* Dad Buyuklian was present with the Lord, waiting for that last trumpet to sound.

———————◆———

After the funeral we all returned to our own lives, our own responsibilities, our own plans. For Phil and me this meant a flight back to Vancouver to continue our preparations for Africa, some short eight months away. These were busy times as we were deciding what we would bring and what we would put in storage. But it was more than just dealing with the stuff; it was also dealing with many emotions as we began to realize the step before us. Phil had his lists and was ticking each line off one by one. Of course, I was also kept busy with our precious little three year old, who was at the age where she got into everything. Some days as I would look at her I would try to imagine what Africa would be like for her. *Were we crazy to be taking her so far away? Away from her aunts, uncles, and cousins?* As I saw the tiny scar on her toe that remained as a reminder of how God had spared her life on that September day, just over a year previous, it was with gratitude for how God had protected and kept her.

Alysia had just turned three years of age and we had been trying to have more children, as we had always envisioned a family of three children. But even before the accident I had had a miscarriage and then several months after the accident another one, right after a *Day of Discovery* with the insurance lawyers. Now that our plans were in place to leave to go to Africa within eight months, it did not seem to be the best time to have another child, so we had put these plans on hold. In the years to come we would have to face the reality that with everything we had been through, our quiver was happily full with our one daughter. While, at times, we felt regret that she had no other siblings, God seemed to always provide what she needed in terms of friendships and other positive role models.

During this time I was also continuing to see the doctor regarding my ongoing candida infection. Because of the broad spectrum of antibiotics, which I had received after my accident, both the good and the bad bacteria in my digestive system had been destroyed. This released an overgrowth of yeast which caused various symptoms, such as extreme fatigue, constant sore throat, menstrual problems, and dizziness, among others. Ultimately, this led to the development of various food allergies, which would take years of discipline with a special diet to overcome. Through God's strength, the steady hand of the surgeon, and the wisdom He gave the doctors, my life was spared, but in the years ahead I would also need God's grace and healing so that I would again be brought to a place of wholeness again – physically, emotionally and spiritually.

The emotional weight of my father's murder was an added burden that I carried during this time. But with the busyness of our preparations and the excitement surrounding our impending departure, this emotional burden was pushed into the background. But I began to notice that I could not cope with the same level of stress that I previously had and I even found myself become more easily angered, over even small issues. The spring had left my step. I did not dwell on these symptoms, though, thinking that in time they would pass. But in spite of my best efforts, instead of just "passing," the added stress that we were going to encounter in the years ahead was going to bring it all to the surface again.

7

Jambo Africa!

The driver skilfully backed the semi-trailer truck with the 20' piggyback metal container unto our gravel driveway in front of the little house that we had called home for the last two years.

April had arrived and with it the first real concrete step that we were indeed moving to Africa. Several months before we were actually going to fly to Kenya, we were shipping most of our *stuff* ahead, hoping that it would arrive not too long after we landed in Africa. This meant that for our last few weeks in Canada we would have to live out of suitcases. While it was a great plan on paper and could have worked, the reality was that our container did not arrive until October of that year, months after we had arrived. While it was in transit, the Gulf War had broken out and so all ship traffic through the Suez Canal had been held up, and with it the ship with our container.

The last few months before our departure life had been very busy, as I continued with my construction contracts, speaking in churches, as well as corresponding personally and through our newsletter. While we had not raised as much support as we really needed, together with our savings, it would be enough for our first two years. After all, we reasoned, this was a new venture and we knew that it would take some time to develop credibility. We believed that more funds would come available once we were in Africa.

The day we packed the container was like a good ol' fashioned barn-raising. The container was parked in our driveway on Friday and needed to be ready for pick up on Monday, so Saturday was set for the day to get all our stuff crammed and jammed into it. My brother and sisters and their spouses *volunteered* to take part in the action. Everything had to be packed tightly in cardboard boxes, and then all the boxes, as well as the furniture and appliances, needed to be wrapped in plywood and then custom fitted into the container. Truly a momentous job!

As the *baby* of the family I was blessed to have siblings that not only loved God, but were also an encouragement – even if some of the dreams and ideas their younger brother had seemed a bit "out there." As I had shared with them our planned move to Africa, there was a sense of support and encouragement. It had been my sister Christal who had passed on a *Genesis* brochure to me exactly ten years earlier and my other sister, Anita, who had floated her brother, a poor college kid, the funds to buy his fiancee an engagement ring. My oldest sister, Rita, who lived in Portland at the time, had made my transition to first year in college in Oregon easier.

I will never forget the shopping cart of groceries she and her husband had bought for me, "Buy whatever you want," they had said. Being on college rations, this was music to the stomach! Then there was all the practical help my brother, Bernie, provided from his accounting business and experience, helping set up our small business and, now, a non-profit society. These were blessings that the Lord had surrounded me with in the form of a family, who also had a heart for sharing God's love.

Our driveway soon began looking like a construction site as sawdust was flying, and boxes, furniture, and plywood began disappearing into the container. Their assistance seemed to be just another in a long list of ways they had helped me over the years. Much of what we were able to do was due to the strong shoulders of those closest to us. Since my parents believed in spacing out their children, from first to last, there were fourteen years separating all of us. So it never ceased to astound me that they who had helped change my diapers and babysit me, were able to also treat me as a peer, blessing me as an adult! But it went beyond that, for most had also been involved in full-time ministry at some point, and had an unshakeable commitment to see God's Kingdom expanded. They were not only related, but also partners with us. So it was with somewhat mixed emotions, on that day, that we began the process of saying goodbye. We were not sure exactly what the future was to hold, but we knew that something within us was saying, "Go!"

After all the preparations, for us "Go" would finally mean stepping onto a Pan Am flight from Seattle to Nairobi, via London. What was initially so exciting, was to become only the first of many trans-Atlantic flights. This trip, which included two all night flights as well as a layover in Europe, was to become rather routine in the coming decade. But in the summer of 1990, it still had the air of adventure as we waved goodbye to the entourage of family that had accompanied us to our *ship*. We did not come from a long line of missionaries in our family and so in a way this was a new experience for all of us.

After nine hours of flying from the west coast over northern Canada, the tip of Greenland, and eventually the British Isles, we touched down at Heathrow Airport in London the next morning. Finding our way around the sprawling maze of Heathrow for the first time was a challenge. We had not slept much on the plane and even during our nearly twelve hour layover in London we could not sleep. It had less to do with the uncomfortable seats, and more to do with the excitement and, yes, even a certain apprehension of the coming days and weeks. So with Alysia perched high atop our luggage cart, we finally arrived at our next gate ready to reach our final destination: *Africa!*

There is nothing quite like the feeling of flying over the continent of Africa for the first time. As I gazed out the window and saw the blue waters of the Mediterranean give way to the brown coastline of the African continent, it was hard to contain the excitement. Of course, we also had our share of apprehensions, something that all the inoculation shots and medical reports at the *Travel Medicine Centre* had helped to reinforce. Receiving our inoculations for diseases such as Hepatitis, Meningitis, Yellow Fever, Cholera and, of course, taking our malaria tablets, made us realize that we were indeed going to another world. It was particularly difficult to see Alysia get these shots and trying to teach her to swallow the bitter malaria prophylaxis tablets – a difficult task at three years old.

There were times that I wondered what I was taking my family into. *Going* had become a bit more complicated than hitching a ride on an Oregon interstate, as I had done some ten years earlier. All I had needed then was a backpack and a few bucks in my pocket. Now I had other responsibilities and had to learn to also trust God for my family, something that was going to be a process of growth. Yet, as we were cruising at 39,000 feet over the African continent, these thoughts were not uppermost in my mind. I had wrestled with this as we had made the decision to go and now it was a matter of just doing it.

But before we had even stepped on African soil the enemy was given opportunity to play on our natural apprehension of going to the *Dark Continent* for the first time. As it so *happened,* on the plane we bumped into another *experienced* missionary who was travelling to Africa. While she had been living in Africa for many years, we soon discovered that she had a less than positive outlook regarding *her* mission field. After only several of her horror stories, which basically revolved around death, disease and destruction, I was hoping that she would find her way back to her own seat, without me having to carry or escort her. Nancy, for sure, could not take too much more of this *faith sabotaging* discussion and I had had about as much as I wanted to take of it also. From missionary slide shows, I already had a fair share of snake and disease stories and did not need a graphic account of anything and everything that had gone wrong for this woman in Africa. While we knew first hand that bad things can happen to even good people, we chose to believe that God was faithful to protect and sustain us.

Fortunately, she found her way back to her seat, and I was able to settle back into my own thoughts, as I watching the farmers' fires in the predawn, as they burned off their fields far below. Soon the predawn darkness gave way to the crimson sunrise in the eastern sky, as the sands of the Sahara merged into the highlands of Kenya and eventually the plateau on which Nairobi was situated. *What would the future hold? How was God going to use us?* With all the twists and turns of the last few years, it was almost hard to believe that we would actually soon step off the plane onto African soil. We were actually arriving on *our* mission field.

It had been a year and a half since we had first met Phil Walker at the mission conference in Vancouver. Phil was now in Africa, having returned from furlough. At the time he and his wife were the only ICM missionary couple in Kenya. The Goodwins were in the States on furlough, while another couple was planning on leaving Kenya to pursue further training. While we had not had a lot of conversations after our short meeting at Missions Fest in Vancouver, I had informed him of our arrival time and as I approached the passport control I was sure hoping that he would actually be there!

Of course what we really needed was our work permit, which he had in his possession. There had not been enough time to send it to Canada after it was approved and so the plan was to somehow meet at the airport. As it happened, we were both on opposite sides of the officials. I knew that since we did not have return airline tickets, we would not be allowed to stay in the country without a work permit. As we dragged our carry-on luggage down the dark corridor towards the queues that were forming, I began to become more acutely aware of the serious-looking army troops patrolling the corridors with AK47 machine guns.

As I got to passport control, I did not yet know that it helped to be friendly and use the customary greeting, "Jambo," or "Habari." This would be something that I would learn. That first time, my expectations were much lower. I was merely focussing on survival and hoping that the man with the beard that I had met in Vancouver would miraculously appear. The reality of what I had gotten my family and myself into began to dawn on me. As I approached the wicket, I began rehearsing in my mind how I would explain why I did not have a tourist visa or a return ticket. But just when things seemed to go from bad to worse, I saw the welcome face of Phil Walker on the other side of passport control. Somehow he had talked his way into the passenger area and we were able to get the visa we needed in order to enter the country legally.

From the look on my wife's face, however, I could tell that this had been a less than thrilling experience for her! The muggy air of the airport, combined with the stress of the situation, did not provide the best of first impressions. I am sure the words spoken by the jaded returning missionary, that we had just met on the plane, probably did not help our state of mind either. Hearing "They hate missionaries in Africa" and "You'll sell your first born to get out of here!" were probably not the most comforting words for a new missionary to hear hours before landing for the first time in Africa! Having talked our way past the immigration official we proceeded to get our luggage. From there we made it through customs and began loading everything into Phil Walker's 4x4 pickup truck.

"Great to see you," he beamed and I could tell that he really meant it. It was hard to believe that we had just briefly met in Vancouver and now we were actually here. I had the feeling that Phil could not quite believe it either. I guess we knew that this was the direction God had for us and so without much input or direction had just made our preparations and launched out. It had never occurred to us that it would not work out.

We bumped and jostled down the road, dodging potholes all the way from the airport to the guesthouse where we would stay for a week before heading upcountry. *Africa.* I had countless times tried to imagine what it would actually be like, almost as if it would have characteristics of another planet. Yet here I was in the bustling city of Nairobi, cars jostling for position, as if in a demolition derby. And even though we were in the city, the variety and beauty of the tropical vegetation, were unmistakable. The *rugged* reality of what was daily life in an African city was every present, attacking every one of the senses – the *earthy* smell of the dust mixed with diesel exhaust, the constant sound of car horns, the sight of street hawkers selling their wares by the side of the road – all wrapped up into one glorious extravaganza for the senses! While the bedlam of traffic and exotic smells of street markets, diesel and the odours of millions of people living close together took some getting used to, it was going to be something that I was going to learn to miss – and look forward to every time I returned to what was once called the *Dark Continent.*

The next few days were spent adjusting to jetlag, and experiencing the new sights and sounds of Africa. Phil Walker was busy attending a conference and so he offered us his truck to get around town as we looked for a vehicle. It sounded easy enough, but I was not sure I was ready for that. For starters, everyone was driving on the *wrong* side of the road, since Kenya had been a British colony! Add to this the *kamikaze* nature of the other drivers and that the steering wheel and stick shift were all on the *other* side and it did not seem like such a great idea. But Phil Walker had a convincing way of encouraging you to do things that you *knew* you could not, or perhaps *should* not do. So throwing caution to the wind, we joined the rest of the drivers, who seemed to be doing their best to see how close they could get to the other vehicles without actually making contact. It seemed like real life bumper cars. I was glad I was in a truck!

After about a week of jetlagging in Nairobi we were finally actually awake for most of the daylight hours and able to sleep through the night. We had also found a good used Peugeot 305 station wagon, which would serve us well. Since Phil Walker needed to stay longer in the city, we decided to leave for Kitale the next morning on our own. It was arranged that we would follow the Hayes family, missionaries that were serving with another mission in Kitale, the town that we would also call home. So we began our journey upcountry in our Peugeot early the next morning. It was to be the first of many trips between Nairobi and Kitale and, as with most first experiences, it was very memorable.

From east to west, Nairobi is located in about the centre of Kenya. About six hours' drive east from the capital city is the city of Mombasa on the Indian Ocean. Travelling in the opposite direction, about the same distance, one encounters the western highlands and the small town that was going to be our home for the next two years. Kitale has the feel of a frontier town. It is actually the last real outfitting and staging place for those heading north towards Pokot and Turkana country, a region which borders southern Sudan.

I soon discovered that one of the greatest challenges of driving in Africa, was to be able to drive at highway speeds without hitting any of the people, goats, and cows walking on either side (and even the middle) of the road. I happened to be following a seasoned missionary driver, however, who was oblivious to all this and was very frugal in his use of the brakes. *Very frugal.* In spite of the feeling that I was constantly putting my life and that of my family into danger, we raced on. Within months the driving conditions would also become routine for us and what once seemed like recklessness, would become a *normal* way of life.

Within an hour of leaving Nairobi, we began ascending the escarpment of what is the Great Rift Valley. This massive seam in the Earth stretches 4000 miles from the Middle East in the north to the borders of Mozambique in Africa. It is such a large physical feature that it can easily be seen from space. The view of the valley floor, from the top of the escarpment, stretches for miles, into the famous game parks of Tanzania, only periodically punctuated by extinct volcanoes. It is, indeed, one of the great sights to behold on the planet. But we could not linger long, as we were told it was important to make it to Kitale before sunset. Driving on the roads was dangerous enough during the day; at night it was toying with life itself!

As we careened (remember, no brakes!) down to the valley floor and the city of Nakuru, things began to feel downright desert-like. With vegetation that appeared to have been transplanted from Arizona or Texas, the setting began to look more like one would expect in Africa. Soon after passing the large city of Nakuru, we crossed the equator, going from the southern hemisphere to the northern one. We then began to gain elevation as we entered the western highland country. Winding our way through Cypress forests and the occasional waterfall, it was hard to believe that we were still in Africa, very near the equator.

Then just after the small town of Eldama Ravine, our first trip was initiated with what was to be a common occurrence, a flat tire. By this point we had already passed through fifteen checkpoints along the way, which for the uninitiated were a bit nerve-racking. The combination of the large spike belts across the road, and the AK47's everyone seemed to have, only added to the sense of culture shock. I was not sure if they were looking for wayward missionaries, but it soon became clear that they did not like the washer and dryer that the Hayes were hauling to Kitale. Every checkpoint meant a close inspection of all papers, and a visual inspection of the *pseudo-*

contraband. This tight level of security was eventually to ease up in the months ahead as Kenya wanted to be seen by the world as a more open society on the eve of national elections.

By late afternoon we turned off the main road, just past Eldoret, and headed towards Kitale, which was now only about one hour away. Outside of the game parks, most herds of wild animals have long since gone extinct in Kenya. But on our first trip to Kitale we were treated to see one of the last wild herds of giraffes grazing on the acacia trees by the side of the road. As we drove off the side of the road on to the hard stubble field, to be closer to these gentle giants, it did not seem hard to imagine a time when herds of wild animals roamed freely throughout this land.

We arrived in Kitale in the fading light of the African evening. Our initial home in Kitale was an old British house on an acre of land which the ministry was renting. We would eventually renovate this to become the first Ministry Training Centre, but for now it would serve as our home. After what seemed weeks of travelling, it felt good to stop moving for a while. In the strangeness of the old colonial home, accompanied by a slight musty odour, we unpacked some of our bags and quickly crawled into bed.

Being greenhorns to Africa, there were many surprises and much to get used to. We soon discovered that if we wanted warm water in the morning we had to inform Joram, the gardener, the night before. He would then light a fire under the large outside drum filled with water. Once heated we had heated water on tap! It was not all that efficient, but it worked, mind you *only when you remembered to tell him*. Learning to master the two burner stove and make sure that the gas bottles did not run dry also become very important. Meanwhile, Alysia was having fun chasing the monkeys that would come into the yard to feed on the guava trees. Of course, after the first time, they realized that they were bigger than she and would stand their ground. From then on she would only chase them from a distance, or when Dad was around!

While I basically am *allergic* to all forms of shopping, I soon discovered that the best prices on fruits and vegetables were in the open market – yet shopping there was not for the faint-hearted! But venturing into this world of rude odours, flies, and price bargaining usually meant being rewarded with lots of great bananas, pineapples, passion fruit, mangoes and papaya. My desire for a good deal won over my aversion for shopping, and so guess whose job it became to go to the open market every week! Every day seemed full of new experiences and adventures. Learning how the system worked was half of the challenge, from the post office, to the bank, to shopping – everything had new rules. The days of dark, damp mornings, trying to motivate myself and the crew, seemed a very distant memory.

When it came to weather, there was not even a need for a weather channel (which was good since we could get no channels!). It seemed that every day was similar to the previous one. Kitale, at the 6,200 foot elevation always seemed sunny and clear (before the El Nino years), ranging from a low of about 15 degrees Celsius at night, during the wet season, to a maximum of 30 degrees Celsius in the dry season. From November to February, the dry season, it hardly rained at all. Then during the season of the *long rains* it would rain regularly in the afternoon and during the *short rain* season just periodic afternoon rains. No, a more perfect climate would be hard to imagine.

But what was really exciting was to be on the ground floor of designing the programs that we would begin to use. After years of being *on the shelf* it seemed I had been given a new lease on life. Even the somewhat mundane tasks during the early months, such as daily language studies, learning the culture, finding and renovating a home, could not dampen my enthusiasm. God had brought us to this place against all odds, and I was ready to roll up my sleeves and get to work.

These early days were also spent getting to know Phil and Debbie Walker and their three teenage boys and learning from their missionary experience. They were vulnerable and unpretentious and it was a joy to work together as a team. It seemed like all the pieces were fitting together. After years of feeling like we were on the backside of the desert, God had brought us to a broad place of ministry that fit with our personality and ministry gifts.

As it turned out, within a few months of arrival the Walkers and us were the only full-time "team" left on the ground in Kitale. One couple, that had begun in the missionary training program, had left to pursue further training and other ministry. Myron and

Carol Goodwin, who had begun working with Phil and Debbie on the Kibbutz in Israel during the eighties and were the co-founders of the ministry in the USA, were on furlough in the States. They were scheduled to return to Africa in the summer of 1991.

It was during this time that the vision and focus of the ministry was crystalized. Though it would go through various adaptations, we knew that we were *to serve the church by training and equipping its leaders.* How this was to be done also went through various changes. Being a pioneer at heart, it was exciting to be a part of the process. As much as we appreciated the lessons we had learned on the backside of the desert, we were not quite ready to volunteer to go back there quite yet, if ever!

The early teams with ICM, in the late eighties, were students enrolled in the *Perspective* course and learning missions while doing missions. Eventually staff would get their feet wet by doing outreaches in high schools and other venues. But at the start of the nineties, the focus narrowed to the obvious need around us – training and equipping national church leaders. After the revival had swept East Africa in the mid part of the Twentieth Century, there had been a great influx of believers into the churches. New churches sprang up everywhere and new church movements grew every week. The result of this was that there was a lack of trained leadership who could really shepherd the sheep. The Church had grown wider and not deeper. This had led to falling away, syncretism, and ultimately a weak church. African leaders themselves have described the Church in Africa as being a *lake that is miles wide, but only inches deep.* We felt called to be a part of the solution to this situation.

To start with, we began looking for good materials that we could use and adapt within the African context. It is often easy for others to assume that those functioning as pastors in Africa already have an established position and infra-structure to manage the flock. But typically, in Africa, an evangelist preaches in an area and a group of believers begin to meet. This group often begins to grow rapidly and the needs of the fledgling assembly also begin to grow. Since most attending are still new believers, those chosen to fulfill various functions in the church have very little experience and are often new believers themselves. This also includes whoever happens to become the pastor, leader or preacher of the new church. For his part, this person soon realizes that he has responsibilities beyond his experience, Bible knowledge, or even character development. But now they have a dilemma: they cannot just abandon the new church to get training, yet they need training to take the church further. This is often the scenario among our primary target group, the *African Indigenous* (or *Independent) Churches (AIC'S)*. These churches are growing faster than any other group in Africa with a membership of over 50% of all believers on the continent.

We began to utilize a method called *TEE* or *Theological Education by Extension* to meet this need. This meant that we would travel a circuit, teaching a small group of pastors in various areas of the country, typically each area on a different day of the week. It did not take long for this to grow to the point that we could not physically get to all the various groups wanting training. By this time Nancy and I had moved into another home and the old British home was renovated so that we could hold *Tutor Training* sessions. Our idea was that the only way we could expand our efforts, was to *train the trainers*. We soon discovered that, once equipped, the nationals could do even a better job than we could and the numbers of those involved in the training programs began to mushroom. It seemed that every spare minute at home was spent on the computer developing lesson plans and administrative systems to track students and ensure our training was being effective. Before long there were hundreds of Africans enrolled, spread out over hundreds of kilometres.

The first year had gone by quickly and we had not only begun to adapt to the culture, but also were enjoying seeing the work grow. At the beginning of our second year, Phil and Debbie moved to Kijabe (near Nairobi) to be closer to their children who were in school at the Rift Valley Academy. Myron and Carol had by then returned from the USA and our small team went through changes as we learned to adapt to each other again. Again it was God's timing as Myron and I were able to put our heads together, I on the lesson plans, he on the administrative structures, and manage all the new contacts and work that Phil was continuously creating around the country.

Meanwhile we also continued to teach small groups of pastors. Every Wednesday we would fly to a group of leaders on Mt Elgon. This meant getting to the Kitale airport early, to meet the helicopter, which was operated by *HeliMission*, a Swiss-based ministry. The term *airport* may evoke too generous a description. This large but lonely runway was surrounded by grassy fields with an equally lonely 10x10 foot office that sufficed for all airport matters. There were also some round tin huts that housed airport workers, though their job description seemed rather nebulous.

So with our briefcase of books, papers, and exams, we would meet the helicopter at the airport for the fifteen minute flight to high slopes near the top of the mountain. Mt Elgon's main claim to fame is that it has the largest base of any mountain in the world (that is not a part of another mountain range). It straddles the Kenya-Uganda border and rises from Kitale's elevation of approximately 6,200 feet to over 13,000 feet. While the helicopter ride was fairly short, we knew from personal experience that during the dry season it could easily take over two hours to get there by four-wheel drive. During the rainy season all bets were off; it might take four hours, or it might take four days. On occasion, I would take my Isuzu Trooper to the Wycliffe base where we taught our class, but we did our best to avoid this.

Almost without exception the mornings were invariably clear and sunny. As we would strap ourselves in, the powerful rotor blades would overcome the force of gravity and we would be on our way up the slopes of the mountain. The valley would stretch out as a vast vista before us as we would gain speed in order to ascend up the alpine slopes of the mountain – a mountain which had once been an active volcano on the edge of Rift Valley. In what seemed like only minutes we would pass over the home of the lone Wycliffe missionary on the mountain and land in the clearing across the next valley. As we would disembark, the pilot would always remind us of *the* most important travel detail. He would remind us that, with us or without us, he and the helicopter would be leaving at noon! It was imperative that we head back off the mountain by noon, for by then the winds would usually begin to pick up and the thunder heads would develop. These winds would bring some very nasty weather, really fast. We never worried, for it seemed the pilots always did enough worrying for all of us, as they would constantly keep one eye on the clouds making sure that we left before the weather moved in.

The slopes of Mt. Elgon were largely populated by the Sabaot people. These are an *unreached people group* (an ethnic group that does not have a strong enough church to reach their own people, without outside help) of between 300-400,000 people. They are scattered around the slopes of the mountain on both the Kenya and Uganda side. Our weekly classes were not only a spiritual lifeline, but also a physical one to those whom we had contact with. Class attendance depended on various factors: weather, deaths in the family, and other church commitments. But usually the classes ranged from a handful to a maximum of twenty. In the years that followed, a few of these students would eventually travel to our extension BA program in Kitale and then less than a decade later some of these same graduates would begin the *Mt. Elgon Training Centre*, whose dedication I would attend in 1999. But in those early years, as we would leave the mountain waving as we went, what we were doing seemed so small and insignificant. All we were doing was teaching a few simple truths to a few pastors. But their hunger and thirst and dedication to reach the Sabaot people of Mt. Elgon would have far reaching results. They would one day expand our simple efforts many times over. This is what made our work so exciting. We were not just teaching, but multiplying leaders. Future staff members eventually would partner with Campus Crusade and the Jesus film would be translated into the Sabaot language, which was then used as an evangelistic tool throughout the whole region.

On alternate weeks we would travel into Uganda to teach. Uganda was a whole other world and for some reason I really had an affection for the Ugandan people. I could remember as a teen hearing of the plight of the Christians in this country, who suffered under Idi Amin, one of the most brutal dictators this world has seen. So perhaps it was no surprise that I had a real interest to help train the emerging church leaders in this country. What a privilege it was to meet personally and encourage the believers who had been through so much. So every week we would travel to Tororo, which was just over the Kenya-Uganda border near Kitale, to teach those who would gather. Our goal was to eventually begin a training centre which would meet the needs of in-service training throughout the country.

From Kitale it was about a two hour drive to the border, if the roads were in decent shape. But, even though Tororo, Uganda was just across the border, crossing the border itself could take literally hours. The only way to speed up the process was to learn the system. The "system" required filling out endless forms, talking with several immigration officials, the police, and even custom officials in order to get our Kenya into Uganda and then back again. Though not recorded in the *Guinness Book of World Records*, our personal best was a blistering twenty minutes! Hard to believe I know.

The cardinal rule, of course, was to appear as if you had all the time in the world and had nothing better to do than shoot the breeze with any and every official in sight. To beat the system we often worked in tag-team fashion, dividing up the requirement between us. Myron and I had honed this to an art form. I always had a tinge of sympathy for the obvious "first-timer," who was typically a foreigner. The dazed, lost look of despair in their eyes usually said it all. With no signage or real assistance, a first-timer had no real idea what they were up against. They had no real idea what had to be done, with what official it had to be done, and in what order it had to be done.

Rule number two, of course, was never to get angry. Regardless of how unreasonable the request seemed (the fact that you needed to pay with twenty US dollars, in cash, when at the same time it was illegal to be in possession of foreign currency, seemed to be a riddle too great for us mere mortals to comprehend), or how late we were for the start of our classes in Tororo. At its peak, there were at least seventeen different steps or stages that had to be *conquered*, before one could get through the border. We would often leave Kitale before sunup, getting to the border by sunrise, teach all day, and then try to make it back to Kitale by sundown.

One on occasion we met a young German at the border. He had been pedalling his ten speed bicycle across Africa and had left Nairobi (at least a 6 hour drive by car) with the understanding that he could get a visa for Uganda at the border. By the time we met him he had been at the border some time after being told by Ugandan officials that he could not get a visa at the border (not entirely true, as we had proven many times) and would have to pedal back to Nairobi. Lets just say he was not a happy camper and had lost his composure with the official. Even though his derogatory words were in German, I am sure that the official caught the gist of them! Basically this gentleman had either a couple days of pedalling ahead of him in the hot sun, or he could apologize and let everyone know that he was wrong, yet another misguided foreigner needing direction. Oh, yes, and pull out a crisp twenty dollar bill for the visa (which he would get a receipt for). Getting angry was never effective, regardless of what *rights* someone felt had been violated. It was important (as in all countries) to remember that we were guests and dependent on the good graces of those in authority. What, of course, they were not always aware of, was the fact that we had Someone who directed our steps and would often undertake in the most impossible of circumstances.

Yes, the border was a world all of its own. Besides the steady flow of foot traffic, carrying unbelievable amounts of goods for the public markets on their heads, there were the hundreds of large lorries and their drivers. Some were waiting on the paperwork in order to proceed, others were waiting for new parts (like a transmission) for their vintage trucks, while it seemed others were just waiting. Of course, these truck drivers encouraged a cottage industry of *ladies of the night,* as well as other seedy elements of society. It was definitely not a place you wanted to be after dark, especially if you had skin of a more fairer variety. While navigating through the border became a challenge, which we tried to make "fun," it was definitely an acquired skill. I was always reminded of this fact on those occasions when guests would travel with us. Typically, by the end of the process, they would be somewhat drained emotionally. A case for one person's *challenge* being another person's *trauma,* I suppose.

On another occasion we were coming back after a day of teaching and glided into the first check point of the border to begin the process, when the stick shift went limp in my hands. We had been running a bit late and knew that it was going to be tight time wise in order to be home by dark. Though I am not a mechanic, it was my guess that the stickshift should not do this and it was obvious that it had somehow become detached from the linkage.

Of course I did what most non-mechanics do. I opened the hood and tried to look intelligently at what basically looked to me like a jumble of metal, rubber hoses and electrical cords. As others began to gather around these two *Wazungu* (Kiswahili for *white folks*), to offer their unsolicited help, Myron had begun to pray. It was hard to think of anything much worse at that moment than spending a night in the car at the border – together, of course, with a few hundred of our closest trucking friends. But then as I looked in the general direction of where I thought the gear linkage should be, I noticed a loose bolt laying on a ledge of the car frame. One would have to know the condition of most roads in Africa to appreciate the unlikelihood of this situation. Within an inch of where the bolt was laying (God had to make it real easy for me, being aware of my very limited mechanical expertise!), I could see where it had to be screwed into in order to make the linkage function again. He never colour-coded it – but pretty close!

It was even in such simple experiences that we saw God undertake again and again. While He had done this throughout our lives, it was almost as if it happened more frequently and dramatically in Africa. While we had not suddenly become more spiritual, it seemed God's grace was greater in light of the acuteness of our needs. As we each step outside of our comfort zones we can all experience this, we do not even need to move to Africa! Even in our daily lives we can live with an expectation of God intervening and doing what only He can do.

Our classes in Tororo were held in various locations, ranging from a secondary school, to tents in the schoolyard, to even the local *Rock Hotel*. As the country was still rebuilding during this time, the windows of *The Rock* were still not fixed after being shot out and the rooms could have used some fresh paint. The latter would have helped to cover the numerous squashed mosquitoes lining the walls, who had undoubtedly lost their lives after sucking the blood from some poor soul while graciously sharing malaria with him. But they had paid with their life and had been left to hang on the walls as if as an example to future generations of mosquitos. Supper was also a unique experience. We had learned that regardless of how many promising items were listed on the menu, in reality there was probably *only* chicken and chips. Naturally, we always *chose* chicken.

The catch was that you had to order early and pay upon ordering. This was necessary so that the cooks would have some funds to go into town to buy the unlucky chicken that had unknowingly *volunteered* to be our meal for the evening. Perhaps not the most efficient system, but definitely fresh! As patrons we just had to be prepared to wait for several hours.

It was sad to see the poverty of the people and the lack of infrastructure. It was equally amazing to see what they could do, with so little. But most of all those early days of the ministry were exciting as we were able to serve the leaders of the church which had suffered such persecution. We often would bring many leaders from different groups together, attempting to restore the trust for one another that they had lost during Amin's *Reign of Terror*. In those early years, it was hard for anybody in the society to trust one another.

While the Christians did not have much materially, they did have a hunger for God's Word, which was very humbling. Our initial two years in Uganda were not easy and we often wondered if we should continue travelling there from Kitale. It is an axiom that one of the greatest ingredient for successful missions work is finding the right people to work with. Unfortunately, as it turned out, we were initially working with someone whose motives were less than pure. While we knew this to be the case at the time, he was our only real contact that enabled us to be in the country.

In the early days we would stay on the front yard of his compound in a tent, basically so that we could keep the mosquitos out. Call us weak-kneed, but we also found it easier to sleep in the confines of a tent rather than listening to the rats that would scurry across the rafters of his *living room* and peer down at us with their beady eyes.

On one occasion we had exchanged about $1000 into Ugandan Shillings, which we needed to store in our tent overnight. While this does not seem like too complex of a proposition, we soon realized that with at an exchange rate of 1000 USh to 1 dollar, this was one million shillings! To further compound our dilemma, the largest bank note at the time was the equivalent of about ten cents. This translate into a substantial pile of cash. After filling our first duffle bag at the bank we discovered that we would need several more bags just to leave the bank. It was then that we realized that sleeping with this large amount of *paper* in a tent could be problematic! It represented a small fortune for the average Ugandan. But with some creative stuffing, our pillows and sleeping bags had extra padding that night, and fortunately no one walking outside of our tent (many of which were armed) was any the wiser.

In those early years our prayer was that God would lead us to leaders of integrity so that the crucial work of training could continue. It would take several years for us to see the answer to our prayer. For many years we carried the burden in our heart for the Ugandan people, but we felt that we were merely scratching the surface of meeting the need in the country.

Our vision of eventually having Centres throughout Kenya and Uganda, and eventually other African countries, seemed a long way away. We experimented with various models with the goal of being able to provide training that was accessible, affordable, and applicable to all those in ministry who desired it. At times it was not clear how we were going to be able to run various extension training programs, as well as in-service certificates, diplomas and degrees, given our limited resources. But in spite of the challenges of those early days, life took on a joyous routine. We functioned well as a team and began hearing positive reports from those whose ministries were benefiting from being able to study God's Word, without having to leave their church, family, or community for extended periods of time.

For us, also, it was the fulfilment of a dream. Being able to focus my efforts and abilities to see others deepen in their personal walk and ministry skills, made all the years of being *on the shelf,* worthwhile. While at the time it had seemed like I was doing nothing, God had been using that time to prepare me for our future service. But God also had more things to teach us. While on one hand we were seeing the fulfilment of our vision, in the months that followed we would be tested to see if we would be willing to walk our *Isaac* (the promise),up Mt Moriah; being willing to lay on the altar the very fulfilment of the promise that God had given to us.

Would our love for God be even greater than our affection for seeing his promises fulfilled in our lives? Would we be willing to trust Him again, in what was to be a dark tunnel that lay before us?

8

Late Nights and Flashing Lights

It was just before the dry season in Kitale, towards the end of 1991. After being in Africa for about a year, we had decided to join some team members for a few days of vacation in Mombasa. Part of the experience had been travelling by car right across the country, traversing through Tsavo National Park, before arriving at the Indian Ocean on the east coast of Kenya. It was truly a once in a lifetime experience to be able to snorkel in the warm blue waters of the Indian Ocean, gazing at the incredible variety of sea life below the surface. Alysia, for her part, had played hard in the pool every day, doing what four-year-olds do best.

It was to be several weeks later, on a trip to Nairobi, that we were to discover that besides the sunburn and nice shells, we had also picked up something else from our trip to Mombasa.

I awoke with a start to the screams of Alysia. It took me a few moments to rouse myself from my deep sleep. As I leaned over to touch her small body, I realized that she was burning up. I quickly took off her covers, by which time Phil and Debbie Walker had rushed into our room, attracted by all the commotion. We were all staying in Nairobi at the same SIM/Wycliffe guesthouse which we had stayed at a year earlier when we had first arrived in Africa. We in one room, and the Walkers in the other.

Since we had no aspirin, all we could do was try and bring the fever down by applying wet cloths to her body. As we did this, her small body would stiffen as it would again go into a seizure. It was with a desperation of not knowing what to do that we prayed together in the dark room that night. Even though we were in the main city of Nairobi, it was impossible to find a functioning phone on the compound. Phil and Debbie, who were seasoned missionaries, advised us just to wait until morning before trying to get to the hospital for tests, instead of rushing Alysia there at night when medical services would have been hit or miss at best. So we ended up spending what seemed like a long night applying cold cloths, keeping her small body cool.

We greeted the first light of dawn with relief. Though no longer convulsing, Alysia was still not feeling well and was pink with fever. By African standards, the Nairobi hospital looks pretty good, though for new missionaries it still seemed as if from a previous generation. We waited for what seemed a long time in the green waiting room that was in desperate need of some more paint. While we had all had our fair share of amoebas and other stomach ailments, nothing in the first year had been this serious, but now we waited wondering if indeed this was what we had suspected – malaria. Eventually a nurse came to draw some blood. The fact that the needle seemed the size of a small elephant needle did not help Alysia's emotional state. By the time that the nurse did a *search and probe* mission on her arm, Alysia was already screaming, no doubt with vivid recollections of the inoculation shots she had received before coming to Africa. As any parent, I was feeling bad for our little sweet four year old, even before she looked up at me with those big brown eyes as if to say, "Why are you letting them hurt me like this, Dad?" Of course, all we could do was hold her and repeat what she could not comprehend, that all this was necessary.

I am not sure why one ever bothers with blood tests in Africa. It seems that if anyone had a fever, or anything close to flu-like symptoms, malaria medicine was usually prescribed. So it was with us. Before we began the six hour drive to Kitale, we started

Alysia on the dose of malaria medicine. While it was nice to get back to the familiarity of our home in Kitale, it seemed so much further away from the relative *civilization* of the big city. As bad as the Nairobi hospital could seem to an outsider, the Mt. Elgon Hospital in Kitale seemed to be from another century, let alone another decade. The local Kitale missionary community was blessed in that one of the missionaries was also a nurse. She had been in Kenya for many years and knew more than some doctors, especially concerning tropical illnesses. Yet the six hours by car that separated us from the medical facilities of the big city seemed a long way at times.

Alysia remained sluggish for over a week and was not her normal self. But after a week it seemed that the worst was over. While she had been on prophylaxis for malaria, so that she would not contract the disease, she had apparently picked up a resistant strain. Malaria continues to be the number one killer worldwide, killing more victims than even AIDS. But it still primarily remains a third world disease and comparatively little money has gone into research to eradicate it.

Slowly Alysia gained her strength back. As for us our routines resumed and we continued being busy as the ministry developed into new areas. But after the incident with Alysia, Nancy was a bit more apprehensive whenever I would go on trips, for she did not know what she would do if something should happen while I was gone. Though malaria was not that common at our elevation in Kitale, Alysia now slept under a mosquito net. It seemed that whenever she had a fever or was not feeling well, we would assume the worst. We were going to discover, eventually, that regardless of what happens in our personal lives or even the world at large, we did not need to give in to fear. We obviously still would have a full range of emotions, but we did not need to live in fear.

It was about six weeks later that we again awoke to the screams of our daughter, "Mommy! Daddy! Make the flashing lights stop!"

As we rushed into her room we could not at first figure out what she was talking about. All we knew for sure was that she was again burning up with a fever. Nancy quickly filled the tub with cold water and before Alysia was really fully awake she was being rather unceremoniously dunked into what must have been a rude awakening. As her fever again increased and she would hallucinate, she would complain of seeing flashings in her head. All we could do was pray and try to keep her fever down. Nancy and I took turns holding her and applying cold cloths, as we prayed and paced during that long night.

What was particularly distressing were the seizures that would stiffen her body every time the fever would spike. It was difficult to watch her suffer and yet feel so helpless. *As a father, was I not to protect her and keep her safe?* Yet we were in Africa as a result of my decision. *What had I brought my family into?* These were the questions that tore at my heart, especially as Alysia would look up at me, hoping her Daddy would make it all go away.

As I paced the floor that night, I found myself having once again to lay our only child, our daughter, on the altar of obedience and surrender. Without even being able to understand, we had to release her wholeheartedly into his care. Even at times when it seems there is no other choice, this process can be very painful. As I looked to God that night and cried out to him, I was not questioning his existence or even his ultimate wisdom. Rather I was essentially questioning the justice of the situation. *How could God treat us this way, especially after all we had already sacrificed and been through? Though he had spared her life once, was He now requiring it again?* We knew all the right theology. Our questions were not primarily theological, but originated from our emotions, the very depths of our soul.

It is always amazing how much God can communicate with his children with his apparent silence. Often in our many questions he becomes a good listener. After all, one of his titles is *Counsellor.* Very often we have found that his silence after our many questions indicate that we are asking the wrong questions. Or that it is not his time to act. In those times we need to gain strength from his presence, which comes in the still small voice, enabling us to continue through the process we are in. He promised to always be with us, even during those times when we do not understand what we are going through and why. It is possible in our Christian walk to ever be seeking after "words" and "direction" from God, that we fail to learn of Him, of *who* He is. Learning of Him typically occurs during those quiet times (ie. Elijah in the cave, 1 Kings 19). We have learned not to take his silence to mean a lack of involvement or interest on his part, but often a quiet confirmation of the fact that we are on the right course. God never wastes words. By his apparent silence He is often communicating something profound with his children – those who know Him. The deepest communication is when He shares who He is; something of his very nature.

As I paced our bedroom in that small African town that night, it seemed as if He quietly reminded me that he too had laid his only Son on an altar. But unlike Abraham with Isaac, there was no substitute ram in the thicket, his Son *was* the sacrifice. Yet he was willing to sacrifice his Son so that many would have access to the Father. I sometimes wonder if we have stopped believing in a Gospel that requires any sacrifice or at the very least any inconveniences to our agenda? Have we forgotten that we are still called to join in the *fellowship of his sufferings?* Or do we now believe that our obedience or "level of faith" is evaluated merely by outward results and material success?

All the great dreams and ideologies ring hollow in the face of the finality of life and death. Obedience only has meaning in the present, not the past, or even the future. Walking down the aisle at a campmeeting some twenty years earlier in response to the pleas of a missionary were not enough on that dark night in Kitale. Even saying *Yes* to God in a small Mexico town on Christmas day some ten years earlier was not enough. I was again needing to offer the sacrifice of obedience, through faith, to Him whom I served – the One who had sacrificed all for me. A faith that said, *Though you slay me, though you even may require my daughter, I will still serve you.* Though not in vogue, particularly in our western brand of Christianity, it is really one of the great foundational stones upon which the mission of the Church has been established throughout the centuries – to follow the Master in obedience, regardless of the personal cost.

One day, Jesus turned to the many following him and said, "I tell you the truth, unless you eat the flesh of the Son of Man and drink his blood, you have no life in you. Whoever eats my flesh and drinks my blood has eternal life and I will raise him up at the last day." (John 6:53-54). He was speaking to those who loved to see his miracles, those who had experienced his blessings in the past, those who were sure He was going to finally overthrow the Romans who occupied their land. From other Scriptures we learn that to *take part in his blood and his flesh*, meant to be obedient to him. We also discover that this did not go over too well with those who were following him. After hearing this, many disciples turned back and no longer followed him. It was not merely those on the fringes who turned away, but some of the very ones who once following him and were called his disciples. . . it was a hard saying indeed.

Holding the small body of my daughter that night, as we paced and prayed, my Master asked me that same penetrating question, *"Will you eat my flesh and drink of my blood?"* Was I willing to be obedient, whatever the cost? If we sugar-coat the cross, varnishing it and taking out all the splinters and pain, we will only have succeeded in deluded ourselves. Obedience never feels good to our natural man, that part of each of us that struggles against God's best in our lives. We would not question the Apostle Paul's spirituality and yet he outlines his personal experiences with this struggle, in his epistles. Resurrection power for living cannot happen until there is a crisis of obedience. And this often occurs only on a splintered, rugged cross, as we willingly crucify our self-interest, vain ambitions, and even our right to the *good life*. The good news is that whatever we give up, regardless of how good it may seem, is nothing more than filthy rags. What we receive in return in spiritual life and fruit, makes the sacrifice pale in comparison. What part of the cross, or our own path of obedience, if you will, have we not been willing to embrace?

If there had been anything that Christ had not been willing to give up, from the glory of heaven and his divinity, to the pleasures and "rights" of humanity, we today would not have access to the Father, and the Gospel would not have the power that it does to save and change lives:

> "Unless the kernel of wheat falls to the ground and dies it remains only a single seed. But if it dies, it produces many seeds. The man who loves his life will lose it, while the man who hates his life in this world will keep it for eternal life. Whoever serves me must follow me; and where I am my servant also will be." (John 12:23-26).

It is not so much an issue of giving up things, but a matter of obedience to Christ. Seeing him clearer than anything else and desiring to pursue him regardless of whatever else needs to fall away. What this obedience produces is much better than anything we could ever give away. This, our act of worship, becomes our reasonable service. In light of what He has done for us it just makes sense.

We discovered that God was in that dark night, even when it seemed that our daughter might not make it. For me to follow him at that point was to endure with perseverance what for me was a cross. Yet it is in just such valleys that fear attempts to turn us from our full obedience to Christ and his will. A fear that is not just a darkness or force, but something that almost seems a tangible presence. Willpower is not enough to release us from this fear. We need to throw ourselves with abandon towards God's will in our lives, motivated by a love for who He is and what He has done for us. Then whatever comes our way we are secure in him, regardless of the external outcome of our particular situation. Without this abandon, the *seed* remains by itself, and will not be multiplied in the lives of others; it will not bear fruit.

This is a paradox. Particularly from the perspective of the seed. How can dying produce more fruit? Jesus showed us the way. *He, who for the joy set before him, endured the cross* (Heb 12:2). While Jesus *embraced* the cross, it was also something that he had to *endure*. We do not see a masochistic Jesus looking forward to the cross with glee. Rather, it was a despised thing, an ugly thing, a painful thing. Yet it was God's will. So why did He endure the cross? What was that *joy* that was set before him? That joy was you and I. His death and ultimate resurrection was going to bring a multiplication of the one seed as it went into the ground to die. Your face and mine are among the faces of those He saw while hanging on the tree. It was the promise of reconciliation that kept him hanging there in that place of shame, not the iron nails that a Roman soldier had hammered through his wrists and feet.

The joy was that you and I would come into a right relationship with the Father. For this purpose He *endured* the cross. Taking up our cross is also a process of obedience, yet it also entails endurance which will develop perseverance in our character. While the ultimate goal will be joy as we see the results of obedience, in the short term it can also be associated with pain and suffering. This is something we often do not want to admit, especially with other Christians. It may make us seem less than successful in their eyes, or worse yet, less "spiritual." Yet we must not make the other mistake of assuming that suffering, *in and of itself,* holds any redeeming value. God is not impressed with our *sacrifices,* but rather with our *obedience.* But obedience will inevitably lead us to taking up *our* cross.

That remains the power of the Gospel to this very day. We need not, or indeed cannot, suffer in any way to achieve what Jesus achieved for us. His payment on the cross for our redemption from the curse in its many forms was final. As his ambassadors on earth, we now have the privilege of willingly laying down our lives, our selfish desires, personal plans, and vain ambitions, so that others may also be redeemed from the curse that binds them. As his Body around the world willingly pays this price, the seed of the Gospel will not remain alone, but will bear much fruit. So often we wish that there was a more convenient, efficient, and perhaps even more comfortable way. Yet the testimony from the pages of the Bible, as well as the lives of saints throughout church history indicate otherwise. Before the joy in the morning comes the cross. The New Covenant teaching of the priesthood of all believers contains this truth. We each now have a priestly function to serve others in this self-sacrificing fashion. He as our High Priest is our example.

As morning was beginning to dawn, it did not seem that Alysia was getting any better. After scouring the book, *Where There is No Doctor* (which is not a real faith builder!), it seemed that the seizures associated with malaria could indicate cerebral malaria, which required immediate medical attention. After consultation with Karolyn, our friend and resident medical expert, we decided to see if we could hire the helicopter operated by a local mission group to fly to Kijabe, a large mission hospital near Nairobi. They confirmed that it just so happened that an appointment had fallen through and so the chopper was available. We quickly packed some things, and headed in the pre-dawn darkness towards the compound where the chopper was parked.

By the time we arrived, the missionary pilot had already filled the fuel tanks of the helicopter from the forty-five gallon drums and the rotor blades were beginning to spin. Within minutes the pilot had the three of us safely off the ground and we were heading towards the Kijabe Mission Hospital. With all the activity and the strain of the previous night, Alysia was now wide awake. The sun was still casting long morning shadows over the beautiful African landscape. As we lifted off, Mt Elgon dominated the landscape as its gentle slopes framed the view to the west. But it was not long before we had left the forests of western Kenya and crossed the Great Rift Valley on the way to Kijabe, a small community which seemed to hang on the very slopes of the valley escarpment. Finally, the crater of the now extinct volcano, Mt Logonot, passed as a silent giant beneath the helicopter and we landed at the helipad of the Kijabe Hospital. The Walkers, who were now living in Kijabe, met us as the rotor blades of the helicopter spun to a stop.

After a long night, it was reassuring to see familiar faces again. Though we had only known them over a year, the pressures of life on the mission field and the sharing of common vision had seemed to weld our hearts together. After checking Alysia into a hospital room and making her comfortable there was nothing to do but wait for a visit by the attending doctor. But as God so often does, He had prepared a little surprise, just to remind us that He knew where we were and that even in the midst of the valley, *He was still in control.* Regardless of how dark it may seem, He knows his children and is right there with them. Nothing escapes his gaze and nothing occurs in the believer's life that He is not aware of. It must first pass by his desk, accompanied by his knowing nod, before arriving as an event in our lives. Yet He is not an austere manager, removed from us, merely giving detached approval – no, having felt all that we feel, He then walks through the valley together with us.

As Alysia was laying in bed, weak from her long night, we heard a knock at the door and a doctor walked in. As we saw him and he saw us, I am not sure who was more surprised, he or us! In the middle of Africa, feeling miles from anything familiar, we actually knew one another! But not only did we know each other: the doctor who walked into that hospital room in the the middle of Africa was none other than the same doctor who had delivered our daughter into this world some five years earlier in Abbotsford, British Columbia, half-way around the world! It was another one of those divine *God-incidences* to bolster the faith and hope of one small family who felt all alone in the middle of nowhere.

Dr. Lewis was now retired and had volunteered his expertise at the mission hospital for one year. I am sure mathematicians could calculate the odds of that *just* happening, though I'm sure it would be comparable to a person getting hit by lightening on a clear day. With his British accent and fatherly manner, he had always been appreciated by us as our family doctor. Little did we know, so many years previously, how we would be so appreciative again of his calming manner in a far away African hospital. After several days of treatment it was determined that it had not been cerebral malaria, and that the convulsions that Alysia had experienced were probably due to her young age and the speed at which the fever had spiked. By this time, Alysia was not only on malaria medication, but also on Valium in order to keep her body relaxed.

Several days later we were again back on our way to Kitale by car and Alysia was again on the mend. As it seemed that she most likely had the type of malaria that could recur, the doctors advised us to watch her for signs of this over the next few weeks. Sure enough, nearly six weeks later she again came down with another malaria attack, though this time there were no seizures and the fever was not as severe. We had also become stronger in dealing with the unknown, trusting her into God's care. Through a local doctor we learned that giving the same malarial treatment over several days would most likely completely eliminate the malaria from her system. Even after returning to Canada we continued to be concerned whenever she would have an unexplained fever, but God had touched her and she never had another recurrence.

During the last year that we lived in Africa, issues were also beginning to surface in Nancy that needed to be dealt with. While I was feeling as if I was hitting my ministry groove, emotions and feelings were surfacing in her that had their roots in her father's murder and the grief process which had been truncated by our trip to Africa. The tribal unrest, which essentially had a political motivation in those days, contributed or even accentuated the issue. While my personality saw the added unrest as a challenge and just part of a truly gritty missions experience, these added strains were beginning to wear on my more sensitive (and more normal!) wife. There were times when the unrest seemed closer than others. On our last Boxing Day (a Canadian holiday, the day after Christmas Day) in Kenya, we hosted an afternoon of playing volleyball with a barbeque in our yard for the missionaries in the community. However, early in the afternoon gunshots were heard from the direction of town and this together with the real potential for unrest and rioting, resulted in the disbursement of our party. The missionaries, as well as the general population, were more on edge during those days reflecting the social unrest. Continuing a gathering under the circumstances did not seem like a good idea.

More regularly we began to hear of Africans we knew who were getting their homes burned down and our neighbours of Asian descent (Indian subcontinent origins) were also being threatened, attacked, and even killed in their own driveways. At this time the American embassy had also issued a warning that all foreigners should be on *stage two alert,* which meant having a bag packed in case one had to flee quickly. Now, of course, those of us in Kitale knew that the only option of flight would be in the direction of Uganda, since "fleeing" to Nairobi would be analogous to jumping from the frying pan into the fire. But we also knew that neither option was really that realistic. Though it was not something that preoccupied us, the fluidity of the political situation did raise the stress level among everyone, as well as for Nancy, who already had a lot on her emotional plate. Taken as a whole, these events served to precipitate what would result in a necessary change of our initial mission plans.

While I could rationalize that I was too busy with the work of a new ministry, as well as taking care of the family, and even preoccupied with Alysia's bouts with malaria, the fact that I did not fully grasp the depth of what my wife was going through is to my shame and embarrassment. I did not fully grasp the depth of her pain. Even if I had, I might not have been able to do all that much, other than listen. But even this would have been a good start. The following years were to again bring some painful lessons about "dying to a vision," re-evaluating the priority of ministry or my life's work and calling, and learning to be content in being obedient, even when it seemed to make no sense at all.

Obedience in the next few years was going to seem far from exciting, far from the mission field and even downright mundane.

9

Irreconcilable Differences

While Phil was out slaying his *giants,* there were inner *giants* that seemed as if they would overwhelm me. Before leaving for Africa I had thought that I had dealt adequately with the pain of the circumstances of my father's murder, but my experiences in Africa were going to prove that this was not the case. The pain of my father's death, and particularly how he died, really began to surface and hit me hard about six months after we had arrived in Kenya. It is not that uncommon for culture shock to bring to the surface unresolved issues, which in my case was grief. This often can happen without even realizing what is occurring and one is often not prepared for it.

While Phil did not seem to need much time to adapt to the new culture, the reality of living in a developing country was a real challenge for me. I had the feeling that everything that was familiar and secure had now changed. From my relationships, places to shop, and the routines of life, everything had changed. Going shopping, preparing food, even going to the washroom, everything was different. It was as if I had arrived in another world in which

113

all that was familiar and all the things that had brought comfort were stripped away. This seemed to bring those things that were deep inside to the surface – issues that were still loose ends in my life, on top of the added pressure of the unknowns in a new culture. Over time, these unresolved issues would also have surfaced if we had stayed in our own culture but it might have taken longer. It is often easier to stay busy with all the familiar things of our lives so that we do not listen to what is going on within us. If we are in our familiar context, we usually know where to access the needed support mechanisms to help us through a crisis, but in a foreign land such supports are often non-existent.

This is why the full force of the pain that I had experienced, but had not dealt with, surfaced while I was in Africa. Laying in bed at night, as I would pray and read my Bible, it seemed that all I could do to articulate my pain was to repeat, "Oh God. . .Oh God!" God in his mercy began to show me how my Dad's tragic death had affected me. It was as if my chest had been hit with a grenade and had caused a sunken crater there. It was as if I no longer had a heart, for it had been blown into little pieces. I was finding it impossible to function without a heart and I could not put the little pieces back together again.

I began to realize, for the first time, the anger and bitterness that I had developed towards God. You made me this way, God! *You did this to me! You let these things happen to me and my family!* It began to dawn on me, in a way much more personal than ever before, what a sinner I was. This anger, expressed in my words and thoughts, were as a hammer driving the nails deeper into my Master's hands and feet.

Though I saw the ugliness of my feelings and my predicament, I did not have the internal resources to process this depth of grief. As a Christian I had been taught to live joyfully, have a happy marriage, raise productive children, and even endure suffering joyfully. All of these are good and noble goals and attributes, but I could not seem to remember hearing many sermons on grief and trauma. Perhaps it was just in the circles I was in, but I was often left with the impression that if I did not appear joyful and living in emotional victory, I was somehow failing as a Christian. Unfortunately, this only added condemnation to my already grieving heart.

Living in a developing nation in Africa, I was in more direct contact with pain and tragedy which was obviously evident around me. As I would share with other missionaries I began to realize what I was going through. On one particular occasion, as I was sharing my feelings with one of our co-workers, Carol, she neatly summed it up by saying, "Oh yes, that sounds like post-traumatic syndrome." I wondered if that was what I was going through. At one point, when their twins were terribly sick, I remember her husband, Myron, saying, "People think because you are a missionary when your children die it's okay, because you are superhuman and can handle it."

I began to realize that I did not want to admit what I was feeling because, after all, I was supposed to be *super-human;* I was a *missionary. How do we share such unbearable pain and shame when lies like this (there are many others) trap us from getting help?* I was awed when a missionary friend gave me a card before we left Kenya. At the bottom was a scripture portion from Ecclesiastes 3:1 which states, "There is a time for everything. . . ." That simple sentence brought me comfort, understanding and compassion. I couldn't believe she was showing me such understanding when I didn't really understand myself – at a time when I felt as though I was on the verge of a mental breakdown.

My father's life had been brutally torn from me and the feeling of loss was tremendous. The fact that he was killed by my own brother brought up questions for me about my family and our past. Though I was not involved in the physical act, I too was traumatized by this tragic event. It was obvious to me that something was wrong. This, in turn, had affected my whole demeanour. I knew that I needed help, but I also knew that I couldn't get the kind of help I needed in a small town like Kitale, where we lived while in Africa. While there were many blessings in being part of the small, tightknit missionary community, who were from various backgrounds and groups, it was this very environment that made it difficult to get help. There was little privacy or confidentiality, which is what I really needed if I was going to heal. The things I needed to share with someone, by their very nature, were heavy and would have been difficult for someone to bear alone. The burden of not being able to share this with others would have been a burden too great to lay on someone in this small missionary community. Though everyone would have had the best of intentions, it would be conceivable that soon everyone in our little community could be privy to my personal life.

I began to realize that I needed to go back to Canada in order to learn about, and deal with, my grief and begin the process of healing. I also realized how devastating this would be for my husband. I knew he had a call on his life as a missionary and after years of being in a personal *wilderness* time he had found his place and was finally realizing his dream. It seemed that my situation would now not allow him to fulfill it. Because of this, I did not want to tell him and determined that I would just do my best to finish our initial two year commitment. But deep in my heart I knew I would not be able to return to Africa. This inevitably caused me also to feel guilt for needing this sort of help. Due to my improper thinking in this area and my sense of desperation, I did not communicate my need to Phil in a gracious manner. Instead, I ended up blurting it out as we were discussing our plans regarding our time of home assignment in Canada. As if out of nowhere, I blurted, "Phil, I don't care what you do; I am not coming back to Africa!"

Though Phil knew that I was not having an easy time adjusting, there had been many good times. I really loved the people and on my good days had really enjoyed our experiences. So it was a bit of a shock for him all of a sudden to have to deal with the stark reality of my true situation. To be fair, I had not included him in the decision process and now my pain was also causing terrible grief in him. He began to feel the loss of his career and life calling. Now there were two of us struggling with God and with the one that we had chosen to spend the rest of our lives with. I was unable to understand the traumatic events that God seemed to allow, and now Phil wondered how he could fulfill what God had laid on his heart to do. It was a very difficult time for us. It was almost as if we were at odds with each other.

While my wife was dealing with the grief from deep traumas that living in a very foreign culture had accentuated, things for me in the ministry were really beginning to come together. We had found training materials that were affordable and accessible that we could adapt to train pastors who would then be able to train others in the many extension centres that were opening up throughout Kenya and Uganda. I had spent every spare moment writing lesson plans for scores of courses at several educational levels. We were beginning to see the numbers of pastors enrolled in the various programs mushroom. This growth meant implementing tracking systems in order to be able to evaluate the effectiveness of the program. Though the numbers were increasing, our main goal was to see lives changed and leaders equipped so that they in turn could train others.

As we began to develop programs to meet the need, we realized that another bible school teaching theology was not what was needed. What we were hearing pastors and denominational leaders saying was that the best way we from the west could help the church in Africa would be to assist in the equipping and training of its leaders. What was needed was *on-the-job* practical training for pastors that was of a top quality, but was delivered in such a way that they could continue in their ministry and with their families in their community. So often those who wanted and needed training had to travel great distances, often leaving their ministry and family in order to be equipped. After long absences from their community and churches, many were often "lost" by their community, never returning to their place of service after their training. It was our vision to provide practical training in ministry skills while they continued to pastor their churches, without sacrificing the quality that was needed for credibility in their society.

To do this we needed to merge in-service, on-the-job training with accepted academic standards. At that time, the concept of accredited, in-service training was just beginning to be accepted. While it was more and more common in some secular circles, it was still rather rare within the church and theological community. These were exciting times as we were pioneering these in-service training programs ranging from secondary to undergraduate and eventually graduate levels. We knew that this was important, for without this key component, many would still feel that they had to leave Africa to receive ministerial training of such quality. Without providing this, we knew that our ultimate objective *to entrust to reliable leaders truths that they in turn could teach others* (2 Timothy 2: 2) would never be fulfilled. While accredited theological education was the initial attraction, discipleship and mentoring became the result.

By their own admission, this is what the church in Africa needed. So often what was taught to others was a case of the blind leading the even more blind. Yet in order to make this possible for the average pastor it had to be affordable. This challenge consumed many of those early staff meetings. Further training was outside the reach of most people, let alone a pastor who may have had an average income of only thirty dollars per month. So we worked at developing educational agreements that enabled us to bring the cost down as well as find partners who would be interested in sponsoring a pastor in training through *Shepherd Scholarships.*

By this time James and Mary Kamau had joined the team as our first full time national staff. Through the partnership of a Canadian church they were able to give their full efforts and time to the ministry. James oversaw all the *CBBS* or *Church Based Bible School* programs and many years later would be our first missionary staff sent to Tanzania. We were also in talks with another missionary in Uganda regarding partnering together to train Uganda pastors at a college level. It seemed that we were on the edge of some very exciting breakthroughs that had only been dreams and visions up to this point. My personal and ministry struggles of the eighties seemed to belong to another lifetime. I was now in a season of life where I was able to use my experiences and abilities to make a real contribution.

So it was within this context that Nancy's ultimatum landed like a bombshell in my world. It was as if the strong wind that had been filling my sails instantaneously subsided to nothing. Yet it was not a peaceful calm, but the sickening feeling of once again being unable to move in the direction it seemed God wanted us to go. Of course I had known that she was struggling emotionally and needed to process some things, where she felt more at home, but I had assumed that this could all be taken care of in a few months once we were back in Canada. But for all the blindspots my pragmatism could produce, I also could sense the desperation of the situation, particularly after being hit squarely between the eyes with it. I knew by the emotion and finality of her statement that there would be no discussion. Nancy was, by nature, very giving and, by personality, very accommodating. In many ways she had been the optimist and encourager, never being one to whine or nag, no matter how difficult the situation. So on that day, I knew that this was serious and not something time or discussion would change. While I may still have been in a pragmatic mode, she was definitely in survival mode. She was desperate.

It was several days later at our staff meeting that I knew I somehow had to find the words to tell the rest of the team that we would not be able to come back. As self-centred as it may sound, looking back, at the time it was the most difficult thing I had to say. It was as if I would choke on the words. It was as if I was walking up Mt Moriah with my *Isaac*, but I had no faith that there would be a ram in the thicket. Yet, true to form, the rest of the team was very understanding and tried to take the big picture view. I, on the other hand, could not see any silver lining and really did not care too much about the big picture. Without even seeing it coming, my future had altered radically and I could hardly grasp how it could have happened. Even the African sky, that once seemed so bright and blue, now seemed dark and grey. The natural surroundings, such as the constant songbirds and lush vegetation, seemed only to remind me that the fulfilment I had had in ministry for these few years would now be coming to an end.

During the last few months in Africa I tried to keep hope alive. But the reality of having to sell all that we had shipped over and dissolve all that we had painstakingly set up, caused whatever hope I had left for the future to evaporate. The fact that we were not coming back caused the work that had been such a joy to become excruciatingly painful. While I had so enjoyed sitting in staff meetings, planning and discussing the development of what God was doing in the ministry, now I struggled with keeping focussed. Hearing the plans for the future, knowing that I would not be directly part of those plans seemed like cruel and unusual punishment. Some days I even wished I could just crawl away and hide.

Though somewhat introspective by nature, I had never really had to ever deal with depression, even during the years of working in the most miserable weather, and not knowing what God was doing in my life. Somehow, I always believed that He was preparing me for future ministry as He had so many others throughout the Bible and Church history. But in the face of having again to lay down the yoke of service, a darkness began to settle over me that I had never experienced before. Though I continued to function on a daily level, not far below the surface there was a hopelessness and sadness that could not be shared with anyone, including my wife. It was to be a valley deeper than any I had experienced, for it went to the very core of my calling, my family, my very relationship with God.

As staff, we had our last meal together in Nairobi the night we were to fly out. These whom we had been through so much with were as gracious and warm as ever, but I felt strangely disconnected. It was not just that I was leaving, but the unknown as to our continued future relationship together. Of course, I knew I needed to go back and maintain the organization in Canada, so as to be able to continue to channel designated funds to Africa, but even this seemed to lose its meaning in the face of my lack of direct involvement on the field. Everyone tried to put a positive spin on things, but it seemed more like "Goodbye" than "We'll see you again."

With the taste of our last African meal still lingering, we boarded the Jumbo Jet destined for London. Though the rest of the family were excited to see family and friends again, I somehow felt alone. As the Boeing 747 lifted off African soil, it seemed that we had just arrived to Africa days before, full of our hopes and dreams. Yet now, a bit battle worn and slightly wiser, we were on our way back. In the intervening years we had experienced the joys of team ministry and seeing God's hand in our lives, as well as the development of the new ministry. While the rest of the team would carry on without me, I felt an empty feeling in the pit of my stomach. I tried to keep my hopes up that something would eventually work out, but I could not realistically envision how.

Like my wife, though perhaps to a lesser degree, I too was now grieving a loss.

10

Bricks and Barbwire

Eastern Europe had always been a place of intrigue and fascination for me. Perhaps it had something to do with reading scores of books, as a teen, concerning those martyred for their faith and *Brother Andrews'* account of smuggling Bibles across enemy lines in cloak and dagger style. But whatever the origin, on our way back to Canada from Africa we decided to take a week and stop in Germany and specifically, Berlin. So after landing in London, we caught our connecting flight to Frankfurt. Our plan was then to drive by car to Berlin, which only a few years earlier had been behind the Iron Curtain.

Berlin. Of any place that epitomized the Cold War after World War II, this would have to be it. To think that a whole city had been divided for nearly forty years! In the fall of 1989 we had watched with disbelief, along with the rest of the world, as the citizens of East Berlin streamed over the infamous *Berlin Wall.* This became the focal point of what was to be the eventual fall of communism, reaching to the very gates of the Kremlin.

Who could forget President Reagan in front of the

Brandenburg Gate in June of 1987 addressing Gorbachev, the leader of the Soviet Union: "If you seek peace open this gate! Mr Gorbachev, tear down this wall!" Just over two years later, through almost a comedy of errors, East Berlin citizens were allowed an exit visa. Once Pandora's Box had been opened, and it became clear that the Soviet authorities were not going to support brute force to control the masses, the events of those years took on a life of their own.

While in Africa, I had kept abreast of the global developments as each satellite republic broke away from the once mighty Soviet Empire. Who of us would have believed that these things would be possible in our lifetime? What would these events mean for world missions? As the church in the west it seemed we were more focussed on fighting the evil, atheistic regime than we were in preparing for when prayer would sweep the Wall away. Mission groups such as *Open Doors,* who once smuggled Bibles into these lands, began to change their focus and tactics. Other mission groups began gearing up to take the gospel message into lands that had been closed for most of the Twentieth Century.

As a child I was fascinated by the modern heroes of the faith who had served in these lands. The stories of Brother Andrew in his book, *God's Smuggler,* had made my imagination run wild. Together with him, I travelled across mysterious borders and checkpoints, with secret rendevous with members of the Underground Church. I would also read and reread the accounts of Richard Wurmbrand, the Romanian pastor who was tortured for his faith. As a young teen, I read and reread the accounts of the many tortures he endured at the hands of the communist authorities. I was deeply impressed by these men and women who were tortured for their faith, but never renounced their Master and Lord. To me they were heroes, and I would often wonder how I would have endured. Granted, this was not typical teenage reading fare, but these biographies were used by God to fan into flame the burden for the world that began to grow inside of me. Reading these books made it easy for me to imagine working in these lands.

Since we would already be in Europe, I did not want to pass up the opportunity to get closer to these lands that were once behind the Iron Curtain. Berlin, formerly part of the Eastern Bloc, seemed a reachable destination. So as we landed in Frankfurt on our way back to Canada in the summer of 1992, we rented a car and headed for this recently unified city. With Alysia strapped into the black leather seat of the BMW rental, we cruised effortlessly (and quickly!) down the autobahn towards Berlin. Quite a difference from only the previous day when we were dodging the pothills on the road from Kitale to Nairobi!

It had been less than two years since a divided Germany had voted to reunite and so the East-West crossing near Magdeburg, about one and a half hours west of Berlin, was no longer in existence. And yet as we passed by the buildings and towers that were in various stages of being dismantled, my imagination again went back to what it must have been like for Brother Andrew to drive his VW Beetle loaded with Bibles across these borders. There was a certain sense of regret, as I always thought that the Iron Curtain would last at least long enough for me to sneak something through!

Another factor drawing us to Berlin was the fact that I still had distant relatives in the city. While there, I wanted to look up my father's uncle, who had lived in East Berlin since the fall of the city after the Second World War. My grand-Uncle, Gustav, was the brother of my Grandmother on my father's side of the family. While the west side of the city was in fairly good repair, once we crossed over the now imaginary line to what was the former eastern section, conditions deteriorated. Instead of classical, somewhat quaint apartment blocks, the large apartments were arranged in rather institutional fashion – very functional, especially for control of the masses, but not very imaginative city planning. As we wound our way through the city, which resembled a large construction site rather than a city, we eventually found the apartment block that was his home. Using the little German that I could remember from growing up, we were able to communicate and make each other's acquaintance. Being born in 1900, he was now 92, but very chipper and bearing an uncanny resemblance to his sister, my Grandmother. As a teenager, my *Oma* had lived with us and so I had heard a bit of the family history from her. I discovered that not only my ethnic heritage, but also my spiritual heritage had threads that ran through this city.

I was fascinated by the stories of how her parents had been sent on the trains to Siberia, during the Bolshevik Revolution, as they were German immigrants in what is today Belarus and Ukraine. Her brother Gustav, and other sisters, had survived the Soviet Gulag camps and returned years later, but unfortunately their parents had not survived the ordeal. She would tell me the story of how, as a small child, her parents could not support all their children and so tendered them out to work for neighbours. My Grandma Henrietta had worked on one of these farms from the time she was only five years of age.

She also recounted one of the milestones in her early life, when a whole pot of scalding water had fallen on her and she had been completely burned head to toe. Since she was only house help and not one of the family, there had been no medical help made available. She had been left in the corner of the cottage to fend for herself as they thought that it was just a matter of time before she would die from her severe burns. She remembered how she had begun to smell from her rotting skin, yet she had somehow miraculously survived. In God's providence, it was through her that the message of salvation came to my father and eventually to me.

In the late 1920's she and her husband had lived in what was then West Prussia, or present day Poland. From here, in 1930, my Grandpa and his son, who was then fourteen years old, emigrated to Canada in search of a better life. On their way to the Bremen docks, they spent a couple of weeks in Berlin, waiting for the departure of their ship. This young teenager, who accompanied his adventuresome father, would later become my father. As an immigrant in Russia, my grandfather was exempt from being drafted by Germany in World War One and then as a recent immigrant my father was also exempt from being drafted by Canada in World War Two. So my Grandfather and father were spared through two world wars, who by virtue of their ethnicity were on the wrong side of both.

My father and grandfather established a homestead on the Canadian prairies, writing their mother and wife to join them some five years later. During this five year separation Grandma Henrietta remained in Germany. It was while there that she had a personal encounter with God at the Baptist church on Hauptstrasse #125 in Berlin. When she eventually joined the rest of the family in Canada, she shared with them the message of this Good News. My father embraced this message and had his own personal encounter with God as his Saviour and Lord at one of the many Gospel meetings that travelled through the small rural communities of the prairies during the thirties and forties. So the threads of my spiritual heritage were woven through Berlin, a city that had such a fascinating and yet complicated history.

After the Second World War, the city itself was divided into quarters by the four victorious armies: the Soviets, Americans, British, and French. Within a few years of the War, the Soviets installed a total blockade of West Berlin, essentially making it an island in the middle of East Germany, an hour and a half by road from the West German border. This led to the airlift by the other three western powers to keep the residents alive. Eventually on August 13, 1961 units of the GDR (East Germany) circled West Berlin with barb wire and begin to construct the wall, which became the front line in the stand off between East and West for nearly three decades.

Amazingly, my grand-Uncle, Gustav, survived it all and I was now able to walk these streets freely and personally see what I had only seen in movies or imagined in the theatre of my mind. Little did we know that one day this city would play a direct role in our lives and ministry. But in 1992, after playing the tourist – buying an *actual* piece of the wall (so they said) and a Soviet hat – it was time to head back to Frankfurt to catch our plane to London and Vancouver. Though a nice diversion, it was to be several years, a few more lessons, and even a couple of deep valleys, before Berlin and Central Europe were consciously on our radar screen again.

The trans-Atlantic flight from London was rather uneventful and we arrived back in Vancouver to the warm welcome of family – the very ones that had helped pack our shipping container and sent us off from the Seattle airport two years previously. But now, since we had either sold or moved everything to Africa, we had to again start from scratch in setting up a home. From where to live, purchasing a vehicle, getting pots and pans, beds and sheets – everything had to be done again. Yet within a few weeks we had the basics and settled into a rental home in Delta, a suburb of the

Greater Vancouver area.

We began attending and getting involved with the new church planted by my brother-in-law. It was hard to believe that it had only been two years earlier that we had left this fledgling church family. At the time of our departure to Africa the church had moved from small home meetings to Sunday services. Even though they themselves were a new church plant, they had faithfully supported our ministry and it was a joy to share with them what God was doing through the ministry in Africa. It was also exciting to see the growth in the church in the intervening years.

As to our ministry, we set up an office in one room of our home and I continued to share the vision of what we were doing as well as engaging in the various administrative tasks that were required. While we knew, intellectually, that it required people on the home front to enable others to be on the field, I was not sure I was ready to be one of those "called" to be on the home front! We determined that it would make sense to change the name of our organization in Canada from *Global Outreach* to *International Christian Ministries (ICM)*, in order to share a common name. At this point ICM was also getting its own incorporation in the USA.

So on one hand, we were very busy retooling as a ministry with a new name and also sharing the vision of what God was doing in Africa. We realized that we needed to transition the mission society from merely supporting a couple on the mission field, to developing into a ministry that would truly be a mission-sending organization. This would be important if the ministry was going to have any longevity and grow beyond the founders.

On the other hand, I felt like a failure and was beginning to wonder if I had missed God. Being back in Canada, it was hard for me to see myself as a "missionary," let alone others seeing us as such. Yes, the work needed to be done, but my heart was still overseas. Though most tried to be subtle, it was not hard to hear the real questions behind the question, "When are you guys going back?" In those days it seemed the answer was, "Never!" but this did not seem like the answer most were anticipating.

Meanwhile, I was scheduled to be back in Africa early in the spring of 1993, for we had return tickets which I could only get refunds for by personally doing so from Nairobi. So while it was easy to make the talking point of the day that I was going back on a ministry trip, I secretly began to wonder when everyone else would find out what I thought I already knew: I was a failure in ministry and I didn't have a clue what God was doing in my life! All the while, I harboured the ever present sense that Nancy, who had always been there through thick and thin, seemed no longer to be at my side. I did not necessarily fault her, as I knew she had been through a lot (some of which was of my making) and had nothing to give now. But I also knew that without her support and assistance there was no way I could ever be effective in ministry – it was a joint effort.

It began to be very clear that things were not *business as usual* in our marriage. After ten years of married life and all that we had been through, I had assumed that we had weathered the storms fairly well. And in many ways we had. We had been the kind of couple that could always share what we thought with each other, but at the end of the day could also accept our differences. But more and more I felt as if I no longer knew this person whom I had married. It was as if the strains of the last few years had changed even my wife's very personality. While she was struggling to deal with her grief and rebuilding her faith in a *good* God who had nevertheless allowed all these things to happen, she was no longer able to be in my corner as she had so faithfully been over the years. Though this turned out to be temporary, at the time it seemed permanent, and I could see no light at the end of the tunnel. I could still remember the encouragement she had given to me as I earned my undergraduate degree, even though it meant her doing the menial task of cleaning other's homes. Or the encouragement of sticking with me and trusting me and even overcoming her own fears and going to Africa with me – she had always been there for me. The apparent loss of this compounded the challenges that I was dealing with in the ministry and was one of the scariest, unsettled times of my life.

I only knew that I had to do what I had always known to do in a dark tunnel – to keep going in a straight line – in the dark continue to do what I had heard to do in the light. I'd learned that, in the darkness, when it seemed that God was not saying anything, it was not the time to make sharp turns to the left or right. I knew that trying to "help" God guide my life would only produce *Ishmaels* (my solution instead of God's) that could haunt us for a long time to come. Many times I had written announcements that this was indeed the last ministry newsletter readers would receive and I was going to pursue a *real* career, a *real* job. But every time I would throw the premature announcement into the wastepaper basket by my desk. While I did not seem to have much faith to carry on, there was always something that would not let me completely throw in the towel, at least not yet.

During this time we continued to live on some savings we still had, though we realized that this would not last too much longer. It seemed that the more we shared the vision, fewer and fewer donations would arrive in the mail. It came to the point that our personal support level bottomed out at only a few hundred dollars a month. We had never been in debt and I was not prepared to start, so I pursued various entrepreneurial jobs such as trying to sell telephone calling cards and doing odd desktop publishing jobs – anything that would generate some income, short of starting up my construction contracting business again. Going back to construction seemed at the time like "going back to Egypt" and admitting total failure; the mere thought of returning to planks, ladders, and jobsites was depressing.

Donations were covering most of the costs of the ministry, but while I tried to keep focussed on the ministry, my part-time efforts were not producing enough money for us to live on personally. I knew that I would have to make a major decision if things did not change after I got back from my trip to Africa, in the spring of 1993.

11

Return from the Abyss

While Phil struggled with being in Canada again, for me it was great to be at home with friends and the now familiar Vancouver area; nevertheless, I soon discovered that there were few people whom I knew at the time who knew how to support us emotionally. This was understandable as few of the friends that we knew at the time had gone through what we had. So I decided to try and get some professional Christian counselling. Unfortunately, the person I was referred to did not really connect with me for various reasons.

My first visit was indicative of my experience. I was immediately handed a sheet of questions, one of which was, *What are you doing to sabotage your life?* But at that point in my pain I really needed a different approach. During those months, as with most people in deep pain, I was just overwhelmed with the pain and could barely sense anything else. It was like smashing your thumb with a hammer; you can think of nothing else; the pain in your thumb has your full and undivided attention. *Yes,* it felt like my life was being sabotaged, but I needed answers and a way back from the abyss, not

129

questionnaires and pat answers. I knew all the *right* answers, but I needed to begin a process in which I could receive God's healing for my hurting, questioning heart.

Fortunately, at this time, a group of people I knew were starting a small group focussed on grief recovery. We began working our way through, *The Grief Recovery Handbook* together. (It is an excellent book on grief.) Learning what I was dealing with was the first step in a long process. I needed to learn what grieving meant, the lies that we all tend to believe, and then the stages of grief and how to process it. So often I wished that there was a shortcut. But what I discovered was that I had to do a lot of soul searching, learning to recognize my true feelings, even towards God. Through the process of journaling, talking, going for walks, and even developing a hobby that I enjoyed doing, I was able to pray, cry, release the pain and come to a point of wholeness again.

During this time I had many well-meaning acquaintances who tried to help me with comments such as, "You just need to relax." I began to discover that a traumatized person cannot "just relax." I found God calling me to discipline myself and to fast, not just relax. Other loving people would say, "You just need to praise God!" However, whenever I would try and praise God, I would just cry! I had grown up believing that crying showed weakness, but I needed to accept the fact that crying was okay and helped to bring healing.

Perhaps the classic advice was, "You just have some choices to make!" I am still not sure what choices they may have meant, but I did not have the resources in myself just to "snap out of it" or "will" myself better. In spite of the excruciating pain I was carrying on the inside, I thought I had made some pretty good choices. I had chosen to stay with my husband and daughter. I had also chosen not to end my life, which at times no longer felt worth living. Through this process I began to limit my contacts to only those who could understand what I was going through and knew the steps to get from where I was to where I needed to go.

I remember one particular night during this period. Phil and I were talking and I explained that I felt everyone was just telling me to "act normal. . .just act normal!"

"But how can I act *normal?*" I shouted. "My brother killing my dad is not *normal* is it!? How can I just act as if this happens every day!?" My dad's life was snuffed out before he really got to know his only grandchild! And my brother was now in a psychiatric prison. But I was just to act *normal,* whatever *normal* was. For most of us *normal* usually means, "please act in a way that does not make me feel uncomfortable or ask the hard questions of God."

After my outburst that night, Phil just held me and said nothing as I sobbed. Comfort does so much more than words. A younger lady whom I barely knew gave me some wise advice during those dark days – advice that I have never forgotten. As I told her what I was going through, she told me her story of how when she was eighteen, her boyfriend committed suicide. Though not that profound, she just let me know that she understood my feelings and that it was okay to be sad, as long as I needed to be. It is hard to describe what a relief that was in those dark days. . .those days when, as the Psalmist David said, *"my bed always seemed wet with my tears."* It was okay for me to grieve.

In a Christian culture that seems very uncomfortable with sadness, grief and anything that does not seem like *instantaneous success,* I have discovered that it is impossible to move on if one does not adequately grieve. The fact is that you can change the outward appearance, but you will remain sad until you have exhausted your grief and gone through the process. None of us enjoy pain, myself included, but as painful experiences are allowed to touch our lives, it is only as we fully grieve that we can be brought back to a place of wholeness. As long as we attach an *unspiritual* label to healthy grief we condemn people to living less than whole lives, for it forces them to pretend to be something that they are not.

More and more I realized how terribly angry I was at God. I made a conscious decision not to turn my back on Him, though in Kenya I had seriously considered giving up being a Christian (if theologically possible!). But I realized that I would be worse off. It was very curious to me how I could be in relationship with God while at the same time having such anger towards Him. It is only through his grace and mercy. I began to be aware of the bitterness in my heart and that I was blaming Him for all the unfair events in my life. Yet I felt powerless to change it. Finally I began to accept the reality of where I was at and realized that I had to accept myself right where I was, in the mud hole. Once I did this, I could finally begin the process of again receiving God's love and comfort.

For the greater part of a year I felt a heaviness on my chest and there was nothing I could do to relieve it. I could not sigh enough to release the pain. I felt so much shame for what my brother had done. I wanted to shave my head to match the feelings of shame and emptiness which I felt on the inside. *After all, what would people think of me, the sister of a man who had killed his own father?* Surely they would think the problem would run in the family. I believed that they would judge me for what my brother had done and would see that I had fallen from my position as a *joyful, victorious Christian.*

A particularly helpful *Christian*, who felt it her duty to give me unsolicited advice, encouraged me with, "They say if you stop going forward in your Christian walk, you are really going backward." For someone who was already feeling very low, this was just another blow. Trying to hide the hurt she caused by her lack of perception, I merely replied, "Oh yeah," in a nonchalant manner, trying not to let on that I knew that she was directing her comments at me. Apparently from my tone of voice she figured that I hadn't quite gotten her point and so she felt she needed to tell me a couple more times! Those who are grieving often have to endure all sorts of such foolishness from those who, though well meaning, do not really have a clue what the grieving person is going through. Those who have not themselves been through tragedy, often try to help in the most clumsy of ways. While they want to fix the grieving person, the fact is that those in pain cannot be *fixed*, only comforted. This is what begins the healing process.

While it may seem as if those in the valley are going backwards, often exactly the opposite is true. As we are open to God in these situations that He allows in our lives, we can become more beautiful through the process. We are just like a seed, which looks its very worst just before it begins to sprout. Grief can be a very ugly process, often combined with times of shock, anger, and denial. Many people, and sad to say even many in the church, do not have the courage, insight or, for that matter, the desire to walk through this process with someone. Considering our own human nature, which enjoys comfort and not pain, I suppose this is not too hard to imagine. Even when we have one or two people who can relate with us in our pain, ultimately only God can go through our pain with us. Yet during those times I often thought it would have been nice to have someone call me every day just to check on me. All they would have had to say was, "How are you doing today? Are you making it?"

During those years I may have responded with, "I don't know, I just don't know." But just being able to say those words every day to someone else would have helped. Though it sounds strange, it would have brought relief and a sense of being cared for. So often we do not know the little insignificant things that are within our power to do for others, yet which would make a huge impact in their lives. I now better understand the Scripture which says that even bringing a cup of water in the Father's name will be rewarded.

For me it was very important to know that someone else identified with my grief. So much so, that I began to question God, "Who, God, do I know that has faced something like this?" It was almost as though I was acknowledging the unfairness of it all. After all, my Dad did not deserve a criminal's death. He never beat us, was never drunk, and never in jail, or in trouble with the law. He was a very good man. In the intensity of my questioning, I heard God, my heavenly Father very tenderly respond, "My own children killed my Son." He, God, actually felt the exact pain I did; how that touched my heart in those dark moments! It was so cleansing as the tears began to flow.

I also began to realize that these events in my life had also taken their toll on my faith. How could I believe God still wanted to do good things for me? My faith muscles were so weak. I wanted to believe and hope in God, but something inside was broken; it was as if my fight was gone. One night as I lay in bed, I began to tell God, "Yes, I believe in you and that you are working in my life." I was making a conscious choice to believe in Him, even though my emotions told me I couldn't. With these words, I felt as if I were trying to lift a hundred pound weight, but only had the capacity to lift five pounds. I continued to repeat, "I believe, I believe. . ." It was a very important exercise for me in winning back my faith, something that the enemy had tried to kill along with my father.

"I believe. . ." It seems simple now, but peace came over me. It was as though I had just taken a big step in the healing process. It was a definite turning point. The enemy of our soul wants to bring evil upon us, to hinder and destroy us. He then wants to keep us trapped, imprisoned or stuck emotionally, so that we cannot be of any further benefit for the Kingdom of God. For Phil and me, this was our desire – to move forward in God's Kingdom and benefit others. Yet in those years, it all seemed hopeless. *How could we ever function as a content couple and family again, let alone reach out to others?*

As I look back to that time when my emotions were raging, it was even difficult to receive encouragement or strength from God's Word. It often seemed as only words on a page, unable to penetrate my heart. The Psalms had always brought me comfort and for years I seemed to camp there with David, particularly those passages where he was grieving, as in Psalms 6. I had noticed I didn't trust God as I had before. I didn't trust that He would or *could* do things for me. I felt I had to rely upon myself. Before my father's murder, I had never fully given myself emotionally in my friendships, as I did not want open myself to be hurt by someone else. But during this time something changed. While it can be unhealthy to look only to friendships to bring comfort, instead of looking to God, I began to gain comfort from friendships. I recognized my own humanness, and that I actually needed people. I learned to trust people again, to let them in and rely on them. I learned how to find people whom I could trust with my frail emotions. I actually wanted intimacy in relationships, something that I had not known to that degree as an adult before. I even learned to relax with my own failures.

I came to the realization that I could not control all the events in my life, my husband's life, or my daughter's life. Romans 8:28 proved itself to be true, "And we know that God causes all things to work together for good to those who love God, to those who are called according to his purpose." The very destruction these events were meant to bring had actually inspired intimacy in my life. Not that my Dad's death was a good thing of itself, but God is so powerful that He could take these really terrible events and build some wonderful things into our life as we co-operated with Him. Through the ugliness of this event, God has brought much good, including a closeness with my sisters and a greater intimacy in my relationship with my daughter and husband.

At one point during the process God showed me a picture of four war cannons, which were all fired at the same time. I felt that He was saying, "Your accident, your Dad's murder, Alysia's bout with malaria, the stress of the tribal clashes while in Kenya, were all Satan's attempt to destroy your life." Then I saw the four exact same cannons firing back in the opposite direction at the same time. God spoke very clearly: "As healing comes and you are a testimony to others, the cannons are turned back towards the enemy." Nothing, *absolutely nothing,* is in vain for the Lord. Every ounce of pain and grief we are willing to endure for Him is not in vain. It will all be used for God's glory. This has brought joy to my soul in the midst of the pain.

Of course this process is not particularly pretty, especially for those closest to us. The most difficult part of all this was that both Phil and I were dealing with a deep loss at the same time. This sorrow put a lot of stress, not only on us and the ministry, but also on our marriage. Phil was dealing with the feeling of the loss of his future and not understanding what God was doing in his life at that point. Because of this, he failed to have the resources to understand how to best help me. At times I also did not even know what I needed. It was a new road for both of us. Many times I just needed him to wrap his arms around me, but he was on the other side of the bed, aching with his own pain. *Where was his future? What was he to now do?* It seemed that right when we needed each other most, we each had the least to give.

This caused a bitterness in me towards him, for it seemed that he had nothing to give me. I was to learn that my bitterness was just a form of deep pain that had not been dealt with. At times I would think, *I have always been his cheerleader, but now when I need one, where is he?* Of course, he was dealing with having to accept the fact that his life had been changed through no apparent choice of his own. But even in the midst of these troubled waters, Phil continued to do the stabilizing things he had always done, regardless of whether we lived in Canada or Africa. While he may not have had the emotional resources to deal with what I was facing, he provided for our physical needs in the best way he could, so that there would not be the additional pressure on me to meet the needs of the family, as I was trying to get better. This brought me great comfort and stability, as I don't think I could have handled the pressure to do both at the same time.

I continued over those years to cry out to God for the easy way out. "Kill me!" was one of my favorite *faith-filled* prayers! The other was, "Take the pain away, now!" Neither was answered. God continued to require discipline of me in the midst of all the excruciating pain. "How could God be so cruel?" I thought. But He wanted to teach me the process, not just fix me, as we so often want to do with each other. "Go on a food fast" was what I regularly heard from God during those years. "I can't, I can't, I can't, God can't you see I'm dying emotionally?" was what I often felt.

But God wanted me to enter into the battle with Him – to fight for my own life, for the life of my family, for the future well-being of our daughter. But I had lost all my fight. I know now that we need a sense of fight in order to become healthy emotionally. So in my desperation I began to fast. I fasted in different forms – sometimes no food at all for a day or for a few days; at other times just a meal or no sugar for weeks; sometimes just eating vegetables. As I fasted, insights came. The self-help books I was reading were also used of God. He would emphasize principles I needed to apply or know. I read books on grief, books on relationships, books on trauma. I realized that the ways I had functioned and related to others previously did not work in a time of grief, for they were not healthy patterns. I had to also learn new ways of relating with Phil and our daughter.

One of my husband's attributes is that he has always been open to my suggestions. He has always been willing to learn from me, and willing to change if need be. I began to tell him some of the things I was reading. Slowly we incorporated more of these dynamics into our relationship. Gradually we became more and more intimate again. Statistically, the likelihood is very high for relationships to dissolve when couples have had three or more major stressful events that they have not adequately dealt with. That was exactly where we had found ourselves. We had to learn how to process the pain or it would destroy our marriage. We had to learn to allow each other to be angry without being offended. For me this was a big step. I learned to listen to why he was angry, and he learned to listen to why I was hurt. We began to learn to better listen to each other.

I had to humble myself many times with my daughter. "Alysia I was wrong, I'm sorry." Or just inform her, "I am not angry at you, I am just having a bad day, I'm sorry I didn't mean to hurt you." Alysia in turn learned to do the same with me. I thank God for the great grace we learned within our family unit. While I did my best to appropriately shield Alysia from the worst of my feelings, I can still remember her trying to crack jokes to make me laugh. Even at her young age, she so wanted to make Mommy happy again. But it was only God who could do that.

The importance of us sharing the good, the bad and even the ugly of what we have gone through, is not so that people could look at us and say, "Wow, look at them!" or "I knew they had a problem with that!" but so that what we have gone through may be helpful for others. While there is a risk in being vulnerable, our purpose is that you may have the freedom to be honest with yourself and your situation. Our joy is in seeing others receive healing as they begin to have hope birthed afresh in their hearts, knowing that they are not the only ones who have felt the way they do or the only ones who have gone through such experiences. Even if you feel that your situation is hopeless, I want you to know that there is hope. Even if your life looks impossible right now, you can make it. Hang on to God. Believe, trust and obey Him in the middle of your darkest hours. He will get you through. You will feel his peace and contentment again.

Of course coming through to the other side is usually a process, not an instantaneous event. Having been there, I in no way want to make light of the effects these traumas can have on our lives and personhood. They leave their impression upon our spirit, our soul and even affect our physically body. But as we obey the Lord during this process He will lead us out of the maze of the emotions and their effects, even though they may take years to process.

Reading helpful books enabled me to understand this process of loss and grief and the effects that it can have. Having an understanding friend during this time that one can share one's feelings and grief with is also invaluable in the healing process; though seeking professional help may also be needed to help one come to terms with processing the emotions in healthy ways. At those times when I was frustrated that I was not "over it" yet, I also discovered how important it was to remain patient with myself, for God was working in my life and there would be brighter days ahead.

Unfortunately, due to these deep traumatic valleys, there can be the loss of the drive to live and the temptation to just give up in the struggle – the energy and effort required seems too great. On a human level this is very natural and, depending on the degree of loss, it can be a real struggle to regain this will to live, yes, *even as a Christian*. As Christians we are not "above" these feelings and should not condemn ourselves or others for them. The difference for us is that we know Who our ultimate source of strength is who can help us climb out of the pit. We can be aware of what is happening and know where to go for the answers that will not just cover up the issues, but deal with them at the deepest levels.

On a very practical side, I discovered the value of finding something that I enjoyed doing, like going for a walk or perhaps doing some form of art. These sorrows of our lives will often trigger great creativity and doing something we enjoy will help us to see something productive come from our efforts. Though during the valley all we see is bleakness and "shadows of death" it is important to continue to do even the most mundane of daily tasks. Though life may feel empty, staying engaged, even if it may seem to be the smallest of baby steps, can help us through. As we have observed our friend whose wife was taken from him by death, we have been impressed with his determination to continue to function. He chose to remain faithful, motivated in large part by the needs of his three teenage children. In time, he was slowly – and with great pain – able to move forward. Putting one foot in front of the other is not a substitute for dealing with the inner issues of loss, pain and even anger, but dealing with these deeper issues can best be done as we continue to take even what may seem like the smallest of steps. While all we may feel like doing is closing the curtains and staying in bed, in time this will only lead to a downward spiral that is even harder to come out of. If you find yourself in such a place, with God's help, you too can come through the other side – step by step.

Before I came to this point of understanding and wholeness, however, it seemed as if emotional alarm bells were still going off all the time, almost as if I was always alert for further tragedies and danger. It was very exhausting. So much had happened to us that in a relatively short period of time, until we came to a point of healing, it was almost as if we were always waiting for another ceiling to fall.

As Phil was preparing to go back to Africa for several weeks in the spring of 1993, I was still living day to day and in a bit of a state of shell shock. In the midst of all this, without even realizing it, Phil's trip was going to be much more than just another trip – it very well could have been his last.

12

A Permanent Souvenir

The drive to the Vancouver International Airport was fairly quiet. Neither Nancy nor I offered much to the conversation. We both knew that I had to take this trip, but we also knew that it came at a bad time for both of us. I was going back to face the team still not sure if we were going to have enough money to live from month to month. Nancy had to hold down the *fort* for six weeks on her own, the longest we had ever been apart from each other since our wedding eleven years earlier. We had always resolved any tensions between us, especially before any separations. But we knew that this time there were some issues outstanding that we could not quickly resolve before my departure.

In some ways, we were both in survival mode. She had begun to develop her life and I mine. With everything else on her plate, I knew that she could not really deal with the ministry issues that I was dealing with and so I seldom brought these issues up. It was a place that we had never been at before in our marriage. We were hanging on, but were not really together in purpose as we had been in the past. It seemed as if the circumstances of life had stolen away the young lady that I had married; the young woman who had sacrificed her own dreams and goals, so that I could finish my training; the woman who had worked side by side with me in the youth group, always willing to put our family savings on the line in order to fulfill what we felt God wanted us to do. While we were still walking down the path together, it was almost as if we had become strangers. We had become like two porcupines who still wanted to be close, but every time we tried, we seemed to hurt each other.

Knowing that we were not going to be able to deal with all this before I left made my imminent departure even more difficult than normal. So as the very last boarding call was announced, it was with a great deal of reticence that I gave her a hug and then scooped Alysia into my arms to give her one last hug before heading through the passenger gate.

After takeoff the plane headed in a northerly direction from Vancouver and we were already eating supper as we passed over the northern tip of Alberta. Most of the passengers were snoozing by the time our plane crossed over Hudson's Bay and the southern tip of Greenland, before the final leg into London. Since I have never been one to sleep on flights, I let my mind wander back over my experiences during the last ten months since leaving Africa. I had begun to realize that there was a place in North American churches for those of us who had been on the mission field. We, who had a passionate heart for God's work around the world, had something to offer in order to mobilize others to pray, to give, and even to go.

Yet it seemed that thus far I had not been very successful in this endeavour. Aside from a handful of committed supporters, our personal support level had dwindled, and we had not been able to recruit anyone else from Canada for the work. It was clear that it would be even more difficult to see results on the home front than we had seen on the mission field. Knowing the challenges ahead, I realized that it would not be possible to accomplish this goal with the way things were going in our personal lives. While some careers did not necessarily require as much direct involvement from one's wife, full-time ministry – and particularly missions – most certainly did. Missions' work, here or abroad, required sacrifices on Nancy's part, which I knew that I could not ask of her now. But I also knew that it would not be possible for me to carry on with our particularly ministry without her blessings and involvement.

The reality of our situation meant that perhaps I would need to pursue some other type of work. Yet since high school I had not even considered anything else. My choice of bible school over the engineering program at the University of Alberta was a choice I had made as a teen, realizing that it would affect the course of my life. But the events of the last few years had made me question the wisdom of this decision. *Perhaps I had embarked on this course just out of the misplaced idealism of youth. Perhaps I had missed God completely.*

As the inner turmoil of these thoughts churned over in my mind, I could not understand why God had allowed us to go to Africa in the first place, knowing that we would not be able to follow through. While I did not question that he was Lord, I could not reconcile all the dots in my own life's picture that just did not line up. Little did I know that over the next few weeks and months things were going to get even darker before we would see the dawn again. God was not through testing my heart's motives and why I was doing what I was doing.

The apparent glamour of travel is a misconception held only by those who have not done much of it. I did not mind new places, but just tired of the hassle of getting from one point to another. I did not get much sleep during the twelve hour layover in London, which I am sure had something to do with the uncomfortable seats. Still a bit bleary eyed, hours later on another plane, I found myself again gazing down at the reddish soil of the continent of Africa. It seemed as if I had just left, though it had nearly been one year. As the Egyptian land mass gave way to Sudan and finally to the familiarity of Kenya, I began to think about the upcoming few weeks.

Upon my arrival in Nairobi, I was immediately going to be picked up for the six hour drive to Kitale. The next day another six hour drive to Jinja, Uganda was scheduled. Once there I was to help with construct the roof on our training centre there. Before leaving the previous year, we had entered into a partnership with another missionary already working in Uganda. The Centre needed someone to help with the design, building and installation of the roof trusses, which was to be my main task in Uganda. If all things went according to plan, within three weeks we hoped to have the bulk of the project completed.

By the time we rolled into Jinja, Uganda, I had been in motion for some sixty hours with only about one night's sleep. Though still relatively young, *but not quite as young as I used to be,* I was nonetheless dragging. I decided to start popping some antibiotics to help with the horrendous head cold I had developed on the flights. But even with these, I was in a bit of a fog for the better part of the first week. The truss design was still at the paper stage and no wood had even been milled yet (a huge undertaking, in itself, during those days in Uganda). We then had to make a huge "actual size jig" on the lawn of the yard so that we could set the cords of the twisted lumber into place before nailing them together, so that they would hold their shape. Things weren't looking that good in terms of the completion of the roof in only three weeks, especially considering all the strapping and roof tiles that needed to be installed.

Having just come from what was still winter in Canada I was not yet adjusted to the sweltering tropical heat of Uganda, the land known as the "source of the Nile." It was sometimes all I could do just to kick myself out of bed early every morning after another warm, muggy night. At night in the guestroom, I could not help but wonder what in the world I was doing here. Though I had also helped build a roof for our training centre in Kitale, before we left, I was now working on a project with a new team member whom I hardly knew. To say things were less than smooth would have been an understatement. But in spite of the all this, every day I gathered my lunch, filled up my water jug, and laced up my workboots before heading to the job site.

Against the odds, that first week we cut and assembled enough trusses in the yard to start thinking about getting a lorry to take the first load to the site. And what a site it was! I had first been on the property a year earlier and had been captivated by its beauty. While Uganda has a beauty all its own, this particular site overlooking the headwaters of the Nile was spectacular. The facility was situated on a gently sloping plateau, a couple hundred feet above the Nile River. Only one mile upstream was Lake Victoria and about the same distance downstream were the Bugagali waterfalls.

This area probably did not look much different from when Lord Stanley first explored and mapped it over one hundred years ago. It was here that he had finally discovered the source of the Nile. The first time we had visited this region, we were taken out on the Nile River in hand-hewn canoes. Knowing that there were crocodiles in the river, we were very wary as our paddlers got closer and closer to the falls. This, as well as watching the water seep into the homemade canoes, was quickly convincing us that admiring the beauty of the water from the safety of the shore might have been a wiser option. As we were told stories of how some of Idi Amin's henchmen were murdered in this very area, with their bodies left in the caves along the bank, any lingering doubts that it was time to head back to terra firma were quickly removed!

But on this current trip, I had little time to sight-see. We somehow had to figure out how to lift the trusses up on the concrete ring beam that had just been completed. After much straining, and lots of help, we wrestled each large truss into place. The task for the following week was to place them, strap them and install the clay roof tiles. So when Sunday arrived, it was a welcome rest after a full week of working in the merciless heat of the sun.

The following week began with high hopes of getting lots accomplished and by the afternoon of Monday we had all forty-eight trusses in place and had stretched out our stringline, so that we could cut each truss before nailing on the facia. I had been frustrated all day with the particular circular power saw I had been using, as the blade guard had been sticking open. More than once I had gone to put the saw down, only to have the unprotected blade dig into wherever I happened to lay it on. Knowing how dangerous this could be, I promised myself that I would fix it that evening.

It was a particularly hot and muggy day when I received my *free, permanent souvenir.* I had just finished cutting one of the last rafter ends and had straightened up after leaning over the edge of the roof. Actually, at the time I never even realized anything had occurred. My Ugandan co-worker, who had been behind me standing on the top of the wall, had been holding me by the belt to allow me to lean further over the edge of the roof. As he pulled me back towards the building, I turned and saw the look of horror on his face! At first I could not figure out what the problem was, but all of a sudden I felt a very warm sensation on my upper right thigh. As I looked down at my thigh, I saw the deep red of my flesh which had been sliced by the still rotating blade of the circular saw.

The combination of my fatigue and the malfunction of the blade guard had resulted in a life threatening accident. After trimming the end of a rafter, I had pulled the saw back to rest it on my leg before placing it on top of the wall on which I was standing. But with the guard of the blade jammed open, it had sliced into my thigh. Though I had released the power button, the blade of the saw had still enough power to make a deep incision on my thigh, about two to three inches above the knee into the flesh of my thigh. I quickly grabbed the t-shirt of my fellow worker (I am sure it was sanitary!) and wrapped it around my leg. Surprisingly enough, it did not seem to bleed all that much, but it was definitely starting to hurt. I wasn't sure if I had hit the bone or not, but at the time all I knew was that I had to get off the roof and back to town.

Somehow I made it down to the ladder and, with a strong African on either side of me, I was half carried and hobbled the few hundred metres to the dirt road that led to the town of Jinja. Jinja was a twenty to thirty minute drive on this dusty road. We flagged down the first *matatu* (public transport, much like a VW van that holds upwards of 20 passengers) that came down the road with dust billowing in its wake. We soon discovered that the entrepreneurial spirit was alive and well in rural Uganda! For once the driver put all the pieces together – a severely injured foreigner who had no way to town but his vehicle – the basic laws of supply and demand necessitated a sharp increase in the normal fare to town. I left the haggling over the price to my Ugandan friends. All I could think about was that I needed to get to some medical attention as quickly as possible, hopefully while I still had some presence of mind.

As we bumped along the dusty Ugandan road, my mind flashed back to five years earlier when I had accompanied Nancy in the "slow" ambulance after her accident. But this young driver was going at breakneck speed, not seeming to care very much for how many potholes he was hitting! For my part, I was beginning to hope that we would all just get there without injuring anyone else in the process. As we jostled and slid along, every bump seemed to jar my leg. Being in the middle of Uganda with a large gaping wound, all

I could think about was not contracting AIDS. Somehow I felt I had to stay coherent enough to ensure that I was not poked with any unsanitary needles, almost as if I had to ward off anybody that would try to get close to me. The reality was that I was probably more at risk from the filthy shirt that I had clumsily wrapped around the wound.

Once we got to town we first headed toward the missionaries' home to inform them and get their advice, since they knew the area. I had remembered hearing that there were some Chinese doctors in town who worked out of their own home instead of the local hospital. Since I had heard enough horror stories about the local hospital I figured it might be best to take my chances with the Chinese doctors. As we came into the compound of our co-workers, all the commotion brought Dianne running from the house. As she joined us in the vehicle, I began to relax a bit having someone present whom I knew and felt I could trust. I repeated my concern to her – that I be poked only with needles that came out of new packages! She understood and reassured me she would make sure of this.

The wound was so deep that I had needed to hold the two halves in place as we bounced down the rough roads towards our destination. The cut was about 6-8 inches long across my thigh just above the knee. At the centre of the gash it was about an inch and a half deep, having less depth on either end, matching the circular blade of the saw that had done the damage. It was obvious that it was going to take a bit more than a few simple sutures to close this wound. As there did not seem to be much blood loss, I assumed I had not cut any arteries, nor did it seem that the blade had hit the bone.

Holding the pieces together was getting harder and harder as it was really beginning to burn in the equatorial sun. It had been nearly an hour since we had begun this journey from the outlying rural countryside. After a quick ride through town, we arrived at the compound of the Chinese doctors. As we entered the front gates and saw the apparent lack of facilities, for a moment I reconsidered the Jinja Hospital option. But we were now committed and time was becoming of the essence.

It was now late afternoon, and as the doctors came out of the house, it looked as if they had just awakened. As a few of them gathered around the vehicle, I was sure hoping that at least one of them was a *real* doctor, not just exiles sent there by the Chinese government! The eyes of one of the thin Chinese men widened considerably as he looked through the windshield at my leg. The look on his face did not inspire my confidence level and, again, I felt like making a run for it, but realized that that might not be such a good idea either! As I got out of the van and leaned against the garage, I resigned myself to whatever might transpire. Standing there waiting, I was beginning to wonder where the operating room was.

It seemed like an eternity to be left standing there holding my leg. I was not sure what the hold up was, but the throbbing in my leg was getting unbearable. To compound matters, black smoke was still puffing from the tailpipe of the van that had brought us. I heard others trying to get the driver to turn off his engine, but he logically explained that since his battery was dead, he would not get his van started again if he shut it off. The best I could do was try and shield my open wound from the smoke. I was hoping that they would quickly decide where they could stitch up my leg, as I was beginning to feel a bit queasy.

It was then that I noticed some commotion to my left as two wooden garage doors were flung open. This was immediately followed by the flailing and squawking of several chickens that had apparently called the little garage home. It seemed that this was going to be the *operating theatre* for the afternoon. Sure enough, someone began sweeping the floor, sending clouds of chicken dung dust (*not a Chinese meal*) in my direction. A wooden table was pulled in and, presto, an operating theatre was created! As I lay down, the Chinese doctor and his helper came in. This time they were completely covered in white from head to toe, white gowns, gloves and masks. They so looked the part that I began to believe that they might just be real doctors after all!

After a few needles of local anaesthetic, they proceeded to stitch up the cut. Since this was not a *real* hospital, I was able to actually watch the whole procedure. No hospital restrictions here! They seem to get the pieces together, but as our family doctor in

Canada remarked several weeks later, "They definitely were not cosmetic surgeons, were they!" At the time I was just glad to see my leg back together. Though it seemed even more painful now, there was a certain relief in no longer seeing an inside fillet of my leg!

Soon I was back at our co-worker's home with my bandaged leg. One tetanus shot later from another visiting doctor signified that all there was left to do was rest. All I could now do was lie there alone with my own thoughts, processing the events of the last few hours. Other than Nancy's injuries a few years earlier, the cut looked worse than anything I had ever seen up close. As they had stitched up the wound, the doctors had confirmed that the blade had indeed just missed the bone. It had cut about one and one half inches through the flesh into the muscle, but had not reached the thigh bone. Knowing the mess it could have made had I cut my knee or hit a major artery, all I could do was just thank God for his faithfulness once again. Considering where I was, it did not take much imagination to realize what could have happened had I gone into shock, lost a lot of blood, or hit a more vital area.

As it was, I was able to recover while in Uganda, without needing to be airlifted to Nairobi, which would have been the case had I needed any other reconstructive surgery. With how susceptible wounds are to infection in the humidity of the tropics, the biggest concern now was that the wound may become infected. After years of construction work, injuries were not totally foreign to me, but I had never had one quite so serious. Even the time, while tar and gravel roofing, that I had fallen on the same knee from a height of eight feet paled in comparison. It had really damaged my knee at that time, but being young I was proud that I did not even have to take any time off work . . .not the best of ideas as I was to find out in following years. But I knew that this time there would be no going back to work the next day. For that matter, I was beginning to wonder how I was going to make it back to Kenya and eventually Canada. As I lay there that first night, home seemed far away and my greatest wish was that I could somehow be miraculously transported there.

Just as with my wife's accident, there was so much to be thankful for. I had been able to make it off the roof and into town and was able to get my leg sewn without incident; all were definite acts of

God's grace and faithfulness. Yet in spite of the blessings, there was the inevitable *Why* question. *What was the purpose in all this? Why here? Why now?* After all the years of construction and crazy risks that I had had to take at times in the past, it seemed unbelievable that this would occur now on a missions trip.

And what about the waste of time and resources this accident would mean? The money and time to be here – all was seemingly wasted. Of course, intellectually, I knew the right answers, but on an emotional level it did not seem to make much sense. I was obviously not going to get the project done, and most of my trip was now going to be spent on my back. In the midst of the deepest waters in our marriage and all the personal struggles we were going through, this had happened. It had been less that a year earlier that I had left Africa with so much of our future uncertain and now this accident on my first time back. While we had never relied on our circumstances as reliable indicators of God's will, this sure seemed like a closed door. Without wanting to, I began to feel myself slipping into a resigned despair. Though I tried to put a brave face on, this hopelessness would stay with me as I went back to Canada.

The idea that, ultimately, God does not really *need* us is a hard reality for some of us to accept. In the final analysis, our lives, and even world missions, is all about Him, not us. At that moment I felt very dispensable. It is not that God does not value us, but it is He who gives us the value, not we who produce it through our many deeds – regardless of how noble they might be. *Why was I doing what I was doing? Whom was I doing it all for?* These questions can only truly be answered in the fire of testing. Lessons I had learned in the past, and had lived to a certain degree, were now being tested at an even deeper level.

Of course, at the time, all this was not so clear. My feelings at the time were a bit more raw in their honesty. In spite of the odds that we had felt against us, I had still travelled to Africa to help out. Yet God had let this happen. And all this had hit us at a time when we were still struggling to put the apparent incompatibilities of our marriage together. It seemed that to follow my path in ministry meant sacrificing my marriage, which I knew was not right. Yet to love my wife and meet her needs meant that I might have to leave what I felt was God's purpose for my life. I could not square that circle. The prospect of returning to dangling from the side of a building on planks, installing siding, was not appealing. I had this image of being a sixty year old toothless man with a stubbly beard, bent over, carrying ladders around a job-site!

During those dark valleys of despair, self-doubt, and self-condemnation, the enemy was a master at setting the CD player to *Track Repeat*. He wanted me to hear the same song over and over. He knows which one best plays to our particular insecurities, fears, and doubts. Perhaps most insidious of all are the refrains that play to our false concepts of who God really is (*"Did God really say..."*). I had returned to Africa after *trying* to make things happen in Canada. While we were still in the process of establishing the mission – this accident had happened. Now it seemed that even what I tried to do in Africa was going sideways. Perhaps God was closing this door permanently.

Simultaneous to my struggles, our programs in Africa were expanding and we had just added the college level. But as I was recovering and hearing the rest of the team continue to strategize and make plans for the future, it seemed that I was even more disconnected from God's purpose than ever. The walls seemed to close in around me, and all I could do was lie in the next room waiting ... waiting desperately to go home. Placing a phone call to Canada had proven to be fairly difficult, so I had not yet informed Nancy of my mishap. Then, since the worst seemed to be over, I rationalized that there was nothing Nancy could do from Canada except worry for the remaining two weeks before I was scheduled to return, so I decided to wait before calling her. Those two weeks seemed like an eternity.

After another week in Uganda, the time to return to Kenya finally arrived. As much as I loved Uganda, under the circumstances I was anxious to begin this first step in the long journey back to Canada. With lots of help I hobbled to Myron's blue Peugeot station wagon and slid into the middle of the second row of seats. We had logged many miles together in the *Blue Peug* from Nairobi and Kampala to points in between. Though I was up and walking around right after the accident, it seemed that a week later, any sudden movement such as standing up and moving around made my head spin. Just standing made my leg throb with incredible pain and so it felt good to stretch it forward between the bucket front seats for the trip to Kitale. With as much effort as this took, I was beginning to wonder how in the world I was going to get to Nairobi and then be able to transit on my own through Europe back to North America.

As we headed towards Kenya, the tropical vegetation of Uganda slowly gave way to the farmland and maize fields of the Kitale highlands. The air became cooler and the afternoon rains that had returned were a welcome relief from the sweltering heat of Jinja. As we passed the Kitale airport on one side and the huge Eucalyptus trees lining the highway on the other, trees that the British had planted during colonial times, I knew that it would only be a matter of minutes before I could again stretch out on a bed at the Goodwins, our co-workers in Kenya. Once back in Kitale I began to feel that I was getting a bit closer to where I could get the situation with my wound monitored. Our missionary friend, Karolyn Schrage, who was a nurse and had always helped us with medical advice over the years, willingly helped change the bandages. Within a couple days she began to notice that the area around the wound was looking pretty red, and it seemed that it had developed an infection. But since I was scheduled to leave for Nairobi in a week to catch my plane, we decided to do nothing just yet.

A few days later, I was visiting with the Schrages in their home. While living in Africa we had appreciated our friendship with this couple who had been in Africa for many years, beginning in a mud hut while ministering to a tribal people. Though it seemed like an eternity ago now, it had been less than two years previously that Nancy and I had gone with them to the *Rondo Retreat Centre*, which was in the middle of the last rain forest in Kenya, the Kakamega Rain Forest. We had fond memories of spending the better part of two days sitting on the veranda sipping tea and visiting, with only the view of the lush green forest and the sounds of exotic birds as company. It was to be years later that this retreat centre, which traced its historical roots to early colonial times, would be the venue for our International Staff meetings.

As Karolyn looked at my leg again after supper, it was apparent that the infection was getting worse and she thought it would be best to call a doctor in Nairobi. As two years earlier, our former family doctor from Canada was still serving at the mission hospital in Kijabe. After a short discussion with him, she announced that the stitches had to come out . . .now. She explained that the doctor had confirmed that if they were not removed, the infection would only get worse. The infection needed to be drained from the wound. I was a bit dubious, as it seemed one week was not nearly enough time for the wound to heal enough to take out the stitches. *I had visions of it flopping open again.* But with no thought of further visiting, she returned with scissors and whatever else was needed to take out the stitches. So laying aside the game we were playing, right in their living room, she proceeded to take out the stitches. While it did not completely open up, the scar left by the wound eventually became much wider than it would otherwise have been, but it did help to alleviate the infection.

While all my regular plans for the Kenya portion of the trip had to be abandoned, over the next few days I was able to visit with various team members from the permanent position on the couch. Yet all I could think about was getting back to Canada and getting better. A few days later, we repeated the process of loading up Myron's blue Peugeot for the drive to Nairobi and my eventual flight home.

The morning we left Kitale was a typical Kitale morning. While it would rain in the high country in the afternoons, the mornings always seemed to begin with wall to wall sunshine. After passing through the farmland between Kitale and Eldoret, we wound our way through the hill country surrounding Eldama Ravine, before passing through the scrub land surrounding Lake Nakuru. As we climbed the escarpment we could see Lake Naivaisha come into view. As usual, it was covered with what looked like faint pink foam, but which were actually resident flocks of thousands of flamingoes.

On the top of the escarpment we made a short detour down to the Kijabe Hospital to see Dr. Lewis again. As we wound our way down to the missions facilities, one could just make out Mt. Logonot, the extinct volcano which rises from the valley floor. It was hard to believe that it had only been two years earlier that we had flown over the mountain on our way to take our daughter to this same hospital for her malarial treatment. Again, the familiar face of Dr. Lewis was there to greet me and look at the wound on my leg; assuring me that I would live to see another day. After picking up a few pain killers, we continued towards Nairobi. It was later that same night that I said goodbye to Phil and Myron and was wheeled to the gate to board my flight. Settling in to my bulkhead seat, with a large cushion to prop up my leg, I tried to get some rest on the nine hour flight to Amsterdam. The morning start from Kitale already seemed like a long time ago.

Once in Amsterdam, airline staff assisted me in getting to my connecting flight to Canada. It was only then that I discovered that I did not have a direct flight to Vancouver. I would have to change planes in Toronto. The flight from Amsterdam was rather uneventful, but once in Toronto, I had only a few minutes to catch my connecting flight to Vancouver. Though I had again been provided with a wheelchair, there was no way I could make the connection. This meant waiting another four hours for the next flight to Vancouver. Not having been able to sleep since the morning that I left Kitale two days before, it seemed that this long *day* would never end.

My leg by this point was causing my whole body to ache and I was feeling nauseated. It seemed I may never make it home. While I was looking forward to my own bed . . .*any* bed would have been welcome. Returning to the same situation at home that I had left only a few weeks earlier did not make things any easier. Instead of clarification in my own life and work, it seemed that the events of this trip had made things even less clear. But the brush with potential catastrophe that I had had made me realization afresh how much I loved Nancy and Alysia and how important these family relationships were. In spite of all the turmoil both of us had been through, we had not stopped loving each other. Yet we still were not sure how all the pieces could fit together.

Perhaps the worst part of the trip was the last five hours of the domestic flight from Toronto to Vancouver. Not having enough room to stretch my leg out in front on me, the pain became almost unbearable. But, mercifully, the plane eventually descended over the beautiful coastal mountains of British Columbia, cruising over the familiar eastern suburbs of Abbotsford, Langley and Richmond. Minutes later, we were circling over the Pacific waters of Georgia Strait on our final approach to the Vancouver International Airport.

Until I landed in Toronto, Nancy had not known that anything unusual had happened on my trip. Not wanting her to worry, especially with everything she had been through, I had decided to only call her from the airport in Toronto. While telling her that I had missed my flight, I also *mentioned* that I had cut my leg in Uganda and would be on crutches, though everything was fine. My plan, once I landed in Vancouver, was to leave the wheelchair and meet her on crutches. I figured that this would be a little less shocking than her seeing me in a wheelchair! I was later to find out that she had been awakened by the Lord to pray for me during the night, at the exact corresponding time in the afternoon that I had had the accident in Uganda.

As I saw her again, it seemed she was even prettier than I had remembered! In that moment of our reunion, the unresolved issues and outstanding matters were pushed to the background. Alysia was her same smiley, bubbly self, wanting to tell me everything that had happened in the month I was gone. On the drive home, I detailed what had happened, punctuating the story with humour, so as to try and downplay its severity. Mind you, once Nancy did see the wound, she became aware of the importance of her prayers and God's grace to us again.

Over the next weeks my leg began to heal, though the nerve damage meant that portions of it were to remain without sensation for years to come. Again, we had experienced God's grace in the midst of circumstance that we did not totally understand. As is often the case for those closest to us, it was even more difficult for Nancy to see me in this situation and realize what had really happened.

Yet in every situation, God's primary purpose is that we become more like Christ. Instead of being pressed into the mold of this world, He desires that we allow Him to transform and mold us into his character. As we allow Him to do this, giving Him the freedom to do what He sees fit, we are then prepared to do the task that

He has called us to do. This is not his intention for just full-time ministers, missionaries or pastors; it is his plan for all believers. God has greater purposes for our lives than just our existence so that we can pay our bills. We *all* have a priestly function, for we are all to be *ministers of reconciliation,* reconciling man with God. As ministers, *kings and priests unto Him,* we have all been given the same Great Commission.

In relation to God, it is our highest honour and mandate to worship and love Him above all else. In relation to others, it is to make that love known. Two thousand years ago, Jesus *commissioned* his disciples to go and make disciples of all nations (or peoples). He is still wanting to have his disciples, those that follow Him, take up this same *commission.*

As a family, we now all had had our brush with life-threatening experiences. It would be nice to be able to relate that from then on everything went well and we all lived happily ever after. However, this was not exactly the case. Though we had experienced the barrenness and heat of the wilderness times, and had even passed through the valley of the shadow of death, we were still in the midst of another *Jordan* experience. Yes, we had seen God's faithfulness and mercy and had seen glimpses of his dealings in our lives, but the big picture was still very unclear. *Did God have a new direction for my life? How could we reconcile the apparent incompatibility between my wife's needs and the direction of my life and ministry?*

As all of us must do in such times, we did our best to remain faithful in what was before us, while still not understanding how God was going to put all the pieces together. Doing the right things even when we didn't feel like it; knowing that right feelings eventually follow right actions. But we also knew that this was not something we could do in our own strength; only God could assemble our pieces, connect the dots and make a beautiful picture from the apparent disjointed segments of our lives.

13

When God Still Doesn't Make Sense

Spring was well under way on the west coast upon my return from Africa in1993. Over the next few weeks my leg began to heal and I began to get my physical strength back. But it was clear that nothing much had changed between Nancy and me. In some ways it may have even gotten worse. Nancy was still in the valley of dealing with the grief over her father's death and could not deal with the added pressures of the ministry and the big picture of what I was going to do. I realized that I could not emotionally lean on her, as I had in the past. She, of course, had emotional needs that I was not meeting, and I too was at a very low ebb. At times I not only felt angry at God, but also at my wife. *Why could she not just get over it?*

Donations to the ministry were still not covering our personal salary and our savings were quickly coming to an end. After my leg had healed well enough, I realized that I would need to make more income than was coming in from the few part time endeavours I had attempted. So, as I had done so many times in the past, I pulled my carpenter belt out of storage and began working on a framing crew to cover our daily expenses. This consumed my days, while evenings and weekends were still occupied looking after things that had to be done for the ministry.

As I packed my lunch bucket and put on my workboots every day, I felt as if a few more of my dreams were dying on the inside. Construction work had always come natural for me; I had never thought that it was *beneath* me, nor was I afraid of getting my hands dirty. Actually, I enjoyed the work, and over the years it had always been a great means to an end, helping us pay our bills without burdening the ministry.

But as year turned into year, it seemed increasingly difficult to continually return to the same old routine. The physical strains of the job were also more difficult the older I got. Sometimes it felt as if I were making no progress at all. Having lived in Africa, experiencing the joy of doing what I felt called and equipped to do, made construction work at home even more difficult. I had begun to see the fulfilment of the dream God had placed in my heart as a teen, only to have it apparently removed beyond my grasp. While I knew that I was once again in the process of experiencing the *death of my vision,* this realization did not make its acceptance much easier.

How many times did I need to go through this process? I often wondered. During the previous ten years I had attended college, pastored, founded a missions society, and gone overseas as a missionary. Yet now again I found myself on the side of a house, nailing on siding – with plenty of time to wonder what I had done to deserve being *on the shelf* yet again. *Why had I done so much preparation, attending years of college, only to end up still doing construction?* When younger, I had found it easier to rationalize than now ten years later. During those younger preparatory years I knew that I had lots to learn and, besides, I knew I had time on my side, I was still young. But I had always believed that if I remained faithful, my time of greater effectiveness would come. Yet after that time, as we were embarking in a new direction, the accident had happened in which Nancy could very well have died. I still remember, in those early days after the accident, having to deal with the fact that my wife could have become a paraplegic. I was very grateful that she was alive, but I also wondered how this event was going to affect our future dreams and plans. At the time, it again seemed as if our dreams were dead.

But in the years after the accident, God had begun to rebuild our lives and piece together our shattered hopes. We had met, and eventually joined together with others who had the same passion to train leaders. In spite of the accident and the tragic murder of Nancy's father, we had still somehow made it to the field. But then within a couple of years, we were forced to return with no prospect of ever returning overseas again. While it did not seem the right decision to dissolve the missions society, it seemed pursuing this dream would alienate me from my wife. Each of these seemed incompatible with the other. I knew that losing my family was not a godly option, yet to give up on my dream and purpose was also not that attractive of an alternative.

I knew that if I lost my family, I really would have lost what was of greatest value. I had already seen some of my peers make tragic choices, either motivated by immorality, greed, or some other temptation that, if we are honest, is common to us all. Fortunately, I had been spared any of these, though I was still wrestling with God's dealings in my life. During such times, it is possible to know all the right answers and yet still not be able to process these at a heart level. What I did know for sure was that I needed to provide for the family and so that is how I again began to do what was in front of me, construction. God would have to take care of the rest.

While I knew that there were many things I could not do for Nancy to meet the deep emotional scars she was dealing with, I knew that I needed to provide a setting in which she could be free to get the help she needed. Part of this was to relieve the month to month financial pressure we had been under. Though it seemed impossible, perhaps time would begin to heal the raw emotions and frayed nerves. It was with this motivation that I had joined a framing crew and was once again pounding nails.

Within a few months of working with the framing crew, their contract dried up and I found myself laid off. Though I still had not wanted to make the level of time commitment that it would take to get my own contracts, it seemed I had no choice. While I had a few contacts, I had been out of the business for enough years that I knew it would have to be God's doing if I was to ever get enough work to pay the bills. But as he had in the past, God came through and I landed a contract to install the cedar siding and trimwork on the mega-homes of a rather posh subdivision. This helped with the bills and also gave a sense of stability to Nancy. With all the changes and things that she had been through, it helped her to focus on allowing herself to heal, without the added challenge that living by free-will donations can be. Although my construction work seemed to drain my limited time and energy, we saw God provide for our material needs during this time.

Nevertheless, the underlying sense of loss and pain we both felt was just below the surface. On one level we continued to function in the face of these trials, yet at times it seemed that our very marriage would end up being a casualty. During that two year period, when things looked the darkest, we were each doing our best simply to hang on to that wedding commitment we had made on June 6, 1982 in front of *God and all those witnesses.* We would often say things to each other in our individual pain that we would regret and have to apologize for. Several times it seemed as if we were looking over the very edge of the precipice at the breakup of our marriage. Neither of us really wanted to commit marital suicide, so we would pull back from the precipice every time. Staying together, however, did not mean that the process of finding answers was easy – even with our commitment it took great effort. At times we wondered how we would ever find marital contentment again.

Throughout that winter, our feelings matched the grey skies. We knew that it was too simplistic, or even unrealistic, to expect that there was one easy answer that would make everything better. In many ways, it was not our marriage that was weak. The foundation we had built, as college friends and then as newlyweds, actually held us together. The basic issue was the fact that we were both going through an excruciating time, simultaneously. This stress is what stretched the fabric of our marriage to its very limits. At times it was sheer will power, and the resolve to not dissolve that vow that we had made to each other, that kept us together. Granted, it was an old-fashion vow that included both the *good and the bad times, the sick and healthy times, to be parted only by death.* But as the passion of youth dissolved into the heat of life experiences, it was our commitment that remained strong. We would later discover that the passion does return, but it never would have had a chance had our commitment not kept us together. But fortunately, God was also still working in each of our lives. And because of the very experiences we went through, our intimacy could become even deeper.

While donations to the ministry were covering the direct costs of the ministry, my attempts to grow our personal support base had been less than successful. Consequently, during the day I continued with my work as a contractor and on weekends would speak in churches and missions conferences, seeking to increase the vision of others regarding the needs in Africa. During this time, I had also enrolled in a directed study graduate program, which I was about to complete. Through great effort and God's help, Nancy's damaged emotions began to heal during this time and God began rebuilding her faith in Him again.

It was within this context that I planned another trip to Africa in 1995. Though I was up to speed on all the changes and growth in the ministry overseas, I needed to again see what was happening in the ministry firsthand. My plan was to teach and visit the work in both Kenya and Uganda. Leaving this time was a bit easier than it had been two years previously, for Nancy and I were beginning to come to terms with the reality of the way our life was, not the way it could, or should, be. I came to recognize that my role as a missions director would be different from what I had imagined a missionary would do. One of the unspoken goals for my trip was to hear from the Lord again and to gain perspective on how I could best be involved, considering where we were at as a family.

During our time of personal struggles and sifting, the ministry overseas had seen continued growth. This had necessitated several personnel changes. The ministry had grown and developed overseas at a faster pace than the support base had in North America. As it had grown overseas, it had become harder and harder to sustain the expanded budget from just the pooled resources of the personal income of the missionaries involved. So while the Goodwins remained in Africa to give leadership to the ministry along with the Kamaus, who had been our first national staff member, the Walkers had returned to the United States in order to give direction to the ministry there.

As well as the enrollment in our *CBBS* (*Church Based Bible Schools*) program increasing to hundreds of pastors, the college level program had by now also begun in Kitale. It was great to be back in Africa, especially with both legs working! Experiencing the natural beauty of Africa and feeling the warmth of its people was like health for the bones. But the greatest joy was to be able to visit old friends, share in various African churches and, of course, teach several courses at our Training Centre.

It was exciting to see that which had only been a dream a few years earlier beginning to take shape. Most of the training was now being done by nationals, which had always been one of our goals. More and more pastors and their church groups were enrolled in the various extension courses being offered around East Africa. Other staff had also been recruited from both the USA and Africa to extend the ministry. The vision of being able to expand the training beyond ourselves had truly become a reality. While some of us had ploughed the ground and planted the seed, others were now able to begin to reap a harvest from those first-fruits. Together, we were able to provide greater numbers of pastors and church leaders with biblical training and teaching.

The month seemed to go so fast and before I knew it I was again in Nairobi, days before flying back to Canada. I stayed with friends, who were missionaries in Kitale when we lived there and had now moved to the capital city. It was hard to believe that it had only been two years earlier that I had visited in their home in Kitale, at which time Karolyn had taken the stitches out of the wound on my leg. Though they were going to be gone on vacation, they graciously opened their home for me to use.

As I settled in for a quiet couple days before heading to the Nairobi airport, the events that I had experienced over the last few days in rural Uganda were still fresh on my mind. It had only been days before that James Kamau and I had visited the small town of Sironko in Uganda. It is located on the western slopes of Mt. Elgon, in Uganda, directly opposite Kitale, which is located on the eastern slopes in Kenya. Over the last year, a pastor from an indigenous church in Kenya had been taking some of our materials to help train this group of thirty to forty pastors and evangelists. He had invited us to join them for a day of teaching and to encourage this group who had been studying on their own.

It had been late afternoon and the warm Ugandan sun was washing the banana fields on the slopes of the mountain with its dazzling golden rays. There had been no real signage and so we had gotten lost several times on our way to the little town. After all, it was no more than a small group of buildings on either side of the dirt road. The rainy season had arrived, and after leaving the main road James and I had gotten stuck several times. So somewhat tired, and a bit muddy, we eventually pulled up to the small mud-wall, tin-roof church in the late afternoon. The thirty or so people, who had been waiting since early morning, had given up hope that we were still going to arrive that day. In order to attend the meetings, many had left hours before sunrise, since they lived some distance up on the mountain. For most it was a five hour walk just to get to the meeting. After the seminar was over, they would have to turn around and walk the five hours back, getting home long after dark.

Their commitment and sacrifice were moving. It may also explain why their churches were growing. As we taught and shared from our hearts over the two days, their hunger for God's Word was remarkable. For hours they would sit on wooden, backless benches and take copious notes. They had not come because we were famous or well known, but because they were drawn by their hunger for God's Word. It was a humbling experience and one I would never forget. Over the next few years I would visit them on several occasions and each time would leave more enriched myself. While we came to give, we often left having received from them.

Hearing how much this simple training had helped this group of churches confirmed the need and benefit of training and equipping church leaders. After the fall of Idi Amin the country had begun to rebuild and the churches had begun to grow. But most leaders had no training and so were hungry for anything that would help equip them to teach God's Word and meet the needs around them.

It was with these memories of having rubbed shoulders with some very special members of the Body of Christ that I prepared to go to bed in Nairobi, on my last night in Africa.

Yet instead of a good night's sleep, I merely tossed and turned. After having again experienced all the joys (and some struggles) of our work in Africa, the fact was that I now had to go back to the realities of my construction work. It was not that I minded the manual labour for there was always a certain satisfaction that came with finishing a project and knowing that you had put in a honest day's work. It was very a tangible arrangement. One could see the job that needed to be done, and when it was finished there was the satisfaction of a job well done – and usually a happy customer willing to pay for the service.

But having to burn both ends of the candle was becoming more and more difficult. Ever since my late teens I had been able to function with very little sleep, yet now it was getting more difficult to keep up that pace. It was also becoming increasingly difficult to juggle ministry, the construction company, as well as my graduate studies. I had begun to feel that I could not keep up this pace. I could not continue doing both ministry and construction full-time. While I did not question what I felt I *should* be doing, I needed to have a confirmation from God that this was indeed his idea. It seemed that to follow this direction meant that Nancy and I would continue going in separate directions – something I did not want. But until we had more support partners it would be impossible to give more of my time to the ministry. It was a mixture of these thoughts that sabotaged any ideas I might have had for sleep that night.

All alone in our friend's home that night in Nairobi, it seemed that I was again walking my *promised Isaac* up Mt Moriah. Like Abraham, I was having to again lay what God had seemed to have promised me, on the altar again – and not pick it up. God would have to provide a ram in the thicket, as it were. I would not, and could not, continue just to *make it happen* myself. What this meant for me was that I would not manipulate others or circumstances in any way, merely to prolong my involvement in the ministry. If God did not raise it up and confirm that I was to carry on, it would have to die a natural death. I had done this before, particularly after it seemed that we were *on the shelf* after our time as youth pastors, but now I needed again to lay my ministry on the altar also. I had no interest in just having a position. I knew that the only way I could be effective for the Kingdom was to be doing what God had designed me to do.

Sometime during the night I found the book by Dr. Dobson, *Holding on to hope. . . When God Doesn't Make Sense* laying on the coffee table and began to read it. I soon found myself identifying with many of the thoughts expressed in the book. While I had made a decision to follow the Lord at a very young age and had never turned from that, I had also grown up with the understanding that to follow Christ did not mean a bed of roses and most probably meant some sort of sacrifice. Yet the combination of the events of the previous years had made me wonder how what was happening made any sense – from Nancy's accident, to the death of her father, to my accident, to Alysia contracting malaria. It was not a question of losing my faith in *who* God was, but trying to understand *how* it all fit together. *Did He really control all these things?* Perhaps the hardest issue to reconcile was the apparent fact that to pursue the call I believe He had placed in my heart, it seemed I would lose my marriage, as Nancy could not share this vision. *Why did He seem to lead us together in the first place, if this was how it would end up?* It was getting harder and harder to connect the dots. The big picture of my life seemed to be as disconnected as random dots on a page. Perhaps they did form a picture, but I could not see it.

It was about 3:00 AM when I finally finished reading the book, but instead of trying to go back to sleep I spent the rest of the night wrestling with God. I knew I needed to come to a point of accepting who I knew God *was*, even though it seemed that I could not understand what He was *doing*. While God is God and can do whatever He wishes, I, as the clay on the wheel, needed to move from mere *resignation* to his will to a willing *acceptance* of his will: to an acceptance that believed that He was indeed working to *will and to do of his good pleasure* in our lives.

It was not a matter of *if* I would serve God or not, for I honestly felt like one of the three Hebrew children of old who were thrown into the furnace. They believed that they would be rescued, but they had resolved not to bow to idols in any case – whether God rescued them or not. That night I came to the point of accepting that my role as an active missionary on the field might be over. As hard as it was for me to accept, I realized that my role as a mobilizer on the home front was perhaps what God had for me. Though it did not seem that I would be as directly involved on the foreign mission field as I had once thought, God began to give me a contentment – a contentment that only comes from *acceptance* of his will, not mere *resignation* to it. Having come again to the place of *dying to my vision*, I knew that if there was to be a resurrection it had to be through his direction and power. While one could argue that, since God is in control, this would happen anyway, there seems to be a spiritual principle that it is our alignment to his will that frees Him to do what He desires to do. We must exercise our free-will – to be obedient to his will in our lives.

As I poured out my heart in the stillness of that African night, a peace began to grow in my heart. While the transition from deep valleys and desert places in our lives takes time, that night something happened and the process was begun. It seemed that God was beginning to cause an old forgotten seed that had been laying in the desert of our lives to germinate again. Throughout those desert places of our life it had seemed that there was nothing of significance happening and very little life present. But in his time, God can choose to germinate those things that have lain dormant for years. In his time He can speak life to them, much as He did to the valley of dry bones in Ezekiel. At first they might seem like only one small bloom in a vast desert, but we must be careful not to miss these early indicators. By his Holy Spirit, He can make a whole field bloom where only dryness once reigned.

Perhaps the key is realizing that ultimately we are not in control anyway. Understanding this helps us to live with a new peace in our lives. I've often wondered how Abraham felt as he walked up Mt. Moriah to sacrifice his son, Isaac, the *son of promise*, the one he had waited an additional thirteen years for, after Ishmael was born. Had he learned over the past decades that God would bring to pass what He said He would? Did he have this same kind of strange peace that did not come from understanding the *how* and *why*, but from trusting the *Who?*

Later that day, I boarded the plane at the Jomo Kenyatta International Airport in Nairobi. I had not yet seen the *ram in the thicket*, but there was a peace that comes from no longer needing to strive and make things happen, but just from knowing that God is in control. A funny thing happens when we actually let go. Instead of losing everything, we find that God is now free to work on our behalf. As long as my main concern is to *save* or *gain* my own life, I end up destroying the very thing I am trying to preserve. From that night in Nairobi, I had a sense that somehow a corner had been turned. After six weeks away, my reunion with Nancy was special, though not as dramatic as when I had hobbled in the last time on crutches. In many ways our circumstances changed little over the next months. I continued to do contracting work and my other work for the ministry on weekends and evenings. Yet there was a peace that God was at work and had a plan. I found that I could rest in that. While outwardly the *desert* conditions of our life had not changed much, there was renewed faith that God was germinating seeds that had been laying in the hard ground.

Meanwhile, other staff had been recruited from the United States for the ministry overseas and the work continued to grow. The Goodwins, whom we had first worked with in Africa, were also now transitioning to a different role with the organization in the USA. As a whole mission organization we were also going through a transition. The role of those of us who were first in Africa was changing and the next generation of missionaries were taking leadership roles. While we still provided oversight and direction, others were overseeing the day to day activities on the field.

Though I had come to a point of acceptance, it often seemed odd to me to have earned my MA and have responsibilities as executive director of a mission society and yet still spend most days in the mud of a construction site. But I knew that if that was ever going to change, it would have to be God who did it. He had promised to make all things beautiful in his time. We wanted to be part of his plan, not just fulfilling *our* plan.

The first shoots of growth were almost imperceptible. Without at first even realizing it, we began to receive responses from our newsletter regarding monthly support. Though only a few letters arrived every month, as I continued to speak in churches and attend missions conferences, more and more individuals and churches began to join our team as financial partners.

Our approach had always been to make our needs known, but never to coerce or manipulate in order to motivate others to give out of guilt. To the best of our ability, we had attempted to remain consistent in this, even throughout the lean years, when the temptation to whine on paper was the greatest. Yet after my last trip to Africa, without any outward change in our approach, every month more began to join our support team. While we hope we have learned to communicate better over the years, there was no real logical explanation as to why more began to support the ministry.

It did not happen all at once, but slowly I was able to devote more time to the ministry and only take the occasional construction job to supplement our income. Within a period of a year, God had answered our prayer as to what degree we were to be involved. Not only had He provided materially to make this possible, but the pieces of our marriage were also being put back together. Nancy had moved from her grief and pain to greater wholeness and I had moved from questioning God to an acceptance of his good and perfect will.

Flowers were beginning to bloom even out of what seemed to be the driest deserts of our lives. Even without my being able to figure out how to connect the dots, God had been working to arrange them to form a picture that He had designed. His ultimate plan was to *restore us and make us strong, firm, and steadfast* (2Peter 5:10).

14

Barriers of Fear –
Bridges of Forgiveness

While I had been back on several occasions, since leaving Africa we had never been back as a family. Actually our departure five years earlier, at the time seemed more like an ending than a beginning. With the depth of inner turmoil we had dealt with, a return trip as a family had never really entered my mind.

The issue of us going back as a family first came up in an annual meeting of the Board of Directors, to which I was not initially that open, knowing the background to the circumstances of our departure. Yet returning as a family would give the opportunity to stay longer and teach, as well as travel and see more of the expanding ministry that had not been possible on my shorter trips. More importantly, it would also give Nancy a chance to meet new members of the team and if nothing else bring some closure to her time there.

It had been a couple of years since my all night experience in Nairobi and much had happened in our personal life. During the intervening years God had slowly begun to rebuild our shattered emotions. Having walked through deep personal valleys and barren wildernesses, we were again beginning to pull in the same direction as a couple. Even so, I was not sure that it would be such a good idea, or that the family would even be open to it. Since it seemed that the added stresses of our time in Africa were catalytic for much of the pain since, I did not want in any way to jeopardize the stability we now had as a family. Above all, I did not want to initiate anything that might not be of God. I had no interest in *dragging* my family to the mission field. In many ways it had have been far easier to just go alone during the intervening years.

However, as we discussed a return trip, not only was Nancy open to the idea, but began looking forward to once again being in Africa. With no great initiation on my part, that which I had never thought possible was happening; we were going to be in Africa again as a family. With the decision made, our plans were set to leave in the spring of 1997. As for me, I was still somewhat astounded that it was actually happening.

Alysia was now ten years of age and so was included in our decision-making process. Though she had only been four years of age when she had experienced the malaria attacks, she still had memories of those days. For her, returning to Africa was also a step of faith. We had asked her what she would think of going back and, even at her young age, she had been thinking and praying about it. She needed assurance that God would take care of her. One night, while we were still making our decision, I went into her room to pray with her and say good night. As we lay on her bed, she said, "Dad, I think God wants me to go to Africa." It was definitely one of those spiritual "Kodak" moments for a parent. In spite of the unknowns, she in her childlike way, had faced her fears and chosen the more difficult path.

The months and weeks went by quickly and before we knew it the time to depart was only several days away. Tucking Alysia into bed only days before leaving, we noticed that she had suddenly developed a high fever. While she had not had any recurrences of malaria since we had left Africa, we always were a bit more observant whenever she developed a fever. Yet it seemed more than *coincidental* that, only a few days before we were to leave, she would contract a fever. With the suitcases laying half-packed on the floor, I again questioned if I really was doing the right thing in taking the family to Africa. The enemy worked overtime in painting all the worst-case scenarios in my imagination. Days before leaving, we again had the opportunity to choose whether we would operate in faith or out of fear. As we prayed together and focussed again on what we felt God wanted us to do as a family, his perfect love again began to melt away the fear.

Before Alysia's bouts with malaria in Africa, several years before, fear has never really been something I had thought much about or had to deal with. Even when the carport had landed on Nancy and Alysia, and in the days that followed, fear was not an emotion that I had had to process. Similarly, when I had been in Uganda and had cut my leg with the powersaw, fear was not something that I particularly had to deal with. In both of these crises, there were legitimate concerns, but nothing that had paralysed me into inaction.

Yet the repeated malaria attacks that Alysia had experienced with the accompanying seizures caused me to experience a face of fear that I had not encountered before. As we had paced back and forth in our bedroom on that dark African night years before, we had felt all alone. In between praying and pacing, we had tried to keep her fever down. Not having access to modern medical facilities, and feeling like we could do nothing for our little daughter was a helpless and lonely feeling. This experience had opened the door to fear and was something that I had to fight against during recurring incidents. In the depth of the night, the fear had not been so much an emotion as it was a presence, something that could be sensed.

This had not primarily been a struggle in the natural dimension, but a spiritual struggle to focus on truth – God's truth. The Psalmist David wrote that, in the dark valley of death, he would fear no evil. If the other stresses during the valleys of our lives do not defeat us, then a myriad of fears have the potential to immobilize us. Only as we recognize the source of these fears and apply God's Word, can their power over us be broken.

Fear that is not brought under the lordship of Christ inevitably destroys our faith, for it does not believe the truth about God and his Word. It has less to do with the circumstances and more to do with our belief about those circumstances and who controls them. If we believe that somehow God no longer loves us or has us in the palm of his hand, then fear is free to grip our hearts. The result can be a paralysis in our ability to move forward.

While this experience days before leaving for Africa again brought back these memories and feelings, there was also a realization that we had developed some faith muscles in fighting this type of battle. While we followed the precautions that the doctor advised and postponed our trip by a few days to let her get over what turned out to be the flu, we recognized the source of the attack and stood our ground against the fear.

Heading for Africa this time was also more interesting for Alysia as she was now older. Instead of carrying her through London she was able to do her fair share of carrying the luggage! We once again stayed with our friends in Nairobi. Our initial plan was to be in Nairobi for only a couple of days, but these few days turned into a week as both Nancy and Alysia were quite sick upon our arrival. Fortunately, they waited until we were out of the airport terminal and vehicle before *ejecting* the airplane food! Once jet lag and stomach problems were behind us, we headed up-country for Kitale. The familiar drive was as beautiful as always and it was fun to be able to share the trip as a family. It was hard to believe that we were all there again after leaving only five short, yet long, years before. So much had happened in the intervening time.

We settled into an old colonial house that had a view onto the half-acre landscaped yard. This would be home for the next two months. It did not take us long to discover that a family of rats had also claimed this as *their* home, but with some effort we were able to *convince* them to look for other accommodations! Being in Africa was drastically different from our home in Canada, but the transition was much easier than the first time we had arrived on the continent, some seven years previously.

———————◆———————

In spite of the *nauseating* return to Africa for Alysia and me, caused primarily by a bad combination of airline food and lack of sleep, the beauty of Africa and the friendliness of the people were as I had remembered them. As we travelled upcountry to Kitale from Nairobi and settled into the old colonial house which was to be home for the next two months, our lives took on a certain routine. Phil would leave early to teach and be back mid-afternoon, while I continued to help Alysia with studies and renewing previous relationships and making new ones.

It seemed hard to believe that it had been five years since we had left Africa as a family. So much had happened in the intervening years and I had come a long way in processing the grief and pain that had threatened to destroy me. In retrospect, I could see how vulnerable I had been to Satan's lies during those times of grief. While we all discard improper or negative thoughts everyday, when we are weak emotionally, due to grief, painful losses, or trauma, we can fall into negative thinking and believe that some of those thoughts may actually be true.

At one point I had even begun to believe that God *could* not protect me from evil. The root of this was that I could not rationalize with my mind how He could have allowed so much destruction in my life in such a short time. When I would read parts of the Bible that stated how God protects us, I would find myself unable to believe the truth at a heart level. I discovered that it is so important to learn to identify the lies that have become a part of our thinking during those deep seasons of despair and difficulty. Once we identify them we can then combat them and rebuild right thinking. As we choose to believe the Bible over our own thoughts, emotions, or experiences, our mind becomes renewed. The Word of God can then sink deep into our hearts and we can receive healing. This begins with a conscious effort to read his Word and meditate on it; absorbing its truths into our spirits. This *is* possible even when we do not have a "positive" outlook and even when our emotions seem to be screaming the very opposite of what we read in Scripture.

When we are overwhelmed with sorrow or negative emotions it can be a very confusing time. We have difficulty rationalizing how this injustice has befallen us. Often our emotions are so loud that they drown out God's voice. We cannot hear the voice of love which we so desperately need to hear. A very practical way that I found helped me to quiet those deafening emotions was to fast. Even just fasting from some of the more unhealthy foods (which taste so good!), such as coffee or sugar helped me to focus my attention and sort through my emotions more rationally. These types of food often put more stress on our body, as it must work harder to digest them. Some of us turn to chocolate or sugar when we are depressed and this usually just compounds the issue, particularly at times when our emotions are out of control. While a rather simple practice, fasting can be an effective means to help us focus our attention on God. Without the unhealthy substances in our body, it is more relaxed and able to better process trauma. God deals with us individually, particularly in regards to those specific things we need to do in order to not hinder the healing He desires to do in our hearts and lives.

A key issue for me in releasing the anger and coming to a place of wholeness, was forgiveness. Early in the process of my own sorrow, I never really contemplated the issue of forgiving my brother for what he had done. There was so much sorrow and pain in my heart, that God first focussed on healing my grieving heart. It took some three years of pouring my heart out to God before He began to deal with me regarding forgiving my brother. On one hand, looking back, that seems somewhat strange, but God always knows the right timing and what order we have to deal with all the issues that are in our hearts. During that period of time He just continued to pour his comfort into my wounded spirit and began building my trust in Him again.

When I first became aware of the need that *I* had to forgive my brother, I was a bit dumbfounded as to how to do that. I had forgiven others who had wounded me in the past, but no one so close to me had committed such a hideous crime against me. Against *me,* for my brother had very personally stolen something that was very precious to me. It was still hard to accept the reality that my father had died prematurely in a very cruel and undeserving manner.

I remember clearly driving home after shopping on a beautiful summer day when God gave me the words to help me forgive my brother. Till then all I could think was, "How God, how. . . ?" It was beyond my comprehension as to how I could forgive Tony. Then came the thought, "Tony is valuable enough that Jesus died for him!" If Jesus would have died for him if he was the only human needing forgiveness, how could I not forgive him? *I too could forgive him, even as I had been forgiven so much by Jesus!* This thought sunk deep into my spirit and I was able to forgive my brother for what he did to my father, my family. . .to me. As I took the next step and wrote a letter to Tony (who was in a psychiatric prison, where he remains to this day) expressing my forgiveness. Though he did respond to my letter, in his mental state it is not always clear as to the level of his comprehension of his actions.

Without forgiving and releasing others, we resort to blaming them. This was another hindrance to my emotional healing. For some they may blame their parents, "If my parents would have loved me better, I would have good self-esteem." For others, as in my case, "If God would not have allowed such horror in my life I would not have gotten bitter." The list of who and what we can blame is endless. I began to realize that I was blaming God for the painful things that he had allowed in my life. We must first accept that in this life we will experience injustice, misunderstanding and even deep heartaches – they are inevitable. It rains on the just and the unjust alike. Eventually all of us will have a loved one die – we will all eventually face pain. Our task is to learn to understand what we are feeling, accept the emotions and deal with them, and then learn to let the pain go. Depending on the depth of the loss, the period of time between loses, and our spiritual and emotional condition, this process can even take years. I found it helpful to remind myself that these things happen – I was not the only one that has ever gone through these things.

In that acceptance, God began to help me work through the issues and face my emotions; taking responsibility for my responses. No one "made me feel this way;" these emotions were my reactions and I had to take responsibility for them and learn to deal with them more constructively. Blaming my parents, my spouse, my friends, or even my brother and heaping anger and condemnation upon them would only further complicate the matter. As long as we blame others, we become stuck in a cycle of anger and bitterness from which it becomes more and more difficult to be free. Letting go may be painful, but hanging on is much more destructive.

This inability to *let go* also hinders our flexibility in dealing with others and life. This rigidity caused by the pain in our lives, is motivated by our need to be safe and secure. But this lack of flexibility is a very difficult way to live life. The good news is that this flexibility can return if we pay attention to our behaviour and make an effort to change. This lack of flexibility is often expressed by always needing to get our own way and needing to control our surroundings, including those around us. This can stem from having emotional issues which we are "stuck" on. It is our way of trying to protect ourselves from future pain. Very often it is also a way in which to keep our personal wounds private. We try to cover our wounds and control situations so that nothing causes the tape which we have covered our wounds with to unravel. In this way we try to keep the "ugliness" of our wounds from others. While there are appropriate times and people to share with, we can only stay closed to others so long, especially with those in relationship with us. Before long, it will no longer be possible for those closest to us to allow us to stay in that "comfort zone." For example, while we may be able to control our spouses with our fear or anger eventually our children, as they grow older, will push our buttons revealing the state of those inner wounds. Without openness with those we are closest to, it will be impossible for our relationships to grow and they also will remain "stuck." The book of *James* encourages us to confess our faults – bringing them out into the open and not covering them – praying with each other so that we may be healed. Of course we do this with those who we can trust and who can help, not worsen, the situation. But deal with others we must, which first means that we must face the pain, feel it in all of its ugliness, and then be willing to change and move forward.

The traumas that I had experienced also increased my fears and it has been a battle to push against the limitations these fears have tried to create. While God sometimes instantaneously delivers us from addictions and even takes away the desire for destructive habits, often times deliverance is a process which we must participate in with Him. This process requires a greater surrender to his love, which will then cast out all fear, and a renewing of our minds to right thinking about our situation. After having accepted God's truth regarding my fear, I also found that I had to take practical steps in order to push past my fears. If I believed God, but stayed under the bedcovers, not much was going to change with regards to their mastery over me. Instead of avoiding the fears, I needed to understand the irrationality of my fears and continue to take positive steps to overcome them.

As I get older I want to continue to push the fences of fear further and further from the centre of my life, providing a bigger arena for me to live my life. Don't let the walls of fear press in on you! Push them out, or fear will rule us by confining us into a smaller and smaller prison, limiting us in our relationships and the good purposes God has for us.

Pain has a way of developing qualities in us that cannot be produced in any other way. Endurance, for example, is a character quality often forged in the fires of pain. I never would have developed endurance if I would have known exactly how long my grief process was going to last. So many times I asked the Lord, "How long? How long must I go through this dark tunnel of grief?" The very fact that God did not give me an exact answer or date meant that I needed to continue steadfast – developing more endurance. For these times of life there are usually no quick fixes or instantaneous bailouts. But the grace and faith to go *through* the process is as miraculous as an instantaneous miracle.

Unfortunately, our emotional and spiritual muscles do not get strong through just joy and pleasurable experiences! These come by going through the circumstances that we would just as well avoid. During these difficult times, compassion and understanding are also developed in us. I think of elderly saints, who have perhaps lost their youthful physical appearance, but who exude such a strength of beauty and grace that we are drawn to them. Though they have learned many of these lessons, they don't feel the need to always be pointing out other's faults, they simply love others past their shortcomings. We often wonder, "How do they do that?" More often than not, they have learned this in the difficult school of suffering and pain. I too want to become better not bitter from the painful pills that we must swallow in life.

These lessons (and what God was really doing at the time), were not all that clear while they was happening. But being in Africa again with the perspective of hindsight, it was obvious that God had never left me and that he had been there all along. Though we were in Africa again considering if God wanted us there for another season, my identity and role had never been focussed on our geography. My desire was to follow the Lord and obey Him, wherever we were at. God knew that if it was up to me I would most likely just stay in my own country! Yet I knew that regardless of where we were living, in order to be effective I had to be at a greater place of wholeness.

As I looked back over the last few years, I could see how God had done this. Yet even at that time, as we prepared to return to Canada, I had no idea that soon upon our return from Africa, God would again begin stirring in our hearts the burden for Eastern Europe. That this would even be possible, considering what we had gone through, was a testament to God's faithfulness and grace.

Our time in Africa seemed to pass by very quickly. While Nancy juggled helping Alysia with her studies and all the details to look after the home, I travelling and taught at our various extension centres in Kenya and Uganda. It was a joy to again be able to share with these men and women from God's Word. Being in ministry already, they were very motivated to learn and were actually enrolled in the training programs in order to be better equipped for their ministry.

For many years we had struggled to establish the ministry in Uganda, due primarily to not working with the right people. We needed leaders who could mesh with our ministry philosophy. From those early beginnings, when Phil Walker, Myron or myself would weekly drive to Uganda to teach, things had definitely taken strides forward. David and Zipporah Omalla had joined the team and were now directing the ministry in Uganda. David had been born in Uganda and had fled to Kenya to teach during Idi Amin's reign of terror. He eventually had pastored and then taught at *Pan African Christian College* in Nairobi, before returning with his wife to his home country, which he had been away from for so many years.

Our base in Uganda continued to be Tororo, which was on the border of Uganda and Kenya. It was the same town that we had taught in when we had first made our trips there from Kitale. While back on this occasion, David had organized a pastor's conference for Ugandan leaders from the area, many of whom I had not seen for many years. Uganda itself had also changed in the intervening years. Greater human rights and freedoms were beginning to have a positive effect on the society.

The joy of sharing with these leaders and friends, who we had known for many years made the time fly by. One of our goals for the trip had been to hear from God as to what our role was with the ministry, specifically in Africa. While our role had changed to a more supportive one – communicating the vision at conferences and motivating others for missions – were we to also now consider spending an extended time in Africa again? After the challenges of the past years it was almost inconceivable that this was an option, yet here we were. That it was even an option was in itself a witness to God's grace. After we had left, with all the issues we were dealing with, it had seemed that we would never visit Africa as a family, let alone consider staying for an extended time again. Though from our perspective it seemed we *had* to go back to Canada in 1992, God had used our time back to establish the mission organization there, something that I would not have naturally gravitated to. Left to my own, I might never have left African soil! But God, as always, has the bigger picture in mind and directs our steps, even when it seems to us we are merely *stumbling* along.

Now that God had begun to assemble some of the loose pieces of our lives we seriously considered whether it might be his time for us to return for a longer period. I loved to teach and share at every training level and could easily see myself doing this indefinitely. But over the course of the weeks that we were there, it became clear to us that now was not the time for us to be back in Africa in a full-time capacity. The reality was that the rest of the team, both expatriate staff and nationals, were doing a great job and the ministry was expanding.

By this time the ministry was also in the process of purchasing an empty secondary school situated on twenty acres in Kitale. We had never been that interested in large facilities per se, as most of our training was disbursed in small groups around the country. Yet this facility would enable us to facilitate more training than we were currently capable of. Due to our lack of space we had not been able to respond to all the requests that we were receiving on a daily basis. These facilities would help us operate our various in-service programs, which by this time ranged from a primary to a college level, as well as better administrate all our extension training. Participants were from various areas of East Africa, but since all programs were in modular form pastors could continue in their ministry, coming for only several weeks at a time to get further training. In this way we were able to utilize our centre to its fullest capacity. It was certainly a long way from the clay tile roof I had constructed on compound of the old colonial home we had first lived in when we had moved to Kitale.

With all the exciting new developments in the ministry, it was hard to part with the rest of the team, as our time to return to Canada approached. Yet our departure from the African team was quite different than it had been five years earlier. Though we were physically leaving, we now had a confidence in God's leading in our lives and knew that He had prepared and given us other tasks to accomplish. While our specific role and ministry had changed in the organization, there were now other workers who had the same vision, and were uniquely gifted to serve the African church. We would continue to serve the Continent, yet in another capacity.

As we left Kitale that day, it was with the recognition that we were part of a larger team which had a common focus. God had taken what seemed like loose pieces of our personal lives and woven them into something that reflected his design. He is truly the Master at taking even the most ugly and tragic pieces of our lives and creating something that has beauty and hope.

On the flight home, little did we know how soon God was going to challenge us with a new vision in our ministry – this time on a new continent.

15

Leprosy and Taking Risks

Once back in Canada, the work of visiting missions conferences, meeting pastors and sharing in churches continued. In order for us to be effective we had to be strategic; we needed to mobilize personnel and increase our resources. Mission speakers, such as George Verwer, continued to emphasize at mission conferences the great needs confronting us around the world. This was especially true with regards to the ratio of Christian workers to population overseas, compared with the number of Christian workers in Canada and the US. But ironically, he was noticing that there were many thousands prepared to serve overseas, but were not able to follow through, for they lacked the necessary funds. We could personally identify with this, as this had been a challenge for us as we had sought to be engaged in global missions over the years.

But now it was I who was in the role of attempting to recruit others for the global harvest field. This also necessitated the need to raise further funds. Yet often I discovered that a deeper question first had to be dealt with. This went to the heart of *why* we were to be engaged in this endeavour at all. *Why should we bother anyway?*

*After all, was not the church in many parts of the world stronger than
ours in North America? Should not the needy in other lands be able to
help themselves already? Was it not true that we had more than enough
needs at home?*

Questions were also being raised from other segments of
society such as, *In our western societies, which are becoming more
and more pluralistic, did it not border on fanaticism to convince those
in the rest of the world to believe as we did?* Often those posing this
questions had vivid images of the *Crusades* of the last millennium,
where "Christianity" was forcibly imposed on others, even at the
risk of death, or perhaps as a reaction to the brand of Christianity
that was spread on the coattails of colonialism. Usually this latter
group implies that through the process of evangelizing missionaries
were *destroying* cultures (glossing over the clear facts from history
of the medical, educational, individual rights that a foundation of
biblical principles have brought to every society based on them).

Of course it is beyond the scope of this book to deal adequately
with these questions, although there are valid responses for each.
Suffice to say, it is important for us believers to understand why
we do what we do with regards to world missions. We need to
understand the biblical foundation of world missions, or our
mission endeavours will be motivated only out of mere pity, good
works, or perhaps even guilt. As the book *Perspectives on the World
Christian Movement* (US Centre for World Missions) points out,
our foundation for world missions is first and foremost a biblical
concept. However, it did not originate with the Great Commission
of Matthew 28:19, but thousands of years earlier, with a promise
given to the patriarch, Abraham.

The Lord had asked Abram to leave his country, people and
family and head for a land that God would show him. He then
promised:

> "I will make you into a great nation and I will bless
> you; I will make your name great, and you will be
> a blessing. I will bless those who bless you, and
> whoever curses you I will curse and all people on
> earth will be blessed through you. (Gen 12:1-3)

As we trace the biblical record, we realize that God desired to show *all* nations and peoples who He was, and this was to occur initially through the nation of Israel. While Israel, as a nation, failed in this task, there were many examples of individual Israelites who were a blessing to individual nations surrounding them.

We think of Naomi and the Moabite women, Elijah with the Sidonian widow, Elisha with Naaman the Syrian, Joseph in Egypt, Daniel in Babylon, Esther with the Persian empire and the list goes on. Each was a specific blessing to a foreign people and nation. But as a whole, the Jewish nation was a muted witness for Jehovah. Finally, Christ came to begin a new order – not an earthly Kingdom that could be seen with human eyes, but a Kingdom in men's heart. It was to encompass all those who would respond to the Father's love. This new initiative was to not only those who were of Moses' seed, the Jews, but to all those who were of Abraham's faith; these who were the *children of faith*, as seen in Hebrews 11. It was not based on nationality, but included all those who believed the promises of God – even for a prostitute such as Rahab (Hebrew 11:31) – someone from outside of the Jewish nation, but who was grafted into the true vine by her faith. These were to be the offspring of Abraham's children; not the children of Moses, reflecting a national covenant, but the children of Abraham, a covenant with those who had similar faith.

In Galatians 3:6-9 we see that the Gentiles would be justified by faith and that God "announced the gospel in advance to Abraham: 'All nations will be blessed through you.' So those who have faith are blessed along with Abraham, the man of faith." As children of Abraham, we too have been ultimately blessed through his descendants. This *blessing* is none other than Jesus Christ and all that his coming signified – a restoring of man's fellowship with the Father. *This is the message for all people and is the basis for our mission.*

Don Richardson (*Peace Child, Eternity in their Hearts,* et al) writes regarding the *top line* and *bottom line* component of this passage in Genesis 12. The top line are the three blessings promised to Abraham personally, whereas the bottom line is the last line which promises that, "all nations will be blessed through you." This was the historical and theological context of Jesus' command before He returned back to the Father. We call this address the

Great Commission, "Therefore go and make disciples of all nations, baptizing them in the name of the Father and of the Son and of the Holy Spirit . . ." (Matt 28:19). As the Body of Christ this also is our mandate: to be a blessing to all nations by being *messengers of reconciliation* – not only a reconciliation of our relationship with God, but then as reconcilers of man with God.

God has opened up the door for us to be part of this process. But this necessitates an engagement by all members of the church worldwide. It includes those who *go* and those who *enable* others to go. The latter, or *senders* if you will, may find it even more difficult than those actually *going*. In our hero-crazed culture, we as Christians seldom show enough respect or honour to those who have purposefully and consciously adjusted their lifestyle and creature comforts, in order to be able to release others to go. It is a difficult task for those called to "stay" to swim against the tide of materialism and complacency which is so pervasive in our western societies. Yet those faithfully engaged in intercession and supplying resources to the front lines are just as much a part of this *Great Enterprise* of blessing all nations with the good news of God's love, as those who actually take the message. We must guard against the idea that one must cross an ocean to be involved in this task. While there is a geographic component, it truly needs to be *from all people to all people* -- wherever we may be.

For us personally, the Lord had begun to raise up a team of faithful supporters. This enabled us to give our full efforts to the ministry, which included periodic trips overseas, sharing about missions in conferences and attempting to mobilize others to get involved. While my heart had always remained on the overseas field, there was a growing need in North America to share this message and the importance for western Christians to stay engaged in world missions. At a time when there seems to be a greater focus on the needs within our local church and neighbourhood, we felt compelled to communicate that it was not a matter of *either/or* but rather *both/and*. It has to be a marriage of both local and foreign missions. We need bifocal vision – seeing clearly the needs of those closest to us as well as those on the horizon. *We need to be both near and far sighted.* While each requires varied strategies, both require commitment. We need to remain engaged in what God is doing globally. So after personally living overseas, it was now our privilege to be able share our heart with those on the home front.

In the midst of all my activities, the e-mail I received in the fall of 1997 from Phil was interesting, but I did not initially give it too much thought. Phil Walker, whom we as a team had appointed as International Director, was now based out of the USA office in Bakersfield. The e-mail which he had passed on to me was from a previous co-worker, who had once been in Africa but was now ministering in Europe with another organization. He shared the need for leadership training in Central/East Europe and invited us to explore the possibilities of working in this part of the world.

In subsequent phone calls with Phil Walker, it seemed that perhaps God was leading us in this direction and, at the very least, an exploratory trip was needed. So in 1998 I planned to visit several Central/East Europe countries on my way to Africa. I was joined by a missionary/pastor who had planted a church in Austria, and who was also interested in our ministry. So after making all the necessary arrangements for our six week trip, we left Vancouver.

From Frankfurt, our plan was to meet with various contacts throughout the Czech Republic, Slovakia, Poland and what was once East Germany. From these contacts it became evident that there was a definite need in these countries for pastoral training and mentoring. Many pastors, who only a few years before had been behind the Iron Curtain, were now having to deal with completely new realities. The church as a whole, was not ready for this turn of events and the leadership was struggling to address the needs in their changing society. While these societies were moving towards a *post-modern* perspective – the church was barely addressing the questions of a *modern* mind of a previous generation. This caused the timeless message of the Gospel to seem irrelevant.

As I drove through these lands for the first time, there were many thoughts and feelings. As we crossed borders, some of which still had remnants of the communist era, all of a sudden Brother Andrew's *cloak and dagger* Bible smuggling did not seem so far-fetched. But the situation and needs had changed. I could not help but remember the Macedonian call that the Apostle Paul heard in a vision some 2000 years ago: "Come over and help us!" This was the same call I heard and felt on that initial trip.

Preaching in a small church of less than one hundred members in a small Polish village was a particularly moving experience. Only years earlier, many in the congregation were not able to get job promotions and had experienced various other restrictions due to their faith. (And Poland had been one of the more moderate countries.) The suffering endured by many of these people had been great. In the intervening years, many western mission groups had arrived, often with "their" agenda, without taking into account the historical context or real needs of the nationals. Often these mission endeavours were merely "outside" initiatives, that were completely independent of the local churches. Instead of true *partnerships* developing, these were often merely *parallel* ministries, never intersecting with local initiatives.

Regardless of how small or even weak the local churches seem, we can only be effective long term by helping and assisting those nationals that are already there. The roadside of world missions is littered with groups who have had their own agenda and only worked *parallel to*, but not in *partnership with*, local initiatives. Particularly in Eastern Europe, where the church had a long varied history, it was clear that a long term approach needed to be taken.

As I shared with our International team a week later in Africa, and during my subsequent return to Canada, it was with a sense that this was a new field which we needed to pursue. At that point we had several Canadian couples interested in this new vision and so we began discussions with them regarding joining the ministry. *But by August of that year I had begun to sense something else in my heart.* The burden which I had felt on my recent trip to Eastern Europe, in light of my personal journey, caused me to wonder if perhaps God had uniquely prepared us for this task. Perhaps it had been more than coincidental that we had visited Berlin in 1992, on our return from Africa, or that I had learned German as a child. Years earlier, as we had viewed the remnants of the Berlin Wall, the vacant towers and the borders crossings, we did not even imagine that we might one day be living in this city.

However, within a few months, many of the potential missionary recruits who had been interested in Europe, were led in other directions. As I reviewed the events of the last year, I began to seriously consider if indeed God had specifically prepared us for this new field and wanted us to go again. After initially feeling the loss of not living overseas – on the front lines as it were – I had come to a place of rest in God's will, which seemed to be to share the vision of missions and serve the ministry from Canada. But, ironically, having now come to a place of acceptance of God's purposes in my life and how I could fulfill those without living overseas, that very option presented itself.

Yet especially in light of our past, I did not want to prematurely share what I was feeling with Nancy. As a couple, we had come through some deep waters and were just now strong together again. Quite honestly, I did not want anything to upset this unity. At the very least, I knew that if we were to live overseas again, the Lord would have to speak to my wife *first*. The last thing I wanted to do was to try and make something happen on my own, or cause her to feel any pressure from me. As for myself, I was not yet sure if what I was feeling was really from the Lord either. He definitely would have to confirm it. But as during other times when we were seeking God's direction, we prayed separately regarding the matter, trusting that He would give us both the same direction independently. We often had found that as we would then share together He would confirm the same direction in both of our hearts.

As Nancy tells it, it was while making the bed one day that she felt the impression from the Lord that it was time again to live overseas and that we would live in Europe. As she shared this with me, it confirmed what I had been feeling. Nevertheless I was still a bit fearful of this step. Along with all the blessings, there had also been many personal repercussions for the family from our time in Africa. Quite honestly, I was not sure I wanted to take a similar risk again. Then there were the issues surrounding the stability of the ministry in Canada since we would be absent for most of the year. Was I really willing to jeopardize the present for all the unknowns this decision would mean?

Considering this apparent risk, reminded me of the Old Testament account in 2 Kings 6, when the city of Samaria was under siege by the King of Aram. In verse 24 we read that food had become so scarce that two desperate mothers had made a pact that they would eat one of their sons one day, and the next day the other. Of course you can guess what happened! After meal number one, the second son *mysteriously* disappeared! Upon hearing of the desperation of the situation, the king of the city tore his robes and proceeded to threaten the life of Elisha, the resident prophet. Being the king, his threat was not an idle one. Now Elisha, was sitting with the other elders in his house. As the messenger arrived with the king's threat, Elisha announced to the king that within one day food would be cheap. The king's right hand man scoffed at this promise, retorting that this would be impossible, to which the prophet replied that this official would hear of this good news, but would not personally benefit, due to his unbelief.

With this backdrop, we are introduced to four unlikely main characters. These were the four lepers who were constantly at the entrance to the city and were entirely dependent on the mercy of others for handouts. In today's terms, they would be beggars or street people with AIDS. As lepers, these men had the lowest status of anybody in their society; they were truly in *no-man's land*. They were not only rejected by their own people, but were not even able to get close to the enemy's camp, which had besieged the city for months. They did not fit anywhere. As these four contemplated their options, which were few, they came up with a plan. Their solution to their dilemma was to go over to the Aramean camp and surrender. They realized that the enemy may put an end to their miserable lives, but on the other hand they may have some luck and get a meal for their efforts. Such were the desperate plans of desperate men. One choice, which did not seem like a viable option, was merely staying where they were. While the end result of both decisions probably meant death, at least if they took a risk they may die with full stomachs. Lofty goals, indeed!

So off they headed towards the enemy camp, unsure as to what they would encounter. The city gates, which were the closest thing they had to security, began to get smaller and smaller the closer they got to the soldier's camp. Still they trudged onward. What they were about to encounter in the enemy camp was far beyond their wildest expectations. They were going to do much better than merely receiving a few crusts of bread. Unbeknown to them, the soldiers had heard the sound of a large army during the night and, assuming that it was the Egyptians and Hittites, had headed for the hills. So when these rather sorry looking beggars stumbled into the camp there were no soldiers left, only lots of gold, silver and an overabundance of food. After eating as much as they possibly could, they began to have pangs of guilt for they remembered that they were within a stone's throw of a whole city of starving people.

At first the guards at the gates of Samaria did not believe their news. After all, these were just the poor lepers who had become a fixture at the bottom of the wall. But realizing they had nothing to lose, they eventually sent out a scouting party. As the good news of their reports reached the rulers of the city, the king, believing their report, threw open the gates of the city, and crowds of hungry citizens rushed towards the tents of the enemy camp. Now, as you recall, the King's official, who was now in charge of the gate, had scoffed at the prophet's words that food would be plentiful within a day. And while he did, indeed, learn that there was plenty of food, he never got a mouthful, for he was trampled to death by the crush of people streaming out of the city gates. He did not participate in the sudden blessing, just as the prophet had foretold only twenty-four hours earlier.

True story, happy ending, but what is the point of it? There are a couple of obvious ones. First, it is interesting that the most unlikely of characters were the ones that not only personally received God's miraculous provision of food, but were the very agents that brought the blessing to the whole city. It was not the king, the king's officer, nor even the prophet, but four simple lepers. It was they who were called upon to take the risk, to leave their comfortable, though unprofitable, place at the gate.

Now one could argue that they had nothing to lose, that it was not much of a risk after all. In the vernacular of our day, they were *hooped* either way. But this is the twist to the story that is so remarkable. As believers we often think that we have too much to lose in "risking it all" for the Lord. Yet, whether we live or die, all that we have is really from Him. In light of this, our relative position, be it near or far from the "gate," is rather meaningless. In real terms are we really risking anything of value? While they had to make the choice to leave the gate, they had a realistic grasp of their situation. They were in no way deluded. The king's right hand man, on the other hand, outwardly had everything going for him; he surely was well positioned in the food chain, yet he lost out on it all because he did not believe what was possible with God. We today still have the same opportunity. If we really believe that we have been bought with a price, in the light of eternity what do we really have to lose? Realizing that our God is also the God of the enemy camp gives us true perspective on our apparent security or lack thereof. *If we are willing to live sacrificial lives, we might be amazed at what God can and will do through us.*

But just as a seed that goes into the ground must be willing to die, so must we be willing to die to our own ambitions, egos and securities if we are going to be a blessing to others. I am convinced that nobody is birthed into the Kingdom without someone having been willing to risk something, laying down their lives in some fashion in order to see the blessing of redemption ignite in the hearts of others. Obviously, without the Son of God laying his glory aside and going to the cross, none of us would have received the blessing of the new birth.

In the New Testament Jesus tells a parable showing the negative results form not being willing to take a risk (Matthew 25:14-30). The story begins with a man going on a journey and leaving his property with his servants. One received five talents, one was given two talents, and the other only one talent. All invested their talents, except the servant that had only received one. The others took a risk with what they had been given and by their risk increased their return. The servant with only one talent hid it, wanting to preserve the little he had. When the owner returned he commended the first two and reprimanded the man that had hidden his talent. Was he merely being mean spirited? Did he not understand how hard it was for the man with only one to do anything with it? He could easily have lost the little he had. No, the master was desiring their participation. It is interesting to note that each was not rewarded for the amount of the return, but rather for the percentage of risk they took with what they had.

If we operate in fear and try to preserve what we have, we not only frustrate our ability to bless others, but we also are in danger of losing the very resources that God has given to us to bless others. He desires to entrust these to those who have his priorities and purposes.

It seemed that God was asking us to take a risk again. *Were we willing to step out as a family again? Were we willing to accept the risk of potential failure? Willing to risk our reputation, our past successes, as well as the potential negative impacts on our family?* We did not have much, but it still involved a step to leave the *gate, even* as the four lepers did so long ago. As I shared my thoughts with our Board of Directors, there was a sense of willingness and trust in spite of some of the unknowns. At that meeting it was decided that I would make another trip to confirm the details of any future plans. While there was an understanding that it would be impossible to cover all eventualities, there was a sense of unity in moving forward.

So, in the spring of 1999, I was again on a plane headed for Africa. But this time, the seat on either side of me was occupied by two accompanying board members, David Herrod and Ron Wiebe. We spent the first three weeks in Africa ministering in Kenya and Uganda, as well as participating in our annual meetings. David utilized his gift with music and worship to lead several workshops and concerts throughout Uganda and Kenya. It was amazing to see the power of music and how it could break down so many cultural and language barriers. Several thousand kilometres and a couple of extra amoebas later, each board member had a new appreciation for what they had only previously seen in pictures and stories that they had only heard second-hand. They had now acquired their own first-hand experiences and could better understand my love for this continent.

Three weeks went by much too quickly and before we knew it we were back in Nairobi buying African souvenirs before boarding the plane for Europe. David needed to get back to Vancouver, while Ron was accompanying me on the European leg of the trip. Ron and I arrived in Berlin, with the goal of gathering more information relating to setting up the family and ministry. We had some contacts in the city and the organization that originally asked us about helping them train their leaders was based in the city and so it seemed like the most strategic location from which to launch the ministry in Central Europe. From here we also then travelled to Poland, the Slovak Republic, and Ukraine, in order to further determine the needs for training in these post-Soviet countries.

Years previously, I had met a mission colleague in Calgary and he had shared the need in the country of Ukraine where he was currently serving. He lived in the western Ukrainian city of L'viv and we had decided to visit him. After meeting with a national church leader in the central Slovakian city of Bratislava, we travelled through the rolling countryside to the border of Slovakia and Ukraine. Since the auto insurance company would not insure the car in Ukraine, we had to leave our rental car at the border and use other means of transportation. This meant catching a local bus and then taking the overnight train over the Carpathian mountains to L'viv. With my trusted travel essentials – some cokes, potato chips and chocolate bars – we were off.

But as it turned out, our travel arrangements were not really that straightforward. From the border city of Michalovce, we first had to drag our carry-on luggage and camera bags to the local bus station. We were to find out from a local pastor that, due to the depressed economy, foreigners had been targets for thieves. It was obvious that with all our gear we did not exactly blend in! My travel companion was beginning to have the same look I had seen in others who had joined me on missions trips – the look of *this is more than I bargained for when I signed up for the trip!*

We somehow squeezed into the vintage fifties bus and began rumbling our way towards the Ukrainian border. It soon became clear that everybody else on the bus was part of some informal *underground* smuggling operation. The ring leaders seemed to be the middle-aged, rather large Ukrainian women, who would readily return our smiles revealing a shiny gold tooth or two! We tried to *fit in* and look as *local* as two very out of place western foreigners could under the circumstances. As we neared the border, the true purpose of our fellow local travellers became apparent. Bags began to be opened and cartons of cigarettes and bottles of alcohol began to disappear under their very large looking dresses. While they graciously tried to get us to participate in their *undercover* border game, we felt it best to respectfully decline!

The look in Ron's eyes at the border indicated that this was *definitely* more than he had bargained for. In light of the turn of events, I didn't have the heart to tell him of the upcoming all night train ride! Sure enough, as we all unloaded at the border, the game of cat and mouse began. Guards peered inquisitively at the ladies, periodically prodding the massive skirts for contraband. In spite of all this, it was we two Canadians who were detained and the last to board the bus, proving the old adage again that it is not what you know, but whom you know. It was obvious that the further east one got, the tighter the border and the fewer the foreigners. While not as strict as during the communist era, officials were still rather suspicious and wary. While the border officials saw many foreigners come through the airport in Kiev, my guess was that not too many foreigners regularly passed through that small border. Though the border was "freer," it did not take much imagination to envision this border only ten years earlier. The oil alleys for checking under cars were still there, though they had since been filled in with gravel.

Since the officials were detaining us at some length, our stocky, muscular bus driver with the tattoos, whom we had affectionately named *Vinnie the mole,* came looking for us. He seemed to know what to say to the officials to free us from their bureaucratic grasp. I, for one, knew that I did not want to get on *his* bad side. But we were glad for "Vinnie." Though his only interest was to get us on his bus so that he could continue, we personally felt that the end justified the means! Moments later, we were back on our rickety bus, with its swaying curtains, broken seats and colour scheme from a bygone era.

As our bus arrived in Uzhorod, Ukraine, according to the crude map the pastor (who seemed worlds away by this time) had drawn, we only had a five minute walk to the train station. We scurried through the cobblestone streets, dragging our luggage, all the while trying to look like *locals,* but not quite succeeding. Once at the train station, all we knew to look for was the destination, L'viv, the letters of which, we soon discovered, looked quite different in Russian text. But we took a chance on the only destination that had four letters that started with an "L".

As I entered the turn of the century (*last century*) station, it was as if I had been transported into another world – a world where everyone else knew the rules and I had to learn them really fast, hopefully before our train left! The late afternoon sun was beginning to stream through the high ribbon windows at the top of gabled roof of the station, as I looked on the schedule board trying to see when our train left. We knew that there would be only one train out that night and we did not really have a plan *B*. But as I looked up at the board, I noticed that our train was leaving in only five minutes! Of course most people spoke either Ukrainian or Russian; unfortunately, I knew nothing of either. But our Slovakian pastor had also given us several pieces of paper with translated phrases into Russian and Ukrainian. I just kept hoping that I would give the right piece of paper to the right person! So with my few written phrases and lots of sign language I frantically found the place to exchange some funds, so I could buy the ticket. With only minutes to spare we bought out tickets, dragged our luggage over several railway tracks and climbed up the stairs into the cabin car. Before we had even settled into our berth, the train began chugging out of the station.

I had never really grown up with any great interest in trains, real or model. Yet even I could appreciate the history of the train we were on, as it was obviously a vintage Soviet model. With the typical narrow hallway on one side and the berths on the other, it was rather standard as far as trains go. Yet we were to find out that *standard* toilet facilities were obviously not up to *any* standard. There was something surreal about the white lace and deep red velvet curtains, together with rather spartan brown cots and accompanied by out of place western music playing from the speaker in the ceiling. As we rattled and clacked down the track, we explored our berth. This, of course, did not take long as it was two single cots, with hardly enough room between them to change one's mind. We had already had about as much Coke and Pringle chips as we could handle and so we decided to take a risk on the dining car. The only other customers were two young tough looking Russians, who were knocking back shots of vodka, as if they knew of an impending shortage.

After eating supper, we decided to get back to our unlocked room, where we had foolishly left our valuables. We later found out, from a travelling American at another train station, that things were not as safe as it might have seemed to somebody like me who inevitably compared everything to Africa. Apparently, on the train the day before, someone had slipped something into his drink, which had put him out of commission long enough for them to take his camera, passport and other valuables. He was not a happy camper.

As for us, over the next few hours before dark we had a front row seat to rural Ukraine. The smoke curling from the cottages and the horses pulling over-laden carts seemed like a picture from another era. But we were just passing through – silent spectators of another people, another lifestyle. After hours of crawling up several mountain passes and switchbacks, we arrived in L'viv around midnight. *Feeling vulnerable would be an understatement.* We had made brief phone contact with my friend in L'viv from the border town in Slovakia earlier that day, but things had been somewhat up in the air. Now the dim lights of the train station seemed only to accentuate our lack of direction. Dressed as we were, carrying our western style luggage, there was no point in even *trying* to fit in. If the crowd of taxi-drivers that we attracted was any indication, we had *foreigner* written all over our faces! To compound our problems, my friend was nowhere in sight. Ron by this time was well aware of the fact that he had definitely purchased the *cheap tour package*; what he perhaps had not begun to realize was that this was rather normal fare for *Jeske Travels*. He did not seem to appreciate that the added adventure was being thrown in for the same price!

Fortunately I had the name of the hotel that Lloyd had given me and so we gave this to what *looked* like the most honest taxi driver, *or at least the weakest.* Since we outnumbered him two to one, we figured we would take our chances. We began to rattle down the cobblestone roads, with the dimly lit street lights casting covert shadows on the stone buildings lining the narrow streets. It soon became apparent that we were at the mercy of this man, and by the look of his car, we entertained the thought that he could hawk a few of our valuables and live for several months maintaining his current income level. Actually, the shape of his vehicle was much worse than most I had seen even in Uganda. Well, we prayed and decided that, if it looked as if he were taking us out of town, we would *jump and roll* from the car! "All part of the mission experience," I kept trying to convince Ron.

But there is a God (*which is helpful when travelling with me!*) and we arrived at the hotel just after midnight. While Lloyd was nowhere to be seen, we managed to catch the receptionist just as she was walking out the door to go home. We sank into the safety of the down sheets and were just glad that our bed was no longer moving. The next day we were to discover that this historic stone hotel had housed personalities such as Mikhail Gorbachev whenever he had visited the area.

The next morning dawned sunny and clear with the sound of birds chirping on the trees that lined the streets. The uncertainties of the train station the night before were already a distant memory. Looking out of the window of our gothic looking hotel, I watched the hunched over figure of an old woman sweeping the cobblestone street with a homemade broom – it was an scene that brought back images from the nineteenth century. My friend eventually turned up that morning and began to show us the town and share the needs of the area. It was another step in understanding the situation in Eastern Europe and formulating how we best might serve in this region.

Unfortunately, due to our tight schedule (we had been gone from home for nearly six weeks already), we had only one day with Lloyd and so later that night we were again on the overnight train back to the Slovakian border. While it was clear that God was moving in these lands, there continue to be some real spiritual, social, and economic challenges. Lloyd was doing a great job with his organization in providing practical humanitarian help; in the following year I would visit him again, as well as exploring other parts of Ukraine, in order to gain more specific insights relating to the needs for training in the country.

A few days later, as we settled down for the trans-Atlantic flight back to Vancouver, it was with many impressions and memories of our last six weeks. Our trip had started in East Africa and had ended in Ukraine. Upon my return we continued to solidify our plans to be in Berlin by the Spring of 2000, though there were still many unknowns. Yet the call, *"Come over and help us!"* was ever before us. With what we had already been through, it could seem as if we were unlikely candidates to be going overseas again as a family. The thought of packing up again and leaving family and friends was not very appealing. It was only the inner voice saying, *"Go"* that gave us the strength to make all the changes and prepare to pull up roots again. At our weaker moments we rationalized that there was still plenty of work to do to mobilize and undergird the ongoing work in Africa from Canada. Yet it seemed God had other plans for us for the foreseeable future.

If God was saying, *"Go,"* in spite of the obstacles, we wanted to be obedient.

16

The Back of the Cupboard

We have seen that as believers we are *children of Abraham; children of the promise.* As God promised in Genesis, all nations would be blessed through Abrahams's descendants. In the New Testament we see that we as believers have been grafted into this same promise and have been given the same responsibilities. Nevertheless, along the way to fulfilling this in our lives, there are many challenges, often represented by the various *stones of remembrance* taken from our Jordan experiences. There are many side journeys and even temptations that can thwart us from participating in what God wants to do in and through us.

This was definitely true for Abraham. The first step for Abraham was leaving *Ur of the Chaldeans.* Ur was a great ancient city – one of the major centres of the then known world. It was Abram's father, Terah, who, together with his sons, left for Canaan. But in the last few verses of Genesis 11 we discover that, while they had all left for Canaan, they had ended up settling in Haran. Terah eventually even died in Haran, miles from his destination of Canaan. Many of us also take the step and leave Ur of the Chaldeans, only to stop and settle in Haran. We must not only begin that journey of fulfilling God's purpose in our lives, *but we must also complete it.*

In Haran, the Lord came to Abram again and called him out to leave the place his father had settled in. He asked Abram to not only leave his country, but also to leave his father's household this time. Perhaps it had become a comfort zone which held Abram back from reaching the goals that God had for him. Yet in his grace, God renewed his promise to him that he would be *blessed so that he could be a blessing to the nations.* Abram most probably would have known that his father had been on the way to Canaan originally, but that he had never made it. But now God was going to reveal more clearly where *this place* was that He was leading him to. As part of the next generation, Abram was now building on what a previous generation had not accomplished. But this time we read that Abram, now seventy-five years of age and still childless, actually arrived in Canaan.

Abraham believed God's promises to him but, like us, he had his times of doubt and had even attempted to help God fulfill his plan in his life through his own human effort. This resulted in Ishmael being born, a full thirteen years before Isaac, the promised son, was eventually born. As Isaac was becoming a man, God's promise to Abraham that he would be the father of many nations, must not have seemed as far-fetched as it had when he had left Haran as a fatherless, seventy-five year old man.

Then came that early morning walk up Mt. Moriah. A long walk up a lonely mountain; a test of faith. Was the foundation of his faith still on God, or was it now based on Isaac, that which he could see in the natural? *Did he so trust God that he would sacrifice the works of God (Isaac) for the ways of God?* This is often at the root of the test facing us as we climb up our own Mt. Moriah. In the face of the unknown, will we trust that God knows what He is doing? Are we willing to *die* to the very vision that we believe He has given to us?

The narration indicates that indeed Abraham believed that God would provide, yet I am sure he was human enough to have a question or two along the way. We see throughout the Scriptures that, even spiritual heroes of the faith, were very much made of flesh and blood just like you and me. Since his *Ishmael* days, Abraham seems to have learned that God was his true source; not only the One giving the promise, but also the only One who could fulfill his promise.

We are Abraham's children. We are made of the same *stuff.* We have the same promise, but also need our own early morning walk up Mt. Moriah. We need to go through similar processes along the way, yes, even including grief, discouragement and disappointment. But as we learn to see God as our source, we discover that obedience to Him is not a burden, but a joy. We no longer have to fear the difficult times, for we realize that our God is big enough to turn all things for *his* good purposes.

To be *children of promise* and participate in *blessing all nations,* there is always a leaving of the comfortable – a stretching process that we must be willing to endure. This is not just for those called to change their geographic location, but applies to all believers – in every neighbourhood, business, or school where we are missionaries. Once we recognize God as our source and trust that He will never lead us outside of his Presence, anything He may ask of us is no more *risky* than that of a poor leper leaving the mirage of safety (outside the city gates), in order to discover true provisions, even if it be in the enemy's camp. We are not motivated to bless others and do good to others out of guilt, but out of love for Him who has done so much for us. As we grow in this process, our natural man may want to shrink back out of fear or uncertainty, but as we gain God's perspective, we will be effective regardless of the *pain* or temporary inconveniences.

It is a strong temptation to hold onto our own lives, and those we love, too tightly. It is even possible to use this as an excuse not to be obedient to the Lord in some area of our lives. Unless we decide to give up our *comforts* and even the *right*s that may be legitimately ours as believers, we will never be a blessing to the *city,* as those four lepers who were outside the gates of Samaria. Yes, as believers and *children of the King,* we have many *rights* that flow from our relationship with the King. But there are also times that we are asked by our Lord to limit the exercise of our *rights* to achieve the greater good of being a blessing to many.

In the New Testament we see the Apostle Paul willing to place himself at the end of the procession, even as an apostle, though he indicates that no one would be able to accuse him if he were to claim the *rights* that were his. Even today, there can be a tendency to emphasize spiritual rights over our privilege to lay down our lives. Even Jesus, who could have exercised his divine rights, chose to hold his right arm of divinity behind his back in order to die on the cross that we might live. As believers, we now all have a priestly duty to lay down our lives, in order to show others the love of the Father. Without this love being walked out in *flesh and blood*, we will not be effective in reconciling others to the Father. We are the Body of Christ: his feet and hands extended, his voice in a hurting world. This is the power of an incarnate gospel.

For us, obedience meant packing our bags and going again – this time to Europe, not Africa. In some ways the latter would have been easier as it was more familiar to us and we knew what to expect. Through the valleys and wilderness times of the last decade we had seen God put together the pieces of our marriage, our emotions, and our ministry. He had restored the years that the enemy had tried to destroy and had turned the evil plans of the enemy to good. Through his grace we had slowly been able to walk through the darkness and even the valley of the shadow of death. And though we had seen God come through in the past, this new level of risk required a new level of faith.

Yet we recognized the source of that inner voice, saying, "*Go!*" The One who had remained faithful and true, even when we had faltered and doubted. While there was still no detailed road map, there were signposts indicating the initial directions which we were to take. And so we began to take those small steps, not knowing exactly where it would all lead. After my exploratory trips, excitement began to build for the new task that God was calling us to. In spite of the unknowns, we had a growing peace that as we stepped out He would again provide. He was, after all, still the God of Abraham, Isaac and Jacob.

Once the decision was made and the time of our departure neared, the necessary finances were the final confirmation that we needed. As well as ongoing funds to meet the budget for the Canadian office, there were the higher living costs in Europe and funds needed for the ministry there. Knowing how we had struggled in the past to raise enough funds, my faith was not exactly at the "mountain moving" level! I knew it would take divine intervention to make it possible. But faith is a participation activity and God desired to stretch us beyond our past experience. It would be impressive to say that we always enjoyed this process, but of course that would not be true!

We found ourselves in a similar situation as the dead prophet's widow in the Old Testament. This elderly widow found herself in dire need. We read of her story in 2 Kings chapter four, as she approached the prophet Elisha with her desperate situation. She had been the wife of one of the prophets who had travelled with Elisha. But now her husband had died and left her with many debts. Things had become so desperate that the creditors were now coming to take away her two sons as payment. Definitely some harsh measures by the local credit and loan office!

Since her husband had been involved in Elisha's "Prophet School 101," she had come to the prophet so that he might help her out. Confronted with what very well may have been a very frantic widow and mother, he asked her what would seem to be obvious: "What can I do for you?" His follow up question, seems to make even less sense, "What do you have in your house?" It was obvious that she needed assistance and it would also seem obvious that she had no resources to meet the need. After all, she was down to the final option of giving up her children to pay the debt. She had nothing left, no life insurance policy, no "Early Death Prophet Compensation Package," nothing. Things could not have been more grim.

In some ways this is how we felt on the verge of relocating to Berlin. God seemed to be asking us to risk everything again, to lay it all again on the line. Yet even as we were willing to do this, it seemed we had no resources at our disposal in order to pay the bills, let alone be a blessing to others. There was even the risk that we might lose what He had provided for us thus far.

What do you have left in your house? The question echoed against the empty walls. But what seemed like a foolish question by the prophet was not so foolish after all. So when he asked her what she had left at her disposal, she remembered that she had a little vial of oil left in the back of her cupboard. Perhaps she had been saving it for a last meal together with her family. But the Lord had plans for that very last, and only, thing of value that she had left. *He wanted her to use it up!*

This was at the very heart of the dilemma which confronted the widow. The Prophet wanted her to risk the very last of what she had. Not only that, but she was to approach all her neighbours and recycle all their empty jars! I am sure that her neighbours knew of her dire straits and may have seriously wondered what in the world she wanted with all *their* empty jars. She not only had to take a risk that would personally affect her and her family, but also any pride she may have had was also tested.

One thing I have noticed over the years is that God never makes any extra effort to rescue our pride! Actually, usually the opposite is true. He often will arrange circumstances in order to challenge us to remain vulnerable with others – something my *natural man* is still allergic to! Growing up with a strong sense of self-reliance and the value of doing things on one's own, contributed to this tendency. Over the years we had been able to use our own resources to further the ministry and, quite honestly, this had always been easier than asking others to partner financially with us. I had always hoped that I could make enough money to finance the ministry completely on our own. ("On our own" being the operative phrase!)

Yet God had wanted to teach us an important lesson regarding the interdependence of his Body. While in the process of learning this lesson, depending on the Lord through others has never come easy or naturally. While I could see many biblical examples of this principle from Paul, and others in the New Testament Church, my pride in self-reliance had been gradually shrivelling every time others had partnered with us. On the other hand, knowing how hard each person has to work in order to pay the mortgage and other bills caused us to appreciate every sacrifice made. While never taking it for granted, over the years we appreciated this symbiotic relationship between our partners and the ministry even more. We were *their* hands extended.

So into her house the widow went with her sons and all the jars that she had gathered from her neighbours. Imagine what it must have been like for her to begin to pour that last little bit of oil she had been saving for months, while her children were watching. Though she was acting in obedience, I am sure she had the same feeling you and I would have had. I am sure she had some apprehensions and fleeting thoughts of doubt. But as she took that first step of pouring out what she had, the oil began to flow.

I am sure filling that first jar was the most challenging; would the oil flow? But as the oil continued to flow, I can imagine her frantically, excitedly filling jar after jar. Finally there were no jars left and the text says that "the oil stopped flowing." *If only I had gotten more jars!* she may have thought. There did not seem to be a restriction by the prophet as to how many jars she could have gathered, but the Bible does say that once all the jars that she had gathered were full, the oil stopped flowing. She then had enough resources to not only pay off her outstanding bills, but also to then live.

I don't know what this little *jar of oil* represents in your life. But I do know that each of us, regardless of how desperate our situation may be, has something that God will require of us as an offering in faith. Perhaps it may be your last little bit of energy, or a hidden talent that no one knows about. Perhaps it is something else that you are holding on to tightly, almost hoping that it is not the very thing that God wants you to expend for the Kingdom. Even as you read this you can quickly think of many reasons why it would not make any sense to pour out that last bit of oil that has been in the back of your cupboard. But if you are desirous to see God work in your life, be sure to check the back of the cupboard.

God obviously does not *need* our little bit of oil or talent to accomplish his purposes. Rather, offering what we have back to Him is an indication of our willingness to be obedient and trust Him completely. This does not seem all that heroic, especially in a culture that only rewards the famous and multi-talented. Yet the paradox throughout church history is that God has always used very normal people who were more *available* than *able*. He delights in using what may seem to us as negligible to accomplish the impossible. This has a built-in safety feature which serves to guard us against pride – for we recognize that we are only stewards. Often in the zeal of youth, we are sure that God is lucky just to have us around. While our motives may be pure, with a few more years (and pounds) under our belt, we begin to realize just how inadequate *self* really is. Whatever any of us will be able to accomplish for the

Kingdom will only be done through his power, with his resources. We have the important, albeit somewhat unglamorous, task of just willingly pouring out the little jar of oil that He has entrusted to each of us.

This was what we felt the Lord asking us to do as we again planned on going overseas for a season. Though we did not feel we had much to offer, were we willing to risk expending it for the Kingdom? This process is something we have all been called to. It is not just for the special chosen few, who we may think are more important members of the Body. So often it is easy to confuse *function* with *value* or *worth*. We have a tendency to glamorize or make heroes of those in full-time ministry or those particularly gifted. We put them on a pedestal and try to vicariously live our Christian lives through them. Just as the armchair athlete cannot have a real sports career by watching the professionals on television, we also cannot falsely believe that we can live our Christian lives through the pastor's sermons or by hearing the experiences of more *spiritual* professionals. But the fact is that we all need a personal walk with the Lord and have a responsibility for what He was entrusted to us. We are accountable for what He has given us, not what He has given someone else. While we all have different roles in the Body we all need to be about the Master's business. Without an acceptance of who God has created us to be, and the interdependence our gifts create for us, not only will we suffer individually, but the mission of the Church will also suffer.

There is a dramatic story in 1 Samuel 30 which further illustrates this. The city of Ziklag had been attacked and burned by the Amalekites. David came on the scene a short time later and discovered that the women, and everyone else for that matter, had been taken captive. The depth of loss caused David and all his men to weep so long and loud that they had no more strength to weep. David then sought the Lord in order to gain strength to defeat the Amalekites. Next, he took six hundred of his men with him to chase down the enemy. At the Besor Ravine it was decided that two hundred men would stay behind with the supplies, as they were too tired to traverse the ravine. The other four hundred continued on to destroy the Amalekite camp and recover everything that had been taken, including their women and children.

As David and the four hundred shock troops returned to the Besor Ravine, these four hundred men did not want to share the plunder that they had recovered with the two hundred who had stayed behind with the remainder of the supplies. At that point in the text we read that David established a statute that was to be for all time: it stated that the share of the men who guarded the supplies was to be the same as those who went out in battle. I think this is a great principle for the priestly task of reconciliation which we are engaged in. It does not matter so much what aspect of the battle God has called us to be a part of, if we are obedient we will all have the same share in the victory.

We are living in great days of spiritual harvest around the world. The mission fields of only a few decades ago, are now sending missionaries to the four corners of the earth. God is also beginning to stir his church in areas that were once alive spiritually, but have long since become dormant. Yet, in this great task, we must all be willing to do what the Lord of the Harvest has asks of us. Without cooperation, we will not be an effective force. Instead of being about the task, we will spend valuable time squabbling amongst ourselves as to who has a greater stake in the victory. We are all in this task together. Some need to stay with the supplies and others must cross the ravine, but we all have an active role to play and we all will have the same share in the victory. It is not so much about *geography* but *heart-ography*. Our willingness to participate.

Each of us is given the opportunity to offer to God the little bit of oil that is at our disposal. While we leave the results with God, we can be found faithful – available for him to use whatever He has put in our hand. Some are called to *Go* and others to *Stay*, but we are all called to *Participate*. Now is not the time to be pulling back, but to redouble our efforts and be strategic in sharing the Good News around the world. As we each do this, God will take what may seem like only a little in our estimation and multiply it for his Kingdom so that all peoples will be blessed by experiencing the Father's love.

17

Of Ceilings and Floors

Though we have used the backdrop of our personal experiences, our purpose has not been just to tell our story. Hopefully it has been interesting reading (or you most likely would not have read it to this point), but ours is by no means the most dramatic or sensational story you will every read. Our hope is that by sharing God's dealings in our lives you will have been encouraged in your own journey with God.

While the context of many of our experiences has been ministry and missions, the issues and spiritual principles are common to all of us. As we have described some of the *stones* that we have pulled from the *Jordans* of our life, we hope that it has spurred you to remember the stones pulled from your own Jordan experiences. We pray that it has given you a new perspective on some of the *waters* that you have passed through. We also pray that your faith and hope has increased for the days ahead.

Like you, we do not have all the answers and, like you, we still find ourselves very much in the race that the Apostle Paul writes about. We have not arrived and by God's grace have more stones to pile. Many of the deep valleys of our lives have become part of our past and by God's grace we have been able to walk beyond these. But we want to use the lessons learned as we face our current challenges. Our marriage is not perfect, but we are growing daily as Christ renews our mind and forms his character in us. As the manuscript goes to the printer, the ministry began in Africa continues to expand and we continue to serve in Europe, as well as giving oversight to the Canadian office.

We desire that all that God has brought us through will be used to bring Him glory. None of us want to forget what God has done in the past, but we do not want to become "stuck" in the past. Each of our pile of stones need to serve the purpose of helping us move forward. They can then serve to give us hope for the future. The challenge in our day to day lives is to not lose sight of the greater purpose that God has for us.

Yet at some stage of our life we begin to realize that we most likely will not fulfill all the dreams we once thought we would. But instead of having regrets and being discouraged, there is another perspective which gives hope and encouragement. While I had often used the account of Abraham to teach that the mission mandate began in the Old Testament and we, like Abraham, were called to bless the nations, I noticed something else from this account. I noticed that, though he had been given this promise, he did not see it fulfilled in his lifetime. The promise was to be fulfilled through his descendants. I began to see a God whose vision spanned the generations. We see a God who repeatedly refers to himself as the God of Abraham, Isaac *and* Jacob. He is the God of every generation.

Abraham was given the promise when he was in his eighties and Isaac was actually born when Abraham was nearly 100 years old. When the patriarch died at 175 years old, his son, Isaac (the *son of promise*) was about 75 years old. By then Isaac's son, Jacob (Abraham's grandson), was about 15 years old. Abraham saw his grandson as a teenager, but never saw what was to transpire through his descendants. He was beginning to see glimpses of it, but he did not see his great grandson, Joseph, gain power in Egypt, providing a way for his descendants to survive the famine and all that occurred as they returned to their land. And while the nation failed to fulfill a large part of this promise, we as sons and daughters who have been grafted in, are part of the heritage with the potential to fulfil this same promise given so many years ago.

We serve the same God – he still whispers dreams and promises in our hearts. He still sees beyond just our lives to those that follow us. In our youthful zeal we often assume that we will accomplish all these goals, when in reality God may have promised things to us that He knows only future generations will accomplish. This is why it is so important for us to live with future generations in mind. We need to be a blessing to future generations so that they will not be stunted or thwarted in what God desires to do through them. This underlines the importance of being mentors and spiritual fathers and mothers to our natural and spiritual children. As I have had the opportunity to serve in various capacities of leadership in the church, there is something I have noticed: we as leaders often fail in the task of mentoring and encouraging others. Fortunately this is a task for all of us, not just for those with positions of leadership.

We have the opportunity to impact the lives of others who can, in turn, influence future generations. This is part of God's big plan to bless the nations through us. A fascinating story illustrating this is recorded in the Old Testament book of Ruth. Naomi had moved with her husband from their home in Bethlehem to Moab. There she had two sons who eventually married. But instead of living happily ever after, first her husband died and then both of her sons passed away! She heard that things were going better in Bethlehem, and so she made plans to return to their original home.

At first, both daughters-in-law decided to come with her, even against her protestations. She reasoned with them that she was not going to be having any more sons, and that even if she did, her daughters-in-law could not wait that long to remarry! Her advice was that they should stay in their home country of Moab, with their own family and culture. Eventually, one of the daughters-in-law agreed that for her to stay in Moab would make the most sense – but not the other. Ruth made the classic statement, *"Don't urge me to leave you or to turn back from you. Where you go I will go, and where you stay I will stay. Your people will be my people and your God my God. Where you die I will die, and there will I be buried."* (Ruth 1:16)

Once they returned, things were not exactly easy. They had to find a way to live. The author in Ruth 2:1 gives us some inside information about Naomi's family. Apparently she had a kinsman-redeemer in the area, but at this point in the narrative she was not availing herself of this option. It was actually Ruth who asked if she could glean in the field – *any* field. The kinsmen-redeemer was a close relative who agreed to continue the name and inheritance of a deceased relative through marrying and providing for the widow.

It just so happened that Ruth found herself in the field of Boaz, one of Naomi's relatives, though we learn later, perhaps not the closest one. The *it just so happens* coincidences of this small book are perhaps the most remarkable highlights of this story, especially in light of the ramification that these little *coincidences* were going to have on the future Messiah. So she found herself in the field of a man whom she later learned was a relative of her mother-in-law, and he *just so happened* to see her as he was checking on his fields. We discover that the reputation of her faithfulness to her mother-in-law had preceded her and he made sure that she was rewarded for her efforts.

Though Naomi had returned to her land and people, she had returned with a chip on her shoulder. She had felt that God had dealt unfairly with her. After all, she had buried a husband and two sons in a foreign country. But when Ruth returned and told of the kindness of Boaz, Naomi recognized that he also was *her* kinsman-redeemer (*go'el*) and she began to see the significance of God's hand in her life again. To this point, it seemed that both Naomi and Ruth had been just *stumbling* along, putting one foot in front of the other – no great plan, not driven by much more than the need to survive.

But when the time was right (chapter 3), Naomi outlined her plan for Ruth to meet Boaz. She was to approach him on the threshing floor, in order to ask him to exercise his rights as her kinsman-redeemer and take Ruth as his wife. We find out later that everyone understood this to mean that he would look after Ruth, her mother-in-law, and raise up an heir; future descendants that would also become entitled to all that was his. For him, this was not a simple matter.

For Ruth, it was also not the easiest of things to do. Boaz, it would seem, was close to the age of Naomi, as he was a close relative of her deceased husband. Ruth, on the other hand, would have been younger, with the opportunity to marry someone closer to her age. She was under no obligation, but in her love and sacrifice for her mother-in-law, who was apparently past child-bearing age, she was willing to sacrifice her desires for that of Naomi.

The climax of the story occurs in Chapter 4. Boaz approached a closer relative concerning his intentions, as required by the law. The closer relative, who was entitled to be Naomi's kinsman-redeemer, realized that this decision could jeopardize the inheritance of his own sons and therefore declined, allowing Boaz to marry Ruth. While it would be easy to see Ruth as the central figure of this story, it is actually Naomi who has this role. While Ruth bore the son, we see Naomi caring for it; the other women even exclaimed, "Naomi has a son!" What selflessness Ruth expressed by her actions. She had returned to a foreign land with her mother-in-law, she had done the dangerous job of gleaning in the field as a young widow, and she had married an older man in order to bear a son that her mother-in-law took credit for! But as Ruth 4:15 indicates, she was praised for her love for Naomi, and deemed to be better than seven sons!

Not only is this a great literary piece filled with drama, twists and turns, but we see that the plans God had went far beyond anything they could ever have imagined. They, like us, were just trying to be faithful, doing what they could. We see Naomi discouraged and disheartened, as I am sure Ruth must have been at times. They were far too close to the trees to see the forest. But to truly appreciate what God was up to we need to look at the background and see how He put all the pieces together. In verse twelve of the last chapter, their relative Perez is mentioned. The residents of Bethlehem wished for Boaz the same success as Perez had experienced generations before. Though our eyes tend to glaze over when it comes to a discussion of Old Testament names and genealogies, there is much to be gleaned from a brief foray into God's dealings over multiple generations.

As we recall from Genesis 38, Perez was the son of Judah, one of the sons of Jacob. Though Judah initially refused to be the kinsman-redeemer for Tamar, he eventually was tricked into performing his obligation. We see that not only Judah, but also his son Perez and grandson Hezron went down to Egypt with Jacob, though God had plans to eventually lead them back to Canaan (the big picture). But the point for the residents of Bethlehem recounting the family of Perez was probably that he was well known and, like Boaz, a resident of their area. They drew comparisons of greatness – greatness that came by giving and thinking beyond just what was good for one generation, but for future generations.

Boaz and Ruth's son, Obed, was to become the grandfather of King David, from whose lineage came the Messiah! And in the genealogy list in Matthew we see Ruth as only one of four women listed in the lineage of Jesus. And to think it all started in a foreign land, with a young woman who was willing to sacrifice for her mother-in-law – leaving her family and the familiar, gleaning in a stranger's field in a strange land. But it does not end there. She eventually married someone old enough to be her father, so that a son could be born to carry on the name of her mother-in-law's family. While the coming of the Messiah was not dependent upon Ruth's faithfulness and obedience, her choices opened up a window of blessing in her life and also future generations, for she became the great grandmother of King David, from whose tribe the Messiah would eventually come, born in that very same town of Bethlehem.

Four hundred years before the Messiah arrived on the scene, a prophecy was given which we read in Malachi 4:6. Before the Messiah was to come, the hearts of the fathers would be turned to their children and the hearts of the children to their fathers. If this did not occur, the land was to be stricken with a curse. As with many prophecies, it has multiple fulfilments: first, to a time four hundred years after it was given, signifying the arrival of the first coming of the Messiah and, second, to his second coming.

In order for the Lord to bless the nations across the generations, these generations have to be reconciled to each other. As long as the parents are at odds with the next generation and vice versa, the land will not be blessed, but stricken with a curse. We see, from this little book of Ruth, that God has a plan for our lives that extends beyond our own generation. You may be currently preoccupied with just being faithful, or gleaning in a field as it were – going through valleys the purpose of which you cannot yet see. Though you may not be able to see how your life is having an impact on others – it does.

We see in Ruth a reconciler; she reconciled Naomi with her own people and her inheritance. The result of this was that the Messiah would come through her descendants. Today, reconciliation is still our task. We all have the opportunity to bless future generations and thereby affect history. God desires to use us to turn the hearts of one generation to those of other generations. To *bless* them means that we will encourage them, speak well of them, and seek ways to propel them forward. Only as we bless future generations, will they be free to walk fully into what God has for them. Our *ceiling* can become their *floor*. They can start from where we ended, not from where we had to begin. They do not need to go through all the mistakes we went through; they can be raised up as a generation that can do what we only dreamed of. Standing on our shoulders they will see horizons we only imagined. On the other hand, we also have the power to cripple future generations by not blessing them and, by default, cursing them.

Blessing future generations includes encouraging them in their new expressions of worship and giving them the freedom to perhaps experience God in ways other than we did; encouraging them to be effective for the Kingdom through their careers. God works fresh in every generation, for He is always up-to-date and relevant. It is often we who struggle with "the next generation," much as our parents struggled with our "new" expressions and experiences of faith. But we have the opportunity to accept the new things God wishes to do as expressed in the next generation and bless them to be the best that they can be and fulfill the calling for their generation. As we encourage and pray for them, we will discover that they are then open to the wisdom that we have gained by walking a bit further down this road of life. But without this attitude we create a barrier between the generations, which is often then perpetuated to future generations. We cease to have influence and they are cut off from the combined wisdom of previous generations.

Now we can all think of cases where individuals have chosen to go their own way, regardless of the *blessing* which was available for them. But while they may not even desire a blessing, it does not mean that we cannot offer it to them, much as the loving father in the parable of the Prodigal Son. His blessing was always available, even though while the son was wayward he could not truly benefit from the blessings of that relationship. But the fact is that we can choose to bless others, regardless of what their response may be. *Blessing others is unconditional.* The power of the parable is in the extension of the benefits of sonship, even though it was not deserved.

On the other side of the equation, perhaps you have never felt that you have received that blessing from the previous generation – either in your biological family or in the family of God. Perhaps you have never been mentored in your spiritual life. In many ways you may feel that you were held down rather than lifted up. You may feel that you have been *cursed* rather than *blessed.* Unfortunately, what we have received is what we will pass on to others and the *way* we have received is the *way* we will pass it on. It is difficult for us to pass on to others blessing when we have been handed cursing. Yet the Good News of the cross is that we can come to God through Jesus and He will be a Father to the fatherless! Instead of being an orphan you can be adopted into his family and break the pattern of the curse. Regardless of your past history, Christ can be your *kinsman-redeemer.* He will redeem you into a lineage that is far beyond your own. Though you still may see yourself as a foreigner, He desires to even use the scars of your background as a blessing to others. You can be used as Ruth was.

Perhaps the greatest profundity is that this multi-generational God, who spans time and eternity, is willing to include us as part of that lineage – as part of his family, weaknesses and all. I find great solace in the fact the he is the God of Abraham, Isaac, *and* Jacob. It is also interesting to note that He does not identify himself as the God of Abraham, Isaac, and *Israel,* but *Jacob.* In other words, He has chosen to be known and identified even with our very humanity and weaknesses. Though Jacob's name, meaning *deceiver,* was changed to *Israel,* God chooses to be known as the God of who we are even in our humanity. He is the God of Jacob. He does not whitewash over who we were, but uses our past as a trophy of his grace and mercy. It is not coincidental that the human genealogy of

Jesus in Matthew's Gospel is riddled with many imperfect and, at times, even unsavoury characters. It leaves lots of room for us.

But, like Ruth, during much of our lives, we often have no idea the impact our actions are going to have on our life and the lives of others. She was simply being faithful to her mother-in-law, having left her family and culture, when it would have been much easier not to. As a young attractive woman, she was willing to take on the dangerous task of gleaning in the field of the stranger – all in order to fulfil her obligation to Naomi.

Yet God, throughout it all, has a much larger plan. He is still the same God today and has a plan for you that is much bigger than you might believe possible. No, this does not mean that we will all be famous, or heroes by the world's definition. But it *does* mean that, as we are faithful, even though we do not always see the big picture, God is orchestrating something beyond our limited and time-bound understanding.

Let us use our scars, even our suffering – everything – as memorial stones to God's faithfulness to his purposes in our lives. As we pick up a stone from our Jordan may it not only serve to propel us forward in this life of faith, but also many others. May we all bless others with our *pile of stones* so that they may be able to build upon our foundation and do even greater things than we ever could.

18

The Final Stone

We all have that one final stone to carry as we cross over that last Jordan from this life to the next. As no other, this event will provide us with the clearest perspective of the true importance of our earthly existence.

In the last book of the Bible, we are given a glimpse of this eternal perspective. Here, the now aged Apostle John describes his heavenly vision of the future, which he received as an exile on the isle of Patmos. In Chapter 4 and 5 we see the curtain on the first scene rise as a voice invites him to come up and see that which will transpire. Immediately, John sees the throne of God and the One sitting on it shining as the sun, reflecting myriads of colours. Surrounding God's throne is a rainbow like an emerald, with twenty-four other thrones, which each have elders seated upon them. In front of the throne, there are seven blazing lamps. All of this is accompanied by peals of thunder and flashes of lightening. Reflecting all this colour and light is a sea as smooth as glass and as clear as crystal.

Additional sounds filled John's ear, as he heard the four living creatures in the centre of this throne area repeating, "Holy, holy, holy is the Lord God Almighty, who was, and is, and is to come." As this was occurring, the twenty-four elders fell down, casting their golden crowns before the One on the throne, extolling his worthiness. John was given a glimpse beyond the limits of space and time as we know it. He received a glimpse of the purpose of all creation, namely to worship Him for whom all things were created.

But then the tone of the scene changes. A large angelic being, with a powerful voice, comes forward to take a scroll from the hand of the One on the throne. With a powerful voice, He inquires as to who is worthy to open the scroll and reveal its contents. The Apostle weeps, as there is no one to open the scroll. But then there is One who comes forward. John's attention now focusses on a Lamb standing in the centre of the throne area. Yes! He is the One who is worthy to take the scroll! So He comes to take the scroll from the One who sits on the massive throne under the emerald rainbow. With the lightening flashes and thunder pealing in the background, he takes the scroll. Immediately the twenty four elders fall down before the Lamb and begin to sing this new song:

> You are worthy to take the scroll and to open its seals because you were slain, and with your blood you purchased men for God from every tribe and language and people and nation. You have made them to be a kingdom and priests to serve our God, and they will reign on the earth.

Immediately John writes that he then heard a huge number of angels, literally an uncountable number, beginning to sing. They were everywhere, as far as the eye could see. They encircled the entire throne area, all around the sea, which reflected not only their gleaming attire, but also their voices. They were joined by every creature, not only in heaven but also on earth, and yes even under the earth, on the sea and everything in between. They continue to give praise and honour to the One on the throne and to the Lamb. It is an emotionally exhausting scene, which must have taken John's breath away. I am sure he wanted to stay in that atmosphere longer – but then the Lamb begins to open the seven seals of the scroll.

Instantly we are transported back again to a very earthly environment, as each seal is opened and John the Revelator is given a glimpse into things that were to come. Perhaps the most striking and most disturbing is the scene brought on by the opening of the fifth seal (Rev. 6:9-11). Under the altar, the Apostle sees the souls of those who had been slain because of the Word of the Lord and the testimony that they had maintained. It is a rather troubling scene, for it does not really fit neatly into a theological box. John sees them shouting in a loud voice for the Lord to avenge their blood and judge the inhabitants of the earth! But they were told to wait a little while longer, until the number of their fellow servants who were yet to be killed would join them. At first this seems like a rather fatalistic response and no real answer at all. Not only would *they* have to wait longer, but there would be others who would experience their same fate!

This seems to be in sharp contrast to the early scene of the throne, the emerald sea of glass, and the glorious worship. But it is just as real. *Who are these under the altar, who had been sacrificed because they maintained their integrity to the Word of God and had maintained their testimony?* We read in Hebrews chapter twelve that these were part of that great cloud of witnesses. They may be under the altar from the throne room's perspective, but from an earthly perspective they are leaning over the very balconies of heaven, as if to encourage those still running the race.

They are there to cheer us on. But those cheering us on are not mere spectators. They have been in the race and have the battle scars to prove it. They are waiting for ultimate justice. And who are the ones that they are cheering on? You and I. Not perfect or problem-free saints, but ordinary people committed to the One on the throne. These martyred saints are cheering on those who are still in the battle, encouraging them to *throw off every hindrance, and those sins that at times threaten to so easily entangle us* (Hebrews 12:1-2). They are encouraging us to fix our eyes on Jesus, who is the author and perfecter of our faith.

As our great example, He has run the first and most difficult lap. We are now to follow his example and not grow weary or lose heart. Even though there are things that try to entangle us along the way and failures and sin may even cause us to stumble, we must continue in the race. He is counting on us, those who have gone on before are counting on us – future generations are counting on us. This *cloud of witnesses* includes those who:

> conquered kingdoms, administered justice, and gained what was promised; who shut the mouths of lions, quenched the fury of the flames and escaped the edge of the sword; whose weakness was turned to strength; and who became powerful in battle and routed foreign armies. (Heb. 11:33-34)

But it also includes:

> others who were tortured and refused to be released, so that they might gain a better resurrection. Some faced jeers and flogging, while still others were chained and put in prison. They were stoned; they were sawed in two; they were put to death by the sword. They went about in sheepskins and goatskins, destitute, persecuted and mistreated – the world was not worthy of them. (Heb. 11:35-38)

In verses 39-40, we read that both of these groups of people were commended for their faith. The latter never received their final recompense while on earth, but God had not forgotten about them. For them He had an even grander plan. His plan was that these who have gone on before will be made perfect as they are joined by those still running the race. These are mysteries mere mortal minds have trouble comprehending. As contenders for the faith, we all are part of this bigger plan. Some *through their faith* saw God do great things while they were still on this earth, while others *through their faith* laid down their lives for the Gospel. The world was not worthy of these, but they had a special place of honour under the altar.

Like the Author of their Faith, Jesus, they too were willing to endure the cross for the joy set before them. What was this joy? The joy was all of us who he knew would be reconciled, by faith, to

The Final Stone 223

the Father through his action. As ministers of this reconciliation (2 Cor 5:18-19), we now as believers have the same mandate.

This is the big picture. It spans time and eternity. It is bigger than any one of our lives. It spans generations, but it is also bigger than all of human history combined. We are part of this continuum. It extends even beyond the events of our universe as we know it; our time is but a drop in the ocean of eternity. It reaches to the very throne of God, to the very altar under the throne. The ground around the throne is not terraced; we will all stand equal. God is not looking for heroes by this world's standards; He is looking for those who are willing to endure and be faithful.

You have read our story; viewed our *pile of stones*. We are not perfect and by no means extra-ordinary. But that is the power and beauty of the Gospel! If God can use us in some small way for his great purposes and plans, in spite of our weaknesses, failures and besetting sins, imagine what He can do through your life! God is calling you to join the race if you have not already done so, or perhaps make some course adjustments. You can respond to his love and plan for your life and begin living life with purpose. If you have begun to lose heart while running the race look to Him and know your faithfulness is not in vain, nothing escapes his attention. With our Master and Lord as our example, and in light of the many who have gone on before, let us *keep on keeping on.*

You may even find yourself in the valley of the shadow of death. Things may be so dark that you don't even know up from down. Your current pain and the darkness of your situation may even be making it impossible to see the big picture at this time. But you are not alone and you are not alone in your struggle. Do not fear evil or the evil one, God has a plan for you even in the midst of the darkness. He will bring you through in his strength. After you have done all to stand, *stand firm.* While we often define faith and victory as a glorious campaign, for the battle-scarred warrior, victory is at times defined by those who are merely able to stand at the end of the battle; not having given in. Defiantly standing firm to the end is what *real* heroes do.

Do not believe that your contribution is invalid just because you can only see things dimly. As Ruth, it may seem you are merely *stumbling* along, only a gleaner in a lonely field. But stand, even in the face of not yet seeing the evidence of the things you hope for; even during those times of life that seem to be pressing you on every side and for which you cannot see a reason or purpose. Endure the process and you will be a blessing to others, even when you do not yet see how. Greatness begins with a commitment, particularly when you do not see the end from the beginning: when it seems there are more nights than dawns. Continue to do what is right even when things seem to be going wrong. Every night sets the stage for another dawn.

Our prayer is that you will be encouraged to diligently run your leg of the race. If you are in the race but are weary, stand firm. God is not finished with you yet. He is working to fulfill his plans and purposes in your life. He is making a beautiful picture of your life, even if all you can see are disjointed segments and missing pieces; He has the clear picture.

While we are at the end of this book, like you we are still in the race and have a few more stones to carry from the *Jordan's* of our life. In spite of the scars, battles and even imperfections, we want to be among those who will be faithful to the end, for one thing we have discovered is that God can make flowers bloom in the desert places of our lives and can bring something beautiful out of every wilderness.

One day we look forward to worshipping around the throne with those whom we know from various nations, languages and people groups. We also look forward to meeting many whom we have not met personally, but who have been instrumental in our lives and we in theirs. Together, we will have the privilege of throwing down our crowns, and proclaiming that it is only because of Him, the Lamb who sits on the throne, that we were able to do anything of eternal value.

We long to hear the words from our Lord and Master, *"Well done, good and faithful servant, enter in. . ."* We look forward to seeing you there. Finish the race. Gain strength from the memory of your *stones.* Future generations are counting on you, as is that great cloud of witnesses who are right now leaning over the balconies of heaven cheering you on. . .

Final Word

Over the last few decades, as the emerging church has grown around the world, so has the need for equipped Christian leaders. To make a difference in the lives of these nationals is what first motivated us to begin the mission society in Canada. From our early days in Africa, to meetings with leaders in other parts of the world, "Come train us!" has been the consistent plea. In response to this need, the ministry continues to expand throughout Africa and the Middle East.

The ministry in Europe has also found a foothold after several preparatory years. Mentoring has become the key to meeting this need of equipping another generation which God is raising up to meet the spiritual hunger among the younger generation in Europe – both East and West. In partnership with local churches, we have developed a mentoring program which includes both small group synergistic learning as well as pairing participants with others in ministry who can mentor them. The goal is that these emerging leaders may have their unique contribution for the Kingdom maximized.

While we are excited about what God is doing in mobilizing the church in Africa to reach back to the sending nations, we also desire to see new life breathed into the spiritual embers still glowing in Europe. This is beginning to happen as a generation that has never been given the opportunity to respond to a relevant presentation of the Gospel has that opportunity. The coming decade will be key as these efforts bear fruit.

If you would like more information regarding our ministry, would like to receive a newsletter, or would like to partner together with us, please contact us. Also, if our Pile of Stones has been a blessing to you we would particularly love to hear from you – we will then be content knowing that we have not piled them in vain.

Phil & Nancy Jeske
P.O. Box 93011 Willowbrook
Langley, BC.
Canada V3A 8H2
604.771-5689
ThisPileofStones@cs.com
www.thispileofstones.org